The Art of Educating with V Diagrams

Educating is complex. It takes a long time to educate for powerful and significant changes in the growth of human experience. This book explains how educating works. V diagrams, K-12 and beyond, can be effectively used by teachers and students, parents and their children, administrators and their staffs, publishers and curriculum makers, researchers and evaluators. Important aspects of educating are organized coherently in the theory of educating. A computer-formatted program, developed and tested for more than eight years in the Exploring Minds Project, at Tennessee State University, simplifies the complexity while extending the range of possibilities electronically.

D. Bob Gowin has taught at Cornell University for 30 years. He earned his Ph.D. from Yale University and was granted a post-doctoral fellowship in Philosophy at Yale in 1958. He has authored 15 books and monographs and co-authored *Learning How to Learn* (with Joseph Novak) and *Appraising Educational Research* (with Jason Millman).

Marino C. Alvarez is a professor in the Department of Teaching and Learning of the College of Education at Tennessee State University. He received his M.A. and Ed.D. from West Virginia University. His interest in content literacy stems from his years of teaching Social Studies in middle and secondary schools. He is the recipient of both the Teacher-of-the-Year and Distinguished Researcher-of-the-Year Awards at Tennessee State University.

The Art of Educating with V Diagrams

D. BOB GOWIN
Cornell University

MARINO C. ALVAREZ
Tennessee State University

CAMBRIDGE UNIVERSITY PRESS

CAMBRIDGE UNIVERSITY PRESS
Cambridge, New York, Melbourne, Madrid, Cape Town,
Singapore, São Paulo, Delhi, Mexico City

Cambridge University Press
32 Avenue of the Americas, New York, NY 10013-2473, USA

www.cambridge.org
Information on this title: www.cambridge.org/9780521604147

First published 2005
Reprinted 2012

A catalog record for this publication is available from the British Library.

Library of Congress Cataloging in Publication Data

Gowin, D. B.
The art of educating with **V** diagrams / D. Bob Gowin, Marino C. Alvarez.
   p. cm.
Includes bibliographical references and index.
ISBN 0-521-84343-x (casebound) – ISBN 0-521-60414-1 (pbk.)
1. Learning.   2. Self-knowledge, Theory of.   3. Education – Philosophy.
I. Gowin, D. B.   II. Title.
LB1060.G69   2005
370.15′23 – dc22   2004023977

ISBN 978-0-521-84343-0 Hardback
ISBN 978-0-521-60414-7 Paperback

I dedicate this work to my children: Sarah Gowin, Robin Gowin, and John Gowin. I thank them for their love, support, and patience through the many years I was working on my writing.

D.B.G.

This work is dedicated to my wife, Victoria J. Risko Alvarez, and son, Christopher M. Alvarez, who are daily inspirations in my life.

M.C.A.

Education, like invention, is primarily concerned, not with what is, but with what may be.

– Boyd Henry Bode

Contents

Foreword

Why Would Any Reader Desire to Read This Book???
Educating with **V** Diagrams

Dear Reader:

Have you ever wondered how it is that you can grasp a new meaning, a meaning not your own? Grasping a meaning not our own is necessary to the very act of reading. Readers do it easily. Their minds just fly down the pages as they read. Meanings come easily when the writing is clear to us, but what happens when we read and fail to grasp the meaning? What do we do then? We just stop reading. If the puzzling meaning is important to us, then we reread.

Suppose you were to receive a note from your spouse that read, "I'm here marking time for the delivery." The meaning you grasp is, "Why is she leaving me a message about marking the time for the delivery?" This message stops you. You are not reading any more; instead, you are wondering, "What does she mean? Does she mean that she wants to tell me the time of the delivery? If so, why didn't she write it on the note? Or does she mean she wants me to meet the delivery person? Or does she mean that she is waiting for the delivery?" You stop and try to figure out which meaning you want to take from the note. You will act very differently depending on the meaning you grasp.

Reflect for a minute on feelings. Your feelings of being stopped cause many questions to pop up. In the space of one second your mind can flick through seven or eight meanings. Does she want to notify me of the time and/or whether or not to meet the delivery person? Or, is the delivery person late and she is waiting for an arrival? What's the key question? You begin sorting out the possibilities. Maybe then you begin to question the questions – Am I thinking straight? What other possible meanings can I think of? Your mind can fly to the quick awakening of troublesome unease. *Feelings embrace thinking.* These brief moments can be of intense focus. You are stopped, and you pay attention to the stoppage. Total subjectivity dominates. Until you work through your feelings and your thinking, your acting is on hold.

What does this writing mean? What's the meaning for me? In this search for meaning we have the beginnings of learning. We must grasp the meaning before we can learn. Why? Our answer should surprise you. Our answer would surprise even prestigious theorists of learning. The importance of grasping a meaning for learning is that what you learn is the grasped meaning. Put another way, we humans possess language and use meanings as the materials for learning. We literally learn the grasped meaning. Meaning and learning are connected, and closely connected, but they are not the same thing. We learn meanings. Meaning is the stuff of learning.

Educating changes the meaning of human experience. Educating simplifies complexity without denying it. This book, *The Art of Educating with V Diagrams*, explains how educating works.

Teachers make lesson plans using the Telling Questions to cause teaching events to happen. Students study and learn using Focus Questions to make learning events happen. Subject matter disciplines are organized to reveal their Telling Questions to make knowledge-making events happen. Administrators, especially, find their control over educative events enhanced by this theory of educating.

This well-seasoned theory of educating has worked in many practical places of educating – colleges, universities, and public and private elementary and secondary schools. Many graduate students have used this theory to guide their scholarly research. Preparation for the Ph.D. and Ed.D. oral examinations is complete when aspiring doctoral students know their way around the **V**. One department of physics has gone all out and uses the theory to guide research in physics, as well as research in teaching physics. Faculty members publish their research guided by Gowin's **V**.

Who in education wouldn't want to read this book?

Our years of experience with Gowin's **V**, with concept maps, with the Q-5 technique (five questions to ask about any document) gives us strong evidence to support the theory of educating. Using our conception of knowledge, we know that students learn and also know how to learn. Using our conception of knowledge, we know students can analyze and construct knowledge claims. We know our students grasp the most Telling Questions about learning and knowing. The **V** becomes an anchor for all their organized meanings.

Human experience comes to us in a jumble of qualities. In an educative environment we take the pains to begin to sort out multiple meanings. In the preceding note example we see a jumble of possible qualities. In educative events we also begin in the midstream of mixed meanings. A process of clarification moves from immediate events directly perceived, to meanings clarified by thinking, on to learning the meaning we have selected, and then on to making knowledge tested and recorded in our deliberately mediated experience.

Getting clear about the meanings we take from our immediate experience is of central importance in this book. The precise connections of meaning and learning are also centrally important. We use a coherent theory of meaning to guide our thinking about the psychology, the philosophy, and the quality of educating in all our lives.

We know how people get smart. One parent, when asked why she liked what her children were doing with the **V**, said, " . . . if you start to take it apart it all comes together. . . . " Yogi Berra could not have said it better.[1]

Thank you for your attention.
D. Bob Gowin, San Carlos, California
Marino C. Alvarez, Nashville, Tennessee

---

[1] Yogi Berra was a catcher with the New York Yankees and is known for his "Yogi-isms." The titles of his books provide the unacquainted reader with the gist of his quotations: *The Yogi Book: "I Really Didn't Say Everything I Said!," "When You Come to a Fork in the Road Take It,"* and *"What Time Is It? You Mean Now?"*

Preface

This book uses a coherent theory of meaning that goes deep enough to combine philosophy, psychology and, educating. All of the principles of educating are expressions of a deep underlying idea of how meaning comes to us and how we shape and reshape meaning as we learn and grow through life. Shared meaning is the greatest human good. Educating changes the meaning of experience. Like art, educating also changes the experience of meaning. To tell a person he or she is ignorant is usually taken to be an insult of sorts, but if you think about ignorance you can also see that not knowing opens the possibility of new knowing. Being ignorant is a good ground for getting smart. Being smart – knowing and really understanding that you know – is a good thing.

Educating is grounded in shared meaning. In talking things over with each other we come to test our agreements and our differences. We can come to a point of deeply felt significance. The injection of computers into almost all aspects of contemporary life gives us ways to share meaning that were never before possible in human history. Alas, the widespread flood of spam and computer viruses of various sorts is a problem. Mere information is not enough. Information can lead to solid knowledge and cherished wisdom. The value of information for educating us is a supreme test of mere information.

This book addresses the complexities of educating by simplifying the process through the use of a theory that specifically applies to thinking, feeling, and then acting on these thoughts and feelings. School reform will not emerge simply from documenting the problems of schools. Until we understand the phenomena of educating, we will never understand how to reform schooling. The same holds for individuals who desire to become educated. In order to become self-empowered in the learning process we need to have a theory of educating that acts as a map to guide us in the quest for learning about and making new knowledge. In far too many instances, miseducating substitutes for educating, resulting in misconceptions and misunderstandings.

These ideas about simplicity-complexity are examples of the subject matter named "philosophy." This book is an example of using a philosophic maxim to guide thinking, research, and writing. In Chapter 4, you will find an example of philosophic work of "definition." Here we give the defining characteristics of the structure of knowledge. Most of this chapter is a philosophic effort to analyze meanings, to clarify meanings, to give examples of how we intend to use words with a certain meaning.

Philosophy is one epistemic element on the **V**. The academic field of philosophy contains many philosophies in rich array. Every academic subject carries a philosophy of that subject matter. Science carries philosophy of science. A science (e.g., physics, biology) carries its philosophy of science and in the teaching of any science that science's philosophy is relevant for the science teacher. Philosophy is a significant part of the structure of knowledge. Philosophy has a significant role in educating.

Significantly, however, most textbooks in use in today's schools and colleges do not give philosophy much space. Apparently, the educative uses of philosophy are not simple or easy or convenient or popular. We have found, however, that when teachers and students come to this element on the **V** they begin a search for "philosophy" and subsequently learn of the significant value philosophy has for teaching and learning. The more experience students and teachers have with **V** diagrams, the more valuable and useful philosophy becomes. Philosophy of Education, as a field of study, supports some specialists who focus on the functions of philosophy in educative events.

In this book, philosophy is both framework and content. The framework supports the analysis and clarification of the structure of knowledge. Content appears in different places: Definitions of key terms, such as Fact-as-record-of-an-event. Principles are found heading each chapter. Initial assumptions appear early in this book. Giving arguments that raise questions are a central feature of educating. Sharing meaning is a human good of the first order, and when definitions of meanings are clear and compelling, philosophy contributes to the human good in a significant way.

Since its inception, *Educating* (Gowin, 1981), as a theory, has served as a guide for numerous doctoral dissertations, masters theses, and published research investigations. Professor Gowin received a year-long fellowship grant from the U.S. Office of Education based on a national competition. At Stanford University, he pioneered a seminar on philosophy and research. Students were asked every week to analyze a piece of research in their field of specific knowledge. The pages that follow reiterate and expand upon this theory. The **V** diagram is a centering device for the theory of educating. The **V** is a method designed to plan, carry out, and finalize research investigations, analyze documents, and aid teachers when planning lessons; it is also for students to learn and understand the aims of the lessons and assignments. The four commonplaces of educating (teaching, learning, curriculum, and governance) have been expanded to include societal influences and are examined and evidenced in the components arrayed on the **V** diagram. Educating, as a theory, focuses on the educative event and its related concepts and facts as they pertain to a topic of inquiry. The theory is useful in classifying the relevant aspects of the educative event. In an educative event, teachers and learners share meanings and feelings to bring about a change in human experience. This theory stresses the centrality of the learners' experience in educating.

The **V** diagram is a tool designed to unlock the structure of knowledge of a given document, program, or event. The **V** diagram unearths information in ways that cultivate the mind to think and critically examine the structure of knowledge of a work. Its purpose is to evoke thought so that new ideas connect to past information and can be learned. Most of what we read, view, and hear is reflected in records of some past event. The same holds in school situations, where students are required to learn records of events that have already happened; seldom are they asked to engage in learning that takes them beyond what is known to what is either new learning or what is possible to imagine.

The **V** is a symbol of knowledge that is constructed. It emerged as a heuristic device for analyzing knowledge claims of science. The main point is the act of pointing at event reality, with the point of the knowledge **V**. Events and objects of science are the main concern of knowledge claims about reality. Science is about reality that is not science. Science is about understanding reality, the events and objects that make up universal realities.

In our work, more than two decades of critical research has been achieved in the area of science. Science is much more than the scientific method assiduously applied. Some have held that if scientific method is to be improved, the use of the scientific method will improve itself. This view is a failed one. Our view: Critical analysis of works of science, like critical analysis of poems, or novels, or movies, or paintings, will produce the criteria of excellence each field needs. We read art critics, movie critics, and literary critics almost daily. We have science critics also but they seem much less popular.

Science is less popular than entertainment and edification of the arts. But both the arts and the sciences are mainstream in advanced education. Literary criticism, done well, is difficult, technical, and necessary. Science criticism can be well done. Philosophy of science is a field unto itself, dealing more with issues of philosophy than with specific experimental–empirical cases of scientific research.

In our critical analysis we examine clear cases and counterexamples. From these results we gradually formulate specific criteria of excellence.

Then, from these criteria we examine new cases. In our work, analyses of more than 3,000 scientific research works have been conducted. For years, students in seminars analyzed a piece of science every week. We criticized scientific methodology studies, empirical research papers, articles and essays of science, scientific books, science laboratory guides, teaching science essays, and curriculum materials for instruction in the sciences. In addition, philosophic criticism was done on logical positivism, pragmatism, analytic philosophy, philosophy of education, and educational theory. One powerful issue concerns this question: "Is knowledge discovered?" versus "Is knowledge constructed?" Today we find Foundationalists versus Constructivists writing about each other on this basic issue. Other powerful issues relate to these questions: Is science value-free? Do theories in science guide scientific research practices? Does scientific methodology fail because research is method-driven rather than theory-guided?

The **V** diagram was invented in 1977 in a seminar on science education at Cornell University. It was the result of years of analysis of specific works. The heuristic was invented by Professor D. Bob Gowin and published as "Gowin's **V**" (1981). Generations of advanced students used the **V** in their theses and dissertations. Other faculty taught the **V** and helped to develop and refine its uses. Professor Marino Alvarez was one of the first to adopt, adapt, and expand the uses of the concept maps and **V** diagrams.

The **V** heuristic was developed to enable students to understand the structure of knowledge (e.g., relational networks, hierarchies, and combinations) and to understand the process of knowledge construction. Our fundamental assumption is that knowledge is not absolute, but rather it is dependent upon the concepts, theories, and methodologies by which we view the world. To learn meaningfully, individuals relate new knowledge to relevant concepts and propositions they already know. The **V** diagram aids learners in this thinking process by acting as a metacognitive tool that requires users to self-monitor their progress by making explicit connections between previously learned and newly acquired information.

The **V** is a tool that helps us to understand and learn. Since knowledge is not discovered, but is constructed by people, it has a structure that can be analyzed. The **V** helps us to identify the components of knowledge, clarify their relationships, and present them in a visually compact and clear way. Several of the many possible applications of the **V** to education include using it to guide the design of research, to analyze research reports, textbooks, and curriculum material that you may be using when developing and improving the design of educative events. It also helps your audience understand the meaning of a piece of research. The exciting aspect of using the **V** is that it does help us to see more clearly how knowledge is constructed, an insight that is empowering, useful, and lasting.

Examples of **V** diagrams are shown together with instructions for their use and development. It is the intention of this book to serve as a resource for one to implement his or her own constructions using **V** diagrams. A primary intent of the **V** is to stimulate thinking and imagination when confronted with problem-oriented tasks. Although primarily a pencil-and-paper tool, an interactive **V** diagram, explained in Chapter 9, has been developed and is described with examples of students' work using this electronic communication. **V**s shown that have plus (+) symbols after each element have been developed electronically using the *Interactive V Diagram* in the Exploring Minds Network, and clicking on this plus (+) symbol enables reviewers to make comments. A research strategy is presented that provides the reader with a framework to guide an analysis of a work as well as planning, carrying out, and finalizing a research investigation. These questions and statements correspond to the components arrayed on the **V** diagram. A stand-alone version of this **V** has been developed that has the capabilities for educators, students, researchers, and administrators to install it on their computers.

This book is divided into four parts. Part One, "Four Commonplaces of Educating Plus One," offers a theory of educating that encompasses teaching, learning, curriculum, and governance plus the societal environment; it describes the role of simplifying complexity without denying it when confronted with new information. Part Two, "The **V** Diagram," explores the relationship between Educating and the **V** diagram by describing the components of the **V**, the elements that are arrayed on the **V**, procedures and examples for making a **V** and for learning and teaching the **V** by teachers and their students in the classroom. Part Three, "Analyzing, Evaluating, and Conducting Research," focuses on the research process by describing the Q-5 technique as a way to transition into the **V** process and as a "code-breaker" when analyzing and evaluating documents, and it shows examples of research **V**s conducted by elementary, secondary, and postsecondary students. Part Four, "Reasoning with Technology," presents alternatives to conventional instruction through electronic educating and describes how the theory of educating and the use of interactive **V** diagrams are being used in the Exploring Minds Network developed at Tennessee State University's Center of Excellence in Information Systems.

Each chapter is written to convey a clear and concise message for using the **V** in ways that hopefully will evoke critical and imaginative thinking. The principles that guide each chapter are:

Principle 1. Educating changes the meaning of experience.
Educating is a process of deliberate intervention in the lives of students in order to *change* the meaning of experience. *Knowledge is a human construction.* Knowledge is not discovered. Coal, for example, is discovered. Knowledge about coal is a human construction. Begin with the practice of making knowledge. Human beings make knowledge out of their experience – they are trying to make sense of their immediate experience and their mediated experience.

Principle 2. Sharing meaning simplifies complexity through educating ourselves and others.

Principle 3. Knowledge has a structure of parts and relations between the parts.
We talk about the structure of knowledge. Structures have parts and relations. A house structure, for example, has a foundation, walls, roof, rooms, etc. – parts and their relations.

Principle 4. The V diagram is a way to show the structure of knowledge.
A one-page **V** diagram can show the structure of knowledge of an entire scientific research paper.

Principle 5. A V represents knowledge of an educative event formed by human agents interacting in a social setting where the reality of the social constructions vary in complex ways. The V simplifies this complexity.

Principle 6. The V diagram clarifies ambiguities and makes new events happen.
For the teacher, the **V** makes lesson planning more meaningful to the student. The **V** enables students to pursue their ideas, risking failure in the process to success and achievement.

Principle 7. The V diagram of the structure of knowledge provides a basis for evaluating. The developer of a diagram judges worth by criteria of congruence-correspondence, coherence-conceptual clarity, the question-event connection, and the fit between questions asked and answers given.

Principle 8. The V diagram mediates conceptual and methodological research design and practice.

Principle 9. Electronic educating extends learning beyond the walls of the classroom or laboratory and enables meaning to be negotiated electronically in ways that go beyond the conventional paper-and-pencil formats.

The art of educating is a two-fold process. In one we engage ourselves into the thinking–learning process in order to become more knowledgeable in the workings of the world; in the other we inspire individuals through teaching to become self-empowered in the learning process by engaging their minds in meaningful actions. The theory of educating espoused in this book is intended to provide a venue by which these two processes occur. Knowing and applying the four commonplaces – teaching, learning, curriculum, and governance – and taking into consideration the societal environments that impact these commonplaces aid in resolving complexities while simultaneously stirring the imagination. Educating helps us to come into conscious possession of our own powers (and our world), especially the flourishing integration of thinking and feeling and acting. As educative events come more and more under our control, educating becomes self-educating, and that is the goal of education.

To study educating is to become intelligent about becoming intelligent. What intellectual tasks confront us as we seek to achieve this aim? This book moves us in that direction by offering a framework of ideas for conceptualizing phenomena of education. By centering our attention on the four commonplaces of educating and the influence of the societal curriculum, we will come to understand educating as an eventful process. Educating is reeducating. It is a continual process of working and reworking, structuring and restructuring the qualities of human experience interacting with nature.

INITIAL ASSUMPTIONS

We assume that scientific knowledge is keenly relevant to the art of educating. Science is abstract and theoretic. Educating is about direct human experience and is practical, concerned with human goodness; it is also productive, concerned with beauty. We use **V** diagrams as a proven approach to the many ways of integrating these important human events.

We assume that educated human beings appreciate both the value and the difficulty of governing educative events for themselves and for others who are less well educated.

We assume that the most difficult human learning is learning a language, a learning achieved by most 3-year-olds.

We assume that transactions of human beings and computers are desirable and become educative when they are governed by a proven theory of educating.

We assume that organisms organize. Human organisms organize meaning.

Acknowledgment

The **V** diagram known as Gowin's **V** was invented at Cornell University in 1977, after a decade of research in science, science education, philosophy of science, and philosophy of education. Cornell University Press published *Educating* in 1981, with **V** diagrams. I acknowledge with gratitude and admiration all the faculty members and graduate students who participated in various ways. Cornell graduate students: Peter Cardamone, first test of concept mapping in teaching, college mathematics, 1975; Dr. Marco Moreira, first to publish a book on the use of **V** diagrams in physics laboratories, 1980, in Portugese; Dr. Laine I. Gurley, first yearlong field test, "Use of Gowin's **V** and Concept Mapping in High School Biological Sciences," Ph.D. thesis, 1982. I am grateful to their brilliance and their groundbreaking courage. The **V** is generative and its use has spread worldwide.

Barbara Coulson, former North Atlantic Director for Cambridge University Press, has supported my work for more than 20 years and two books, and I give her my heartfelt appreciation. Philip Laughlin, our editor, has been prompt, and demanding, and delightfully optimistic, and our thanks go to him and his assistants. Kenneth Karpinski, Project Manager, provided the necessary accouterments for the book, for which we are grateful. Patty Schurba gave expert computer advice throughout the difficult and complicated joint manuscript preparation; thank you for your friendly support.

Virginia Pugliese and her many children and grandchildren have given me love and personal support through the half dozen years I have spent writing and working on this book. Thank you so very much.

D.B.G.

A book intended to spur ideas and aid in self-educating and simplifying complexity comes to fruition when we reflect on our parents, teachers, mentors, friends, students, and relatives who provide opportunities for us to engage in these kinds of stimulating tasks. Both of us have many to thank for helping to better understand the intellectual processes needed to learn new information, but also ways in which to teach others to become self-educating. For me these persons include Professors John Helfeldt, Judith Thelen, Lawrence Erickson, and Thomas Hatcher. Dr. Michael R. Busby, Director of the Center of Excellence in Information Systems, Tennessee State University, has provided us with constant support during this endeavor, for which we are greatly appreciative. We also acknowledge the support provided by NASA through the Tennessee Space Grant Consortium, Network Resources Training Site (NRTS), and NASA Center for Automated Space Science. Greg Henry and Dr. Geoff Burks have served as mentors to many of the students involved in the Exploring Minds project, and Ms. Goli Sotoohi has been an invaluable technician and researcher in the design of the Exploring Minds Network and creating the images appearing in our book. The teachers and their students are important members of our Exploring Minds project. High school teachers who deserve special mention are William Rodriguez, Lee Ann Hennig, Terry King, and Dr. John Lee.

Lastly, I acknowledge my wife, Victoria Risko Alvarez, who has been an inspiration and companion throughout this learning process. I am thankful for our son, Christopher, who provides the incentive and sparks the need for educating to flourish as an enduring process.

M.C.A.

FOUR COMMONPLACES OF EDUCATING PLUS ONE

1

The Art of Educating

Principle 1. Educating changes the meaning of experience.

How we educate is a complex process. Our task is to simplify this complexity without denying its value. This task requires much thought, careful planning, and individual effort. Educating becomes possible when it is viewed as a social event of shared meaning between individuals. Educative events help us come into possession of our world, both social and natural, and occur as a consequence of human choice, intervention, and inauguration, which give us power over subsequent events. Literally thousands of educative events happen. Examples of educative events include: a teacher and a student working together on a *plan* for a scientific experiment; a coach and a player reviewing a *playbook*; an automobile mechanic explaining to a driver a procedure with the fuel injection system described in the *owner's manual*; a gardener using a *book* on gardening to demonstrate the process of hybrid germination in plants to an interested party; a parent and a child reading about their *family tree*; and a student showing the teacher a *computer programming application*. In each of these examples, we see people using ideas (e.g., documents) to change meanings of events. *As educative events come increasingly under the control of individuals, educating becomes self-educating.*

The **V** diagram helps learners to recognize the complexity and also the basic simplicity of the knowledge construction process. **V** diagrams help first-time learners of the **V** to see that knowledge has structure. From the first learning experiences through all grades and levels of learning, knowledge has structure. Observing that knowledge has structure helps greatly in anticipating new events. Learners at each grade or level come to expect to see the structure and how it is made. The **V** is used to diagram the issues that are produced by claims of knowledge and, through its arrangement of the epistemic elements, reveals its source of conceptual and methodological

3

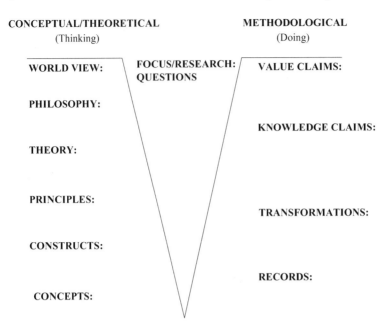

CONCEPTUAL/THEORETICAL   METHODOLOGICAL
            (Thinking)   (Doing)

WORLD VIEW: FOCUS/RESEARCH: VALUE CLAIMS:
                       QUESTIONS

PHILOSOPHY:

                                            KNOWLEDGE CLAIMS:

THEORY:

PRINCIPLES:

                                            TRANSFORMATIONS:

CONSTRUCTS:

                                            RECORDS:

CONCEPTS:

EVENTS AND/OR OBJECTS:

FIGURE 1.1. A skeletal **V** diagram showing its elements.

practices. A skeletal **V** is shown in Figure 1.1. The 12 elements arrayed on the **V** are explained in Chapters 3 through 9.

In describing how to use the **V** diagram for both analyzing and learning about the structure of knowledge we apply Bob Gowin's theory of educating designed to make sense of educative events (social constructions devised by people) using four commonplaces: teaching, curriculum, learning, and governance.[1] This theory of educating is a conceptual approach to problem solving that fosters teacher and student interactions resulting in creating meaning through negotiation of ideas. By centering our attention on the four commonplaces plus the societal environment of educating, we come to understand educating as an eventful process in the reorganization of meaning that becomes a mainstay in our "life's work." This understanding fulfills our intrinsic desire to become self-educated for our own well-being.

---

[1] For a detailed analysis of the theory of educating see D. Bob Gowin, *Educating* (Ithaca, New York: Cornell University Press, 1981). Reissued Second Printing in paperback 1987.

EDUCATING

Educating is a process of deliberate intervention in the lives of students in order to *change* the meaning of experience, and it begins in midstream of important events in their lives. The change educating makes happen empowers students to become self-educating; they learn to take charge of their own experience. This change of the meaning of experience requires teachers to teach (teachers cause teaching). *Teaching* is defined as the achievement of shared meaning. The deliberate intervention in the lives of students is aimed at negotiating meaning between teacher, curriculum, and student to the point of mutual understanding. In this process, the teacher brings something, the curriculum presents something, and the student brings something. All three are involved in contributing something toward the empowerment of students so that they become self-educating.

A concept map with the components of "Educating" shows the relationship between the teacher and the learner in the educative process (see Figure 1.2).

Just as teachers cause teaching, students cause learning. The student is therefore responsible for learning. *Learning* is defined as an active, nonarbitrary, voluntary reorganization by the learner of patterns of meaning. The student learns the new with the power of the old; the new unfamiliar materials must become integrated with the old, familiar ideas and meanings the student already knows. Learning is how the student grows from the familiar to the unfamiliar so that these two are progressively integrated and differences are reconciled. The **V** diagram appearing in Figure 1.3 illustrates one example of an educative process.

In this **V** diagram, the components that make up the concept map are evidenced. This example from sports is a player and a coach negotiating meaning of a play intended to make a difference in a future event (the outcome of a game). It is through this discourse that the sharing of knowledge, and the extent to which the same meaning can be ascertained, is accomplished. The concepts, events, and records of facts are instrumental in this meaning-making process. The degree to which this play's meaning is grasped, understood, and executed will be determined by the exchanges that take place in the practice sessions and the actual game. For educating to occur we work together to achieve meaning through the interaction of thinking, feeling, and acting.

Thinking, Feeling, and Acting: The TFA

Thinking is a behavior not directly observable by an objective observer. Teachers know well the mistake of trying to be certain about a

6

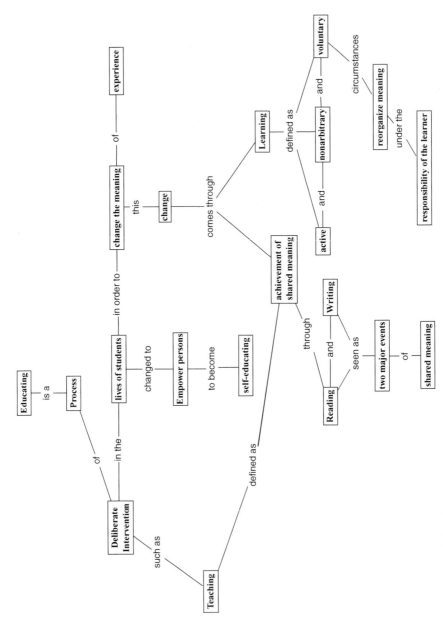

FIGURE 1.2. Educating.

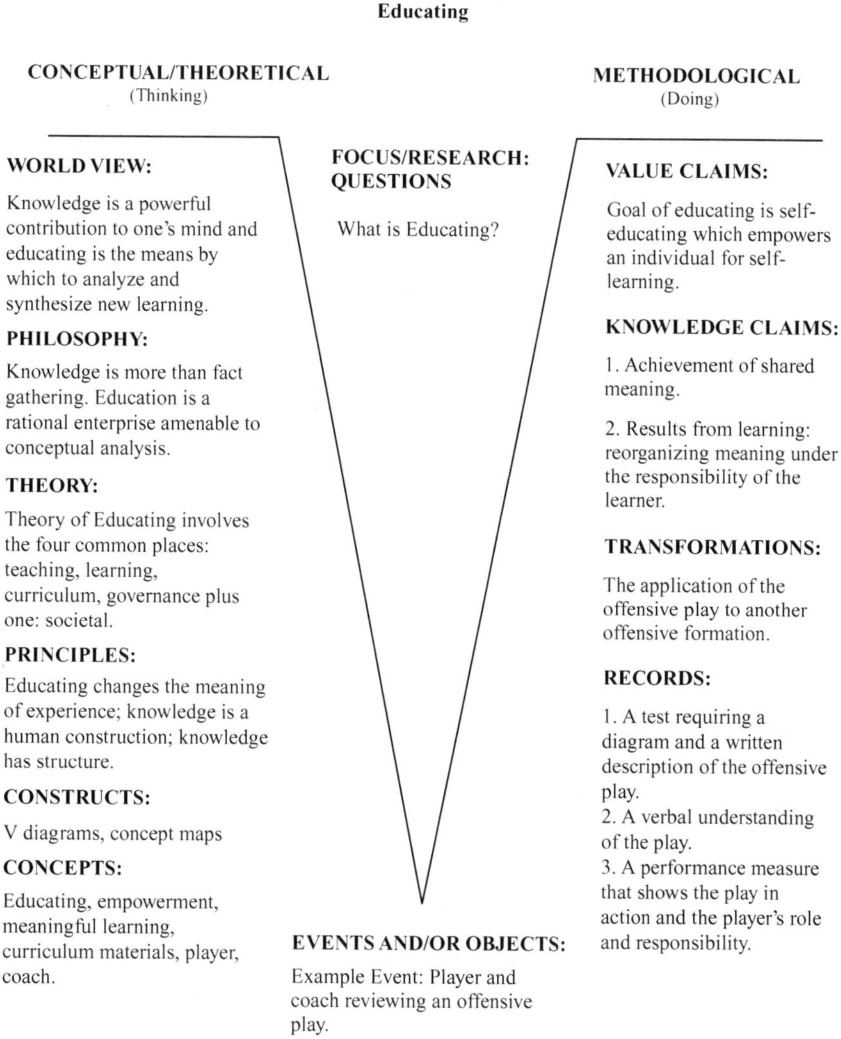

Educating

CONCEPTUAL/THEORETICAL (Thinking)		METHODOLOGICAL (Doing)

WORLD VIEW:

Knowledge is a powerful contribution to one's mind and educating is the means by which to analyze and synthesize new learning.

PHILOSOPHY:

Knowledge is more than fact gathering. Education is a rational enterprise amenable to conceptual analysis.

THEORY:

Theory of Educating involves the four common places: teaching, learning, curriculum, governance plus one: societal.

PRINCIPLES:

Educating changes the meaning of experience; knowledge is a human construction; knowledge has structure.

CONSTRUCTS:

V diagrams, concept maps

CONCEPTS:

Educating, empowerment, meaningful learning, curriculum materials, player, coach.

FOCUS/RESEARCH: QUESTIONS

What is Educating?

VALUE CLAIMS:

Goal of educating is self-educating which empowers an individual for self-learning.

KNOWLEDGE CLAIMS:

1. Achievement of shared meaning.

2. Results from learning: reorganizing meaning under the responsibility of the learner.

TRANSFORMATIONS:

The application of the offensive play to another offensive formation.

RECORDS:

1. A test requiring a diagram and a written description of the offensive play.
2. A verbal understanding of the play.
3. A performance measure that shows the play in action and the player's role and responsibility.

EVENTS AND/OR OBJECTS:

Example Event: Player and coach reviewing an offensive play.

FIGURE 1.3. A **V** diagram example of educating.

student's thinking behavior. Concept maps externalize a student's thinking. Maps provide a shareable document for teachers and students to negotiate meaning.

Feeling is a behavior whose meaning or meanings are difficult to read correctly. We do not yet have any way to ensure that feelings can be correctly shared, negotiated, or reliably repeated. We can ask, "How are you feeling?" The responses we get can lead to further discussions. Up to a point, we can agree that we understand each other's feelings. Up to a point. Mostly, feelings are our own personal, subjective awareness and are no one else's business unless we voluntarily put them on the table for discussion. We each have our secrets we believe are still secrets. We declare our independence of our feelings.

Felt-significance is a key concept in this theory of educating. We believe that learners grasp meanings that are not their own, and we believe learners can *feel* the significance of these grasped meanings. Felt-significance is a powerful moment in educating when grasping a meaning and feeling the significance come together. It is a common human event to "get it" and simultaneously recognize the importance of "getting it." Surprises, novel events, new meanings come at us daily. Some of these events we feel are important enough to keep. "Now I see." "So that's it, eh?" "I got the meaning, and now I feel I understand it." "Makes sense to me. I'll remember that!" "I was blind, but now I see." These events of felt-significance are key to educative events. We name felt-significance an educative value; it is an event that can be recorded in human memory and made a keep sake.

Acting is a behavior guided by meaning. Acting is a combination of energy and information, where information controls energy. Explicit meanings guide and direct overt actions. In the best cases we successfully do what we meaningfully intend to do. Often, however, good intentions result in unintended consequences, and we realize we did not know what we were doing. Purposefully acting in a stage play is a good example of an acting behavior.

Educative events can bring about a flourishing integration of thinking–feeling–acting.

Example 1: An Educative Event (Arithmetic $2 + 2 = 4$ versus Chemical $2 + 2 \neq 4$)

You mean two plus two is less than four? How can that be?

That's not true in counting, you know! So, can you explain your crazy claim? So, tell me. Teach me. Show me! OK, you want me to pour two ounces of water into this measuring cup and then pour two ounces of alcohol into the same measuring cup. Wait a minute! Why doesn't the liquid rise to four ounces?

You mean that when the two different kinds of liquids are combined into one measuring cup that it is less than four? In this case, two plus two is not four? Why does this happen? You say because the molecules that make up water and those that make up alcohol are shaped in such a fashion that when they are combined they are able to fit closer together and therefore take up less volume than when they are separate?

So, you say a counting event and a chemical event are different events? Yeah? Arithmetic deals with numbers. Chemistry deals with factual events of chemical behavior. So? So what? It is very important? Oh. Now I see: The logical and the empirical are two different events. Not the same kind of event.

Example 2: An Educative Event ($1 + 1 = 1$)

Let's see if I can make an analogy to molecules taking up less volume when combined.

I play tennis, and the tennis balls come three in a cylinder. If I had a box that contained ten empty cylinders and a box that contained 30 tennis balls I would have two boxes: $1 + 1 = 2$. But if I took the 30 tennis balls in the box and combined them by putting three into each cylinder I would have one box instead of two. This is because the size of the cylinder holds three tennis balls and takes up less volume, therefore eliminating the need for the other box. I now have two boxes that now are one box: $1 + 1 = 2$, but 2 combine into 1. Wow! I get it. $1 + 1 = 1$. You have boggled my mind!

I GET IT! Using the measuring cup in the first example and then using an example with which I am familiar helps me to better understand this principle than if I just hear it told to me.

There is more? I didn't get it all? You just helped me to understand that $1 + 1 = 1$? One box holds all that two boxes did. OK, so two boxes collapsed into one box. Sure, I get it.

There is still more? Arithmetic deals with numbers. Chemistry deals with factual events of chemical behavior. In this case, the molecules when combined take up less volume. So? OK. What don't I get now?

Oh. Now I see: the *events* are different. The *logical* and the *empirical* are NAMES for two different KINDS of events. They are not the same kind of event. Logical empiricism made a career of that simple distinction. Egad, that's significant!!! I REALLY GET IT NOW! I understand the difference within and between the two examples. Oh, yes but that philosophy's dead, right? Ha! OK. The distinction is still alive, and that's the significance!

In these two examples, the sensation of felt-significance is evident in the thinking, feeling, and acting that take place in these educative events. The person being taught reveals these actions through a series of spontaneous "I get it" reactions, which are so necessary in the educative process.

FOUR COMMONPLACES OF EDUCATING PLUS ONE

The belief that we should seek simplicity but preserve complexity is illustrated in the four commonplaces of educating plus one network of relations between *teaching, learning, curriculum, governing,* and *societal learning environments.* The simplifying comes from integrating complex events of educating.

In these commonplaces of educating, *teaching* is achieving shared meaning through negotiation rather than telling; *learners* are responsible for their actions; the *curriculum* is emergent and constructed rather than given and fixed; *governance* is the way we control meaning to control effort; and the *societal environment* is an important factor to be considered if formal school practices are to be meaningful. Incorporating students' out-of-school experiences into the formal school curriculum strongly influences and has an impact on new learning. This theory is based on the premise of a Constructivist epistemology (the idea that both individuals and groups of individuals construct ideas about how the world works). For educating to occur, we work together to achieve meaning through the interaction of thinking, feeling, and acting.

Teaching

Teaching is the achievement of shared meaning in the context of educating. While it is agreed that teachers are the efficient cause of teaching, they are not the efficient cause of learning. The teacher acts intentionally to change the meaning of the student's experience. The aim is a shared meaning between the student and the teacher. The teacher is responsible for seeing to it that the meanings of the materials the student grasps are the meanings the teacher intended for the student to take away. The student is responsible for seeing to it that the grasped meanings necessary to the student's new learning are the ones the teacher intended. Providing sufficient time for negotiated meaning is important. Grasping the meaning is something that each of us must do; it is not part of what the lesson contains. When learning has educational worth, it requires the grasp of meaning.

The teacher is responsible for providing teaching methods and materials that learners can relate to their experience. These methods and materials are intended to help learners become active minds rather than passive participants. The focus of these methods and materials is for the student and teacher to share and achieve new shared meaning. Together they must agree on the key new meaning. In an educative event, the teacher initiates the event by using meaningful materials and instructional methods to teach students so that they are able to understand the meaning of concepts and facts contained in these materials. The teacher helps students to become aware of what they already know and helps students see the importance of making use of their prior knowledge and experience. Learning connects the old with the new. Explicit expression of and use of key concepts is the most simple and compelling way to negotiate meaning and simplify complexities. *Facts do not explain themselves. Concepts do.* Conceptual grasp leads to satisfying explanations of what is happening.

Educational Episodes. When we think of educational episodes as having a beginning, middle, and end, we can see that the actions of the role of the teacher will vary. This movement through time involves changing meanings during these stages as the teacher's role changes from initiator, to facilitator, evaluator, and discussant. In the final phase of an episode, the teacher assumes the role of a master teacher.

A master teacher organizes the many different roles teachers can play. Any teacher will have many different lesson plans. When these plans of action are drawn up around the **V**, you can clearly see the different questions the teacher must ask and the different events that are required. In these final episodes, the teacher can emphasize the contextual nature of knowledge claims. The fact is that the meaning of knowledge statements is a function of the context of inquiry that produced them. When contexts change, the meaning changes.

Further, the fact is that conclusions have important limits to their generalizability, and there is always the possibility that different ways of viewing the same phenomena might produce an enlightened view. This is an exciting prospect. All knowledge is a good ground for the new conceptual entertainment of unrealized unknown experienced events. New thinking emerges. All knowledge claims can be phrased as questions for further inquiry to answer. The "Parade of Vs" shows clearly these significant changes.[2]

Teaching is consummated when the meaning of the material that the student grasps is the meaning (or sets of meaning) the teacher intends the material to have for the student. The deliberate finding, testing, and explication of meaning found in materials characterize educational episodes involving teaching. If teaching changes the meaning of the student's experience then the student's subsequent experience will be changed also. Two changes occur: (1) a change in the meaning of experience and (2) a change in the experience of meaning. The student's power to better control a later experience is grounded not so much in the teacher's authority as in the student's understanding of how the educative materials enhance and enlarge the range of his or her own experience. This shift in power can cause increased motivation to learn. The teacher's responsibility is to see that what the student takes from the educative materials does in fact help the student in this increased understanding. When the student feels increased power over events, he or she can also feel increased responsibility. Sometimes conflict arises from students' increased power and responsibility. At this point, frankness, honesty, and the openness of negotiated meaning are appropriate. Integrating thinking and feeling and acting takes time and practice. Mistakes will be made. Interesting questions will arise.

The teacher's greater knowledge of the conceptual structure of the field of study permits him or her to judge the difference between an important question and one that is mere piffle. Too often silly and overly simple ideas are thrown in the mix of strong ideas. The student may try to answer the question before reaching this understanding. Any genuine question is about future events. When the questions are clear the next step concerns techniques and methods to be used for answering the questions. Again, the teacher, who may already know what to expect, can assume the role of stimulator by refusing to tell directly the most appropriate and sophisticated methods of work and letting the students try it out and see what happens. By stimulating students to try to find workable methods

---

[2] See Chapter 6 for a description and example of a "Parade of Vs."

the teacher is helping inquiry into uncertain futures. When events are in doubt, a good method encourages exploration of events. Next, assuming that all of the preceding is grounded and working, open-ended questions about the scene, the phenomena of interest, ways of conceiving of the universe, and the like can be entertained. The students work up toward the top-of-the-**V** questions. After all, almost any future is possible. Imagining futures can be exciting.

Additional concern with the agent and the audience and with the kinds of values to be found in the area of study can be explored. Recognizing the sorts of human values one can call on can be very stimulating. Thus over the period of the educational episode, the teacher helps to anticipate possibilities and to find ways to narrow and simplify possibilities for the purpose of knitting them together. Areas in which given knowledge claims are defective, uncertain, partial, or missing can stimulate an exciting animating grasp of future events.

Curriculum

A curriculum is a logically connected set of conceptually and pedagogically analyzed knowledge and value claims. By "conceptually analyzed" we mean what is produced when one places the **V** diagram on primary sources of knowledge. In that analysis we make explicit the structured relations from world-views and philosophy down through theories and conceptual systems to specific events and objects, and then back up through records, data, generalizations, explanations (including techniques and methods), and value claims, including especially the criteria of excellence. Working up a good curriculum can take years.

By "pedagogically analyzed" we mean the concepts of teaching and learning and curriculum that are held while practical field tests of teachability and studyability are conducted. Knowledge of these practical events can take years to develop. The feedback loop of information from these practical tests feeds into the last revisions of materials before they are pronounced ready for use in instruction. Many teachers fill their time away from the classroom making these studies real.

The curriculum is an analyzed record of prior events that we use to make new events happen; the curriculum is to be related to teaching and to learning, but *not* reduced to either. The curriculum refers to a material thing that exists, not the experiences that can be undergone as a consequence of interacting with those materials. The whole of the educative process is not reduced to one part.

Judging the Criteria of Excellence. Every field has its claims for criteria of excellence. In science, two criteria often found together are reliability and validity. The reliability criterion is used to judge the excellence of knowledge claims produced by an inquiry by analyzing whether techniques of measurement pass tests of repeatability or reproducibility. The question asked is whether a scientist using the same measuring device under the same experimental conditions would repeatedly find the same thing. The criterion of validity sets a different task for judges of knowledge claims. A claim is judged valid if it refers to the piece of reality it purports to refer to, and if that portion of reality is thought to be important to the science. Scientific criteria for methods of work are usually grouped into two categories for theories and methods.

Another example is in the field of literary works. The criteria of excellence used in the study of literary works of art fall into groups around four elements: the work of art itself, the artist making the work, the audience experiencing the work, and the universe about which the work evolves.[3] A work may be judged for its internal coherence; the artist judged for imagination, expressivity, and craftsmanship; the audience may judge by standards of edification and entertainment; and the criteria stemming from a concern with the universe include realism, accuracy, and truthfulness. Different theories of literary criticism balance these four sources of criteria of excellence in different ways. This sort of knowledge takes years to develop, and it is a mark of a master teacher to know criteria of excellence.

All experts in all fields employ criteria. One quick way to find the criteria of excellence in any field is to locate the experts, examine the cases they judge, and see how they use criteria to judge them. Experts disagree, of course, but they all use some standards of judgment, and their points of disagreement often significantly illuminate what the whole field is about.

These criteria can be revealed by the method of analysis of claims. When found and explicitly recognized, criteria of excellence are extremely useful as explicit grounds for judging content. Every field is different with respect to these criteria, a fact of great significance. Questions arise about the master subject: Is there one master subject? If not, how are different subjects connected? Is one discipline fundamentally different or just merely different from another discipline? A display of the criteria of excellence used by any discipline helps in answering these sorts of questions.

Five Roles of Educative Materials. Often we think of a curriculum as something that is in some material form – such as a textbook, program, or video – that we can pick up in our hands, something material. Educative materials are reconstructed from analyzed primary sources, and this activity is the analysis and reconstruction phase of what we call "curriculum." Think of a four-year-college major in English as the analysis of primary sources. Getting a grasp on primary sources is made much more efficient in time and money when the primary sources are analyzed with **V** diagrams.

---

[3] Max H. Abrams, *The Mirror and the Lamp: Romantic Theory and the Critical Tradition* (New York: Oxford University Press, 1953).

"Program" is the name for the organization of these materials in antici-pation of their use in sequences of teaching and learning. Program devel-opment can be well-organized with **V** diagrams. The Theory of Educating used in these pages is the best way to connect and integrate the teaching, learning, and curriculum. *Curriculum* refers to the recovery of meaning from bodies of knowledge containing criteria of excellence for use in teach-ing and learning. Curriculum materials have at least five roles. Curriculum materials carry value claims. These five ideas about curriculum work are themselves very significant as

1. vehicles of criteria of excellence;
2. records of prior events used to make new events happen;
3. the authority of the record;
4. conceptual organizers; and
5. multipliers of meaning.

1. VEHICLES OF CRITERIA OF EXCELLENCE. Educative materials are cal-ibrated instruments for use in teaching and learning. They carry with them the criteria of excellence we use to judge that they are what they are claimed to be. The difference between a book, say a novel, and educative materi-als is that the latter carries with it the criteria we use to judge novels as (a) quality novels and (b) useful for educating. It is not merely aesthetic criteria, or criteria of literary merit, that we need, although we certainly need these, but the additional set of judgments about "educability" that we must have.

Good art may be both pedagogically and aesthetically good. For educa-tive materials to carry criteria of excellence, they must pass two major tests: One comes from the standards of the field from which the work originates and the other comes from standards of education. Curriculum analysis consists in bringing these tests to bear upon specific exemplars.

2. RECORDS OF PRIOR EVENTS USED TO MAKE NEW EVENTS HAPPEN. When we, as teachers, think of the curriculum as records of prior events to make new events happen, we get a sense of what we are to do in teaching. Educating is an activity that is in motion. It is a mistake for teachers to rely on others to select the materials, if they cannot specify what events will happen with the use of those materials. Many textbooks fail at this point. *Subject matter should release energy, not block it.* Our efforts should be directed to capitalizing on using records that serve to enlighten further in-quiry. Central to initiating activity is the asking of telling questions, focus questions, personal and social questions. Questions animate events. Text-books change meaning when all the answers are converted into questions. The **V** has a specific place for questions.

3. THE AUTHORITY OF THE RECORD. Conflicts occur in educating. Tension arises when new ideas challenge old and familiar ideas. Genuine

disagreements are found in all disciplines. The experts disagree. Curriculum materials can serve to reduce conflict and tension of educative events when the one-to-one actions of persons are considered. The *authority of record* can be used to resolve conflicts. Records of events are so important that we name them facts. Appeals to the facts of the case often resolve disputes. The *facts* help determine the exact meanings. Another source of conflict reduction comes from the concepts defining and naming regularities in events. Facts are records of events. Appealing to the facts of the case is a powerful way to defuse person-to-person disagreements. The curriculum can serve as a governing device for person-to-person decisions.

4. CONCEPTUAL ORGANIZERS. A conceptually organized curriculum can be of direct help to the thinking of both teachers and students. Human beings think with concepts. To the extent that key concepts and telling questions are clearly in the foreground, these elements serve as "advance organizers." An advance organizer provides ideational scaffolding connecting what learners already know and what they need to know before they begin to learn new material. Advance organizers anticipate future events. Conceptual organizers include advance organizers (Ausubel, 1960, 1963), structured overviews or graphic organizers (Alvermann, 1981; Earle & Barron, 1973), previews (Graves, Cook, & Laberge, 1983), V diagrams with concept maps (Gowin, 1981; Novak & Gowin, 1984; Novak, 1998), and thematic organizers (Alvarez, 1983; Alvarez & Risko, 1989, 2002; Risko & Alvarez, 1986).

A few clear ideas are much better for students than many vague ones buried in baskets of simple information. Much information today is severely simplistic. Lists of disconnected items replace sentences. Flat statements unsupported by meaningful connections often dominate textbooks. The conceptual connective tissue is missing. Students are at a loss to grasp key meanings; as a consequence they can only resort to memorizing without understanding, and learning slows down drastically. A curriculum full of conceptual organizers increases greatly the power of thinking about future events.

5. MULTIPLIERS OF MEANING. Another important role for educative materials is the increase in human intelligence, which the materials permit. Each person does not have to repeat all of human experience to become educated. Selected materials are efficient; they help us get the point in an ordered, direct, clear way. We learn to comprehend a lot from a little. We simplify complexity. Every time new information helps to reorganize the meaning of what is already known, there is added significance. It is the increase in new connections in the pattern or set of relations that *are* the new reorganizations.

The V itself is a multiplier of meaning. Reading around the V, like writing around the V, increases our understanding. It should not feel surprising that we save time and money when we comprehend better.

Are There Fixed Stages of Learning?

Educational stages are qualitatively different in individuals. People learn in many different ways and at many different times in their lives. Whitehead (1929) wrote of a stage of romance, governed by awe and excitement. He thought precision followed romance and that much value is often hidden in precise details. Generalization often occurs from the richness of variety and a satisfaction occurs from seeing the big picture. Whitehead's interesting trio of romance–precision–generalization/satisfaction can be thought of as stages or as just qualities of different events of human understanding. Intrinsic continuity of stages and qualities does not reduce necessarily to sameness. Significant learning is the reconstruction of human experience as that experience changes from a strong feeling of involvement to a strong knowledge yielding power and mastery. Reconstruction need not be forced into fixed stages, we believe.

Is a Concept Map a Firmly Fixed Pattern?

Ranked concepts imply a judgment. A well-thought-out concept map can take the form of a fixed object, but this is not a requirement. We like to think of concept maps as having flexible order. Indeed, we have used the image of a concept map as a rubber sheet. If you pull on the side, or top, or anywhere, you get a new arrangement of concepts. Sometimes taking the bottom-most concept and putting it on top can stimulate thinking in radical new directions. We think with concepts. Thinking changes as concepts change. Thinking with concept maps should stimulate thinking, not stifle it.[4]

Learning

Learning is the active reorganization of an existing pattern of meaning. Students are responsible for an achievement of grasped meaning. Understanding what has been taught or learned as a basis for past ideas is the fertile ground for new meaning to occur. Earlier we wrote that educating begins in midstream with people who already know something. Educating can begin when children learn a language. It is the person's present knowledge that supplies the power for new knowledge to be acquired. For the person as a learner, two things are of utmost importance: what the person can claim to know and what the person can claim to need to know.

The problem of learning can be stated simply: to make connections between what is to be learned (what the learner needs to know) and what one knows already. A person can reveal prior knowledge by either concept

---

[4] Procedures for developing a concept map are given in Chapter 8. A scoring protocol for concept maps is shown in Appendix III.

mapping or by "Laying the **V**" on personal knowledge. Children reveal their grasp of events by talking to us, and to themselves. Ask children what they know about almost anything, and they will tell you. It is surprising what untutored children already know. Television and video games sometimes can be powerfully educative. Too much violence and speed can do damage to young learners' capacities to absorb knowledge that takes a long time to grow.

Learning is precious. A lifetime of learning can begin early in life. John Dewey is famous for his interest in and wisdom on children. He recognized that children do their own learning. We agree. Everyone must do their own learning; no one will or can learn for us. Learning is an act of an individual to connect the new with the old and to work voluntarily to fit them together. The variability in the learning process is far greater than the central tendencies.

Educative Events. Educative events are artifactual and mutable; they are events, and they are eventful. They are inventions; they are social constructions; their realities vary as their constructions vary. They are deliberately set by human beings and depend for their existence on the cultural patterns by which volitional agents relate to one another. Artifacts in education consist of test scores, questionnaires, surveys, and opinions, and therefore they are difficult to interpret as records of events. These artifacts are records of human activity that do not occur naturally. Because humans change their minds, artifacts as records change and are subject to different meanings and interpretations from different people at different times. Learning is an eventful process, an action the learner *chooses* to undertake to change the meaning of experience for himself or herself. This choice to learn can be risky, daring, scary, and uncomfortable. As such it, too, is artifactual, culturally patterned.

Students are responsible for causing their own learning by taking an active part in the event. Learning is a process under the *deliberate* cause of the learner. Teachers do not cause learning in students. It is incumbent on the teacher to connect the known of the students' prior knowledge and world experience to the new information that is being taught. The teacher's role is to help learners to understand the initiating event. Teachers can help students in making connections between thinking and feeling that leads them to act on these feelings and thoughts in their problem solving and decision making. Students can often feel a threat to act for the first time on a new found idea. The future events may be *risky*. For learning to occur, students need to be aware of how to make sense of the materials they are studying. Do I, or don't I act? Learners need to be able to relate their trusted background knowledge and experience to risk new information or a new situation. This requires keen motivation on the part of the learner. When learners are really motivated, answers are sought to questions that deal with the process of learning: the "how" and "why," the future and my grasp of its meaning.

Drill and Concept Learning. Drill is usually disciplined group training based on constant repetition and correction of mistakes. A drill is like an exercise in gymnastics. One runs through a drill (as in a squad) and one runs through warm-up exercises. There is nothing new in these matters. A drill is an action that moves learning in the direction of *overlearning*. When one wants automatic and unthinking behavior, nothing better can be recommended than drilling to the point of automatic responses.

One does not learn concepts through drill, for drill presupposes conceptual understanding. Confusing conceptual understanding with drilling is a pedagogical mistake. Conceptual learning is coming to grasp a new concept in order to think new thoughts. Drill presupposes that the thoughts are clear; it is the doing that needs to be made automatic.

Taking Charge of One's Own Learning. The key idea is the student's individual responsibility for his or her own learning. Although it may seem easy to say that students *have* responsibility, we need to see how they can *take* responsibility. When students learn that they are actually responsible for their own learning, they gain power over the conditions of their lives.

Along with this general sense of responsibility, there are specific responsibilities students have in an educative event. One of these responsibilities is to pay attention so that meaning can be grasped and shared. One pays the cost of learning by paying attention. The student must give back to the teacher some idea of meanings grasped and significance felt. The student is testing meanings at this point as a prior condition for learning them. The student is also testing the teacher to find out if the teacher made a mistake. Both must work together to share meanings, for unless the student takes responsibility for sharing meaning, the teacher is disenfranchised and cannot teach. For the teacher to have the right to teach the student has the duty to share meaning. This reciprocity of rights and duties is part of the condition of governance in educating.

V Knowledge about Learning. The **V** gives us knowledge about learning. It shows us elements of knowledge in their relation to other elements. This knowledge now becomes directive in learning something new. If the point of the new learning is a new concept, then we know we should try to relate this new concept both up and down the structure of the **V**. We know we should try to relate the concept to events by searching for regularities in events to which the concept refers. We further should relate the new concept to other concepts by searching for its place on a concept map or its place within a conceptual structure. So with any new element to be learned, we need to find out what kind of epistemological element it is (a concept, a fact, a knowledge claim), see how that element functions in the knowledge structure, and take appropriate action after this analysis to fit the new to the old.

Knowing the structure of knowledge gives us knowledge about what to do in any new learning experience. We fit the new to the old as we see where it fits the knowledge structure. Having knowledge about knowledge gives us a powerful way to regulate our learning about learning. Once we have learned about learning we have second-order knowledge that can drive powerfully and efficiently our subsequent learning and the creation of first-order knowledge.

Governance

Governance controls the meaning that controls the effort. This formula states that governing events control the meaning that controls the effort put into teaching, into curriculum, and into learning. The definitions in this book of these commonplaces tell what counts and what does not count as an instance of teaching, curriculum, and learning. If, for example, one accepts the view that teaching is the achievement of shared meaning, then that idea tells a teacher what certain actions mean as examples of teaching. The meaning controls the effort. Teachers and students must work together over the curriculum until congruence of meaning is achieved. If learners, as students, recognize the necessary role they must play in the sharing of meaning, then specific actions are guided by this idea. Students who realize "grasping meaning" and "getting the point" and "feeling the significance" in the sharing of meaning will act, as students, very differently from those who do not understand this view of what is involved in educating. A curriculum that reveals the structure of knowledge, and especially the relevant criteria of excellence, will make the specific meaning accessible to teachers and students and will thereby control their efforts. Each of the four commonplaces has a role in governing the others; none is totally overriding of the others – they must interact, for each has a quality required by the others. Regular use of these ideas saves time. A lot of time. In some cases up to or more than 50 percent of the time allotted.

Governance enters the context of educating because of the need to control the meaning that events are to have as educative events. Our main concern is with what we should think, feel, and do in order to control the meaning. Governance is power in a social setting that is required to bring together teaching, curriculum, and learning.

Through education we come into possession of our powers, and that includes power over educative events. When we consciously and deliberately make educative events happen, we have power over these events. But these events are social events, involving teachers, learners, and other persons, and these events almost always involve a sharing of power. Teachers, typically, have power over students, but the curriculum has power over teachers. Students have power over their own learning if it is truly their *own* learning. The sharing of meaning between teachers and learners and curriculum requires the cooperation of all parties. Each of these three commonplaces must be harmonized if the educative event is to happen. The proper representation and protection of special claims and powers is the special power of governance, the fourth commonplace.

Power over events comes from controlling meaning. We govern through mediated meanings. By telling others and ourselves what events mean, we come to make sense of our experience, and we come to have power over nature and experience. Meaning is social. When meanings are constructed so that we "get the point," that arouses our powers, animates our interests, and leads us on to new events; we see connections in events. Meanings are social constructions that enable us to exercise the powers of inference, of self-understanding, and of thoughtful action – all of which permit us to come to agreements, to share purposes, to control events in terms of what we think they should mean. Governance derives from shared meanings, some of which are taken as controlling.

Shared meaning is what makes educating possible and is also particularly important at the points of choice where activities of educating are governed. We have here one basic phenomenon working in two related but different ways. *The construction of meaning not only derives from the social setting, but also works to govern the social setting.* Devices of social control work on this principle. Social control is necessary in educating because educating is a social event. Social events are controlled by controlling the meaning they are to have. As we create meaning out of human experience, we create forms of permissible social interaction. In human history many such forms have been invented. Wars and other disputes of power have followed from the invention of different forms of social control. Fascism, socialism, and democracy are names given to some of these inventions. The important point is to realize that these forms *are* social inventions and social constructions; they exist as social realities.

This theory of educating focuses on changing the meaning of experience, but notice, not only does educating change the meaning of experience, but new meanings work to stabilize further changes in experience. Not only is learning the active reorganization of meaning, but reorganized and reconstructed meanings govern subsequent learning. Thus if we wish to govern educative events, we should look to what we need to think about and do to control the meaning educative events are to have.

For those of us concerned with educating, the quest must be for power over valid meaning. We must learn to write our meaning scripts for ourselves. We must participate in conceiving of the criteria of excellence (rather than success) that help to make sense of nature and human experience. In administration and social governance, control over valid meaning is the most direct control over effort. In a social democratic government, both oppressive power and powerlessness are to be avoided. The task of government is to secure cooperation among people so that mutually shared purposes can be achieved. The task of governance in educating is the same.

Societal Learning Environments

Educating is a social practice that takes into consideration both formal and out-of-school experiences. As learners we need to make connections between our societal learning environments and the formal school-type environments. Older students often work and go to college at the same time. Daily they experience these two domains of human experience. When each contributes to the other, then the learner is making good use of time. These societal and school factors are complex, interrelated, and interactive entities that influence our education. Societal factors include that portion of a person's education acquired outside the formal classroom (see Cortes, 1981, 1986; also Neumann & Peterson, 1997). It comprises the informal curriculum of home, neighborhood, community, peer groups, organizations, occupations, media, and other socializing forces that combine to educate each of us throughout our lives. Also included are cultural and spiritual influences that affect the learning process.

School factors focus on formal in-school functions such as curriculum, school organization, counseling, assessment, teacher expectations, behavior, and so forth. Being aware of the sociocultural context in which students live helps the teacher to make learning a meaningful connection between the classroom and the students' world environment (Alvarez, 1993; Dewey, 1902; Donham, 1949; Erickson, 1984; Sarason, 1990).

There is evidence to suggest that young children are given more chances to explore, converse, share ideas, and ask questions at home than when they are in formal school settings (e.g., Goodman & Haussler, 1986; Hall, 1987; Lipman, 2003; Tizard & Hughes, 1984). Spontaneity is a key that separates home learning from school learning. Children use language at home to express their thoughts and are concerned more with meaning than form. Home-type learning allows for knowledge responsive to the child's curiosity, interest, and a need to understand and communicate ideas that emerge from informal events. Authentic questions and problems are discussed and solved as the need arises. Conversely, structure, form, rules, and memorization tend to be associated with school-type learning. This occurs, in part, because teachers follow guides within published reading materials that contain answers corresponding to predetermined questions. Using the V helps teachers and students to focus on real events happening now in their lives.

Lessons should be planned that take into consideration the relevant question: Does this new information relate to my student's own experiences? To be learned in a meaningful manner there needs to be an association made by the learner with an existing system or organization of experience so that understanding can occur. In too many instances, new information is connected to previously learned lessons, instead of linking it to what the student has acquired in his or her out-of-school experience:

> The teacher says, "Do you not remember what we learned from the book last week?" – instead of saying "Do you not recall such and such a thing that you have seen or heard?" As a result, there are built up detached and independent systems of experience instead of reacting to enlarge and refine them. Pupils are taught to live in two separate worlds, one the world of out-of-school experience, the other the world of books and lessons. Then we stupidly wonder why what is studied in school counts so little outside. (Dewey, 1933, p. 259)

Making connections between what is known and what is to be learned are important considerations when teaching and when learning new information. Taking time to ascertain an individual's societal curriculum makes this process more enlightening and enables learning to occur in ways that are relevant instead of artificial. Artificial learning takes place when new information is perceived by the learner as being not essential or irrelevant and therefore is committed to rote memorization for later retrieval on an examination. This practice of artificiality also occurs when new information is not part of a learner's out-of-school experience and therefore few, if any, connections are linked to make this a meaningful learning experience.

EMPOWERING STUDENTS TO LEARN FOR THEMSELVES

Being empowered is a process for us to come to self-understanding. Self-empowerment is a notion that one can cause his or her own learning while trusting others in the process. As students, we are responsible for and cause our own learning, and we need to be empowered to learn new ideas. As teachers we need to empower our students to learn for themselves.

Teachers can assist students in the learning process. First, teachers can change the meaning of experience for students. By this we mean that students need to be shown how to learn.[5] Learning how to learn is an assumption made by some teachers in that these teachers feel that students already know how to use effective learning strategies (e.g., note-taking, summarizing, writing coherent papers, reading and understanding the special and technical vocabulary of a chapter). Together, the teacher and student can benefit from teacher-assisted and student-initiated strategies by working in a collaborative endeavor by sharing meaning in an effort to resolve confusion and clarify misconceptions. Of course, strategies alone do little to aid the learning process if the materials selected have little relevance or meaning to the student and the topic of study.

---

[5] Joseph D. Novak and D. Bob Gowin, *Learning How To Learn* (New York: Cambridge University Press, 1984).

2

Simplifying Complexity without Denying It

Principle 2. Sharing meaning simplifies complexity through educating ourselves and others.

Simplifying complexity without denying it demands that *meaning must be shared* among a wide variety of persons and concerns. These concerns and issues are on a level of ascension on which meaning needs to be shared. The notion is to formulate connection making among complex ideas and events. *Sharing meaning simplifies complexity* that is brought about by educating ourselves and others. This process begins by requiring that we "put on the table" the meanings we use to make sense of our experiences. The next step is to try to share these meanings, to negotiate differences, *to grasp a meaning not our own.* Our task is to find ways to make the unfamiliar more familiar. By understanding how meaning is constructed out of our experience, we can come to share meanings.

Because human experience is so rich, and learning so idiosyncratic, the diversity of meanings is extraordinary. In a sense, *each of us is the author of our own text.* We know, or think we know, what things mean to us. As we go through educating events (teaching, learning, curriculum, and governance), we are trying to simplify the complex (by extracting net meanings) and to "complexify the simples" by taking extracted meanings to new places to make new events happen.

CONSTRUCTING MEANING

Meaning is constructed when we use signs or symbols (e.g., words, numbers, labels, tags, concepts, signifiers) to "name the world." We use a term to mark off one thing from other things. It is as if we tie a tag on an object ("chair" or "coffee bean") or an event ("raining," "eating," or "talking"). Once labeled, we can next look at the label and see if we agree about its use on this occasion. We may decide to change "chair" to "antique chair" or "Chippendale," or to change "coffee bean" to "Colombian coffee bean." We may change "eating" to "dining" and "talking" to "conversation" or "dialogue." In some circles, each of these changes in meaning marks an increasing sophistication – *an escalation of value*. By this change, we do not lose the first "primitive" meaning, we gain the distinction of the more sophisticated meaning. Some people may object to the judgment that using the more sophisticated meaning (i.e., the making of a finer distinction among objects and events) *is* an escalation of value.

Refinements in meaning do not necessarily increase the value. Without the primitive meaning, the sophisticated refinement would have no basis in events and objects. It is always important to be able to tie meanings back to experienced events. Or, in other words, no matter how long the thread of meaning is, it is important to be sure that the thread is not broken. The human mind is so agile and gifted with powers of inference that we often take for granted the fragility of the fabrics made up of mere threads of meaning, any one of which is easily broken. Warning: We *can deceive* ourselves by the meanings we tie together.

MEANING AND TRUTH

Making sense of experience by constructing meaning does not ensure that such meaning is also *true*. The test of social agreement (Do you and I *mean* the same thing by the terms we use?) is much more immediate. While one test of truth (*consensus gentium*) relies primarily on shared meaning (i.e., consensus), such meaning sharing may not be true, given other tests of truth (e.g., the more strenuous and difficult test of verifying under conditions where falsification is readily possible). So, meaning and truth are different. All truth claims must be first meaningful, but not all meaningful claims are tested for their truth-value. The issues of meaning and truth are discussed in philosophy under the name of "epistemology," the study of the structure of knowledge (see Chapter 4).

CONSTRUCTIVIST LEARNING

Constructivist learning occurs when learners try to make sense of material presented to them. This kind of learning has traditionally been referred to as meaningful learning, or learning by understanding, and is distinguished from rote learning, or learning by memorizing (Ausubel, 1968; Mayer, 2003; Wertheimer, 1959).

Children and adolescents form mental models or personal constructs of how they perceive the world in which they live; the world does not create these constructs for them. As Kelly (1955) explains, constructs are individually built and "tried on for size" as one views world events. These constructs are sometimes categorized into groups of systems consisting of subordinate, coordinate, and superordinate relationships. They are used to forecast events and to assess the accuracy of the events after they have occurred. As learners, we constantly test our interpretations of the world and revise our mental models or personal constructs as we experience and test alternative explanations throughout our lives.

Constructivism is based on the notion that learners are actively engaged in building theories about the world and the way it works. This inquiry often is a natural process that places learners in the role of a detective or scientist who engages in experimentation and problem solving on his or her own. In this view, cognitive structures are not fixed but vary with the development and experience of the individual. When in the classroom, the teacher, can provide contexts that facilitate theory building by using meaningful materials and by making use of students' experiences (Chaille & Britain, 1991).

It seems that an important role of a teacher, when teaching content or subject disciplines such as science, is to aid students' ability to reflect upon what they know about a given topic and make available strategies that will enhance their conceptual understanding of text and science experiments. Developing metacognition, the ability to monitor one's own knowledge about a topic of study and activate appropriate strategies, enhances a student's learning when he or she is faced with reading, writing, and problem-solving situations (see Brown & Baker, 1984). Metacognitive learning occurs whenever individuals are able to self-regulate and control their own learning when confronted with new knowledge. In order for metacognition to occur, one must have strategies for monitoring his or her understanding of a given topic. Recently, strategies have been reported in which students are actively constructing their own concepts. One instructional strategy that may significantly enhance the learner's ability to "know" (i.e., to categorize, organize, and integrate new information) is hierarchical concept mapping, and another is **V** diagrams (Gowin, 1981; Novak, 1990, 1998; Novak & Gowin, 1984). Both of these strategies enable learners to come to know and understand new information in ways that go beyond mere memorizing for short-term retention, toward the application of these newly learned concepts to other situations.

This Constructivist approach to learning focuses on the student rather than the curriculum, the kind of assessment, or the type of technology to aid student achievement. The quality of student learning is of prime concern, not the amount of information the students have acquired. Learning with and using technology as a tool is the emphasis of the Exploring Minds Network described in Chapter 9. The journaling component, notebook section, student/teacher study, and Interactive **V** diagram are some of the features that enable students to share in dialogic exchanges, provide opportunities for analyzing and synthesizing ideas, think about learning, and engage in authentic tasks and assessments in meaningful learning situations.

Learning that is meaningful, rather than rote, enables students to better understand new ideas whether presented in traditional contexts or in educational technology situations. In essence, constructivism embodies the concept of meaningful learning and takes into consideration thinking, feeling, and acting on these thoughts and feelings to bring about a better understanding of how the world works and how individuals can shape its progress.

MINDFUL LEARNING

Simplifying complexity also takes into consideration mindful learning: the ability to view situations or problems from multiple perspectives rather than following one linear path of inquiry to achieve a specified outcome. Simplifying complexity does not necessarily equate to expediency such as in getting to the "right" answer. It demands thoughtful resolution through mindful inquiry, which may or may not result in finality.

Mindful learning is a *process* where meaning is given to outcomes rather than as a means of achieving desired outcomes. Ellen Langer contrasts mindful learning with intelligence by stipulating that mindfulness is a *state* when we implicitly or explicitly (1) view a situation from several perspectives, (2) see information presented in the situation as novel, (3) attend to the context in which we are perceiving the information, and eventually, (4) create new categories through which this information may be understood.[1] Being mindful requires us to be more observant, to evaluate stability, to ask more questions, to take into consideration the context in which the events take place, to be more cognizant of knowledge claims rather than knowledge absolutes, and as Alfred North Whitehead proclaimed to think about and imagine "unrealized possibilities."[2]

MINDING SIMPLIFIES COMPLEXITY

Minding, the process of the active mind, always works to simplify complexities. This is the key to what our minds do – they are minding events the person is actually involved with at the time. Like minding the store or business, or minding the children, we are using our minds to pay attention to unfolding events. We are anticipating new and unrealized possibilities. We are minding the future. We are minding "from" the future as we anticipate new and future possibilities.

[1] Ellen J. Langer, *The Power of Mindful Learning* (Reading, MA: Addison-Wesley, 1997).
[2] Alfred North Whitehead, *Modes of Thought* (New York: Macmillan Company, 1938).

It is this state of mindfulness that we examine the contexts to which **V** diagrams are used to initiate, carry out, and finalize research investigations and evaluate documents, programs, or works; these diagrams are used in the planning of lessons by teachers for their students. Within this context the meaning that is derived from applying the structure of knowledge to educating using Gowin's (1981) theory encompasses the four common-places of educating: teaching, curriculum, learning, and governance.

GETTING SMART ABOUT KNOWLEDGE

If the intent of research is to make knowledge, then understanding knowledge making (epistemology) is important. Studying whatever one claims to be knowledge they have produced creates knowledge about knowledge. The **V** is used to diagram the issues that are produced by claims of knowledge. Through its arrangement of the epistemic elements the **V** reveals its source of conceptual and methodological processes.

School has "trained" people to become single-minded in arriving at solutions. Everyone is working toward a predisposed answer with the majority learning and understanding little of what is taking place. What is more disturbing is that students "don't care" if they understand what is being taught. One student replied, "I don't have to understand – I just need to know it." Serious discussion is diverted into simplistic talk. *Students defy their own curiosity*. They shut off learning, especially if it appears difficult and requires sustained effort. Learning is reduced to its simplest denominator, where learning facts and minimal concepts are the desired outcomes of the system measured by standardized tests for differentiation. Learning demands time, effort, and curiosity to be long-lasting and effective. Students are seldom placed in situations where they are in charge of their own learning outcomes. The **V** enables students, teachers, and researchers to become more thoughtful, more mindful, and more curious when deliberating and engaging in knowledge making.

V DIAGRAMS AND SELF-EFFICACY

Albert Bandura defines self-efficacy as "the belief in one's capabilities to organize and execute the sources of action required to manage prospective situations."[3] Self-efficacy, an internal set of belief systems, enables individuals to monitor their thoughts, feelings, and actions. Being able to derive meaning from their experiences comes from learning from others, reflecting on what has been experienced in the past, and being able to monitor one's own behavior in the process.

---

[3] Albert Bandura, *Social Foundations of Thought and Action: A Social Cognitive Theory* (Englewood Cliffs, NJ: Prentice Hall, 1986).

Students are accustomed to having the teacher "set the stage" for planning a research investigation. Questions are predisposed, materials are provided, and guidelines are given to the student. When students use V diagrams they become in charge of their own learning. This role reversal can lead to frustration if the teacher and the student are not prepared. After all, how often are students asked to direct their own learning experiences? Responsibility is now transferred to the student from the teacher. Likewise, when a teacher/researcher is first confronted with the prospect of developing a V diagram, the challenge is formidable. At first, this teacher/researcher imagines that it is quite simple to "fill-in" the appropriate elements arrayed along the sides and within the V diagram. However, once ideas begin to swirl around, the process becomes complex and provides a stimulating experience for the teacher/researcher to think how the events, concepts, and records directly relate to the research questions. Most of the thinking takes place on the left side of the V. This theoretical/conceptual thinking side determines how well the investigation is conceived. It is estimated that as much as 75 percent of our time in the development of the research process is devoted to this left side of the V.

When students are asked to formulate a question(s) to investigate a given topic, they may be placed into an unfamiliar situation to "act" rather than "react" to one in authority. Students are not accustomed to this role reversal in formal school settings. They encounter these types of situations outside of school in their societal interactions, but not in their formal curriculum. If a trusting relationship is not established between the student and the teacher, this disparity can become paramount to blocking the feelings and thoughts necessary to initiate, carry out, and finalize the research investigation or lesson.

The goal is for the student to become the leader at the forefront of the learning process with the teacher as facilitator. Students are placed in the position of "showing" the teacher what they can do. For many this position becomes a liberating experience that enables them to take responsibility for their own learning by thinking about learning in ways that differ from their previous conventional teaching/learning experiences. Once this trusting relationship has been established the teacher is able to facilitate the learning process by guiding students to achieve meaningful learning outcomes. The V diagram is a metacognitive tool that mediates this transition for the learner to "think and reason" for himself or herself.

V DIAGRAMS AS A TOOL FOR SIMPLIFYING COMPLEXITY

A V diagram simplifies complexity by helping us to see, more explicitly, the processes involved in knowledge creation. It serves as a tool for discussing the meaning and value of research investigations and thereby acts to clarify complexities through meaningful dialogues that enable simplicity to evolve without denying its convolution. Each element on the **V** interacts with every other element and, during this process, we become intimately involved with making new knowledge either through our own research initiative or when analyzing and evaluating other documents.

Joseph Novak (1998) describes the **V** as a Constructivist tool in the formulation of meaning and also of knowledge.

The beauty of the Vee heuristic is its comprehensiveness and also simplicity. It serves to illustrate that there are a dozen or so epistemic elements that are involved in constructing or examining a piece of knowledge, and yet it places these elements into a single structure that helps to illustrate how each of these elements function (p. 82).

The conceptual/theoretical left side of the **V** guides our thoughts and efforts toward knowing and understanding the knowledge and value claims produced on the methodological right side of the **V**. The **V** heuristic is Constructivist in nature in that a piece of knowledge we are investigating depends on the elements that comprise the **V**. If we choose different questions, use different concepts, principles, or theories, make different records or transform records differently, we can legitimately arrive at different knowledge claims about the same events and objects. In short, how we see events or objects in the world depends on how we personally construct our vision of these events and objects.

V diagrams serve the dual purpose of recognizing complexity and the basic simplicity of the knowledge construction process. **V** diagrams enable the user to think creatively when actively engaging with the elements arrayed on the **V**. **V**s can be used individually and also in group settings. During this process, reflection becomes paramount for understanding the how and why the knowledge claims and value claims are constructed in relationship to the focus/research question(s). **V** diagrams serve as an anchor for conceptualizing the elements arrayed on the theoretical/conceptual and the methodological sides, and the focus/research questions and events in the middle. The **V** also serves as a comprehensive tool in both the learning and evaluation process for authentic assessment.

Part One

Summary

Educating is a social event of sharing meanings. Meanings can be shared between individuals – this makes the events of educating possible. The conditions of shared meaning, in the context of educating, have patterns, and thus educative events can be subjected to rational (planned) inquiry, even though the regularities are artifactual (not natural). Making educative events happen is a consequence of human choice, invention, and inauguration. Literally, thousands of educative events happen. Formal education is not only a deliberate intervention in the lives of people but an intervention with a highly selected and refined set of materials. These materials must be tailored for their meaningfulness, and they must embody the criteria of excellence. Furthermore, in formal education we believe that repeated events of deliberate intervention gradually shape habits such that *persons are liberated by and freed from both the intervention and the materials.* As durable and reliable as educational activities are, they are also short-lived and ephemeral; no single characterization will capture completely the whole scene. So, recognizing that we are not trying to define the ineffable, we use the following statement to provide a working sense of direction.

Educating, as an eventful process, changes the meaning of human experience by intervention in the lives of people with meaningful materials, to develop thinking, feeling, and acting as habitual dispositions in order to make sense of human experience by using appropriate criteria of excellence.

The notion of meaning is a foundation in the theory of educating. To teach is to try deliberately to change the meaning of a student's experience, and a student must grasp the meaning before he or she deliberately learns something new. Learning is never entirely cognitive. Feelings accompany any thinking that moves to reorganize meaning. In educating, we are trying to integrate thinking, feeling, and acting.

Believing we should seek simplicity, and preserve complexity, we advocate four commonplaces of education plus one: teaching, curriculum, learning, governance plus the societal environment. In this theory of educating, making sense of educative events is paramount. The key event is *a teacher teaching meaningful information to a student who grasps the meaning of the information under humane conditions of social control.* The teacher initiates the event, the information and materials (curriculum) are guides to the event; the students take part in the event; the event as a social event has distinctive qualities governing it; and the societal environment is an important consideration that encompasses the social milieu of the event. Each of the four commonplaces plus one gets separate analysis but always with a concern for how each commonplace relates to the others.

Educating helps people come into conscious possession of their powers (and their own world), especially the flourishing integration of thinking, feeling, and acting. As educative events come more and more under the control of individuals, educating becomes self-educating. Just as writing is rewriting, educating is reeducating. It is a continual process of working and reworking and structuring and restructuring the qualities of human experience interacting with nature.

To teach is to extend, change, or give new meanings to experience. Changing meaning and changing behavior are contingently, not causally, related in human experience. We distinguish behavior from action by saying that an action is a behavior with meaning. Learning, in the context of educating, stresses that the student should be free to choose to learn. The student is the efficient cause of learning, which means, in part, that the responsibility for learning is the learner's (not the teacher's). The curriculum stands, separately, as an object of inquiry. Knowledge about knowledge is the guide to curriculum inquiry. The curriculum is an analyzed record of prior events that we use to make new events happen; the curriculum is to be related to teaching and to learning, but not reduced to either. Each of the three commonplaces must be harmonized if the educative event is to happen. The proper representation and protection of special claims and powers is the special power of governance, the fourth commonplace. Governance is power in a social setting that is required to bring together teaching, curriculum, and learning. The societal curriculum influences the learner in formal school settings. These societal and school factors are complex, interrelated, and interactive entities that influence our education. Societal factors are the portion of a person's education acquired outside the formal classroom. The learning process is comprised of the informal curriculum of home, neighborhood, community, peer groups, organizations, occupations, media, and other socializing forces cultural and spiritual influences, which combine to educate each of us throughout our lives.

Simplistic solutions to complex problems do little to enhance the learning process of coming to know and understand. If we want to be knowledgeable in dealing with educational problems and situations, we need a theory that is designed to guide us in the process of learning and evaluating what is happening and what has already occurred. The theory of educating espoused in our book deals with the commonplaces of educating and the student's ability to become self-empowered. When confronted with novel problems or situations, we need to be mindful of the various landscapes that the problem or situation offers us. Our goal is to view its complexities without denying them, and to simplify them so that they can be better known and understood.

When judging the end of educating, it may be helpful to make a distinction between ends and aims. An end of educating is self-educating; an aim of educating is to change the meaning of an experience. That is our focus as educators: to aim at those qualities of present experience, which are in themselves educative events that permit educating to happen. In self-educating, each of us *act* – these actions are necessary for educating. Educating and miseducating are universal human phenomena. They are the ways that one generation of human beings shapes the beliefs, behaviors, and actions of subsequent generations.

The chapters that follow describe how the **V** diagram simplifies complexity without denying it. The **V** diagram deciphers the complexities of knowledge and knowledge making. It is a tool used to engage the mind in a thoughtful and insightful manner to know, understand, and clarify the complexities afforded by events. The **V** makes our intentions, processes, and outcomes worthwhile and meaningful.

Seeking simplicity without denying complexity is a principle that requires much thought. The **V** diagram is a heuristic that can be used to better analyze and understand the structure of knowledge of a given topic. Revealing the complexity of a given topic with a **V** diagram enables the user to better understand its structure by simplifying the educative event so that superior knowledge may be attained.

PART TWO

THE V DIAGRAM

3

Thinking around the V

Principle 3. Knowledge has a structure of parts and relations between the parts.

Thinking "around the **V**" takes us up and down the parts of the **V**. We can begin anywhere. A good place to begin is with one's world view. The world view is a name for one's stable system of beliefs and behaviors. It is what you are comfortable with in your living experience, how you set about events, what you know how to do, and how confident you are that you do really know something important and useful. Your awareness of your keenest interests, what you pay attention to, and how you anticipate future possibilities are very important. Your world view will not change very much, or very fast, but it can change and grow with new experiences of new meanings. As you learn to appreciate the power the **V** has to help you get a grip on things, you will change. You will begin to get smart in new ways.

Meaning must be grasped before deliberate learning can occur. It is not enough to know what the topic is about, one must understand why and how new information is related to what is already known. The **V** diagram is one tool that can be used to enable learners to focus on educative events to build upon existing knowledge. It is a tool that can be used by teachers, researchers, and students to plan, carry out, and finalize a research investigation to learn about the structure of knowledge.

V DIAGRAMS: AN OVERVIEW

The **V** diagram was developed as a way to aid in the understanding of meaningful relationships among events, processes, or objects. It is a tool that helps one to observe the interplay between what is known and what needs to be known or understood. Upon completion, a **V** diagram is a record of an event that was investigated. The **V** diagram serves three purposes: (1) planning a research project, (2) analyzing a research article or document, and (3) acting as a teaching/learning tool.

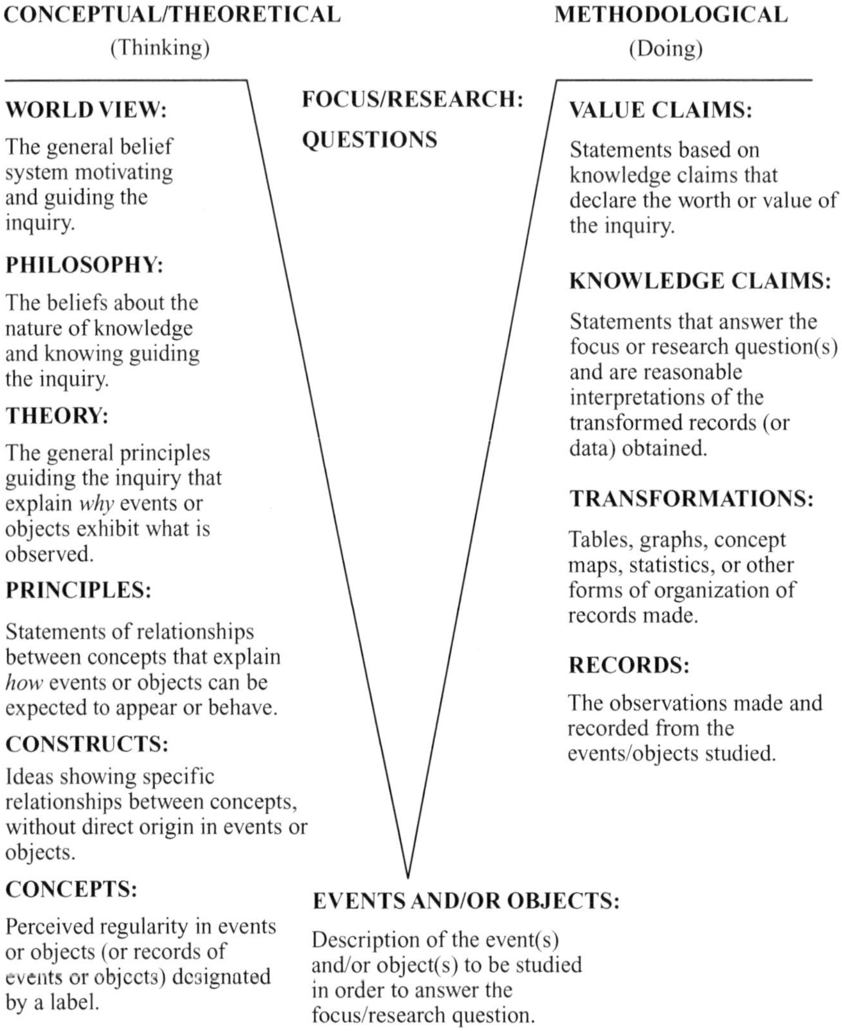

CONCEPTUAL/THEORETICAL
(Thinking)

METHODOLOGICAL
(Doing)

FOCUS/RESEARCH:

QUESTIONS

WORLD VIEW:

The general belief system motivating and guiding the inquiry.

PHILOSOPHY:

The beliefs about the nature of knowledge and knowing guiding the inquiry.

THEORY:

The general principles guiding the inquiry that explain *why* events or objects exhibit what is observed.

PRINCIPLES:

Statements of relationships between concepts that explain *how* events or objects can be expected to appear or behave.

CONSTRUCTS:

Ideas showing specific relationships between concepts, without direct origin in events or objects.

CONCEPTS:

Perceived regularity in events or objects (or records of events or objects) designated by a label.

VALUE CLAIMS:

Statements based on knowledge claims that declare the worth or value of the inquiry.

KNOWLEDGE CLAIMS:

Statements that answer the focus or research question(s) and are reasonable interpretations of the transformed records (or data) obtained.

TRANSFORMATIONS:

Tables, graphs, concept maps, statistics, or other forms of organization of records made.

RECORDS:

The observations made and recorded from the events/objects studied.

EVENTS AND/OR OBJECTS:

Description of the event(s) and/or object(s) to be studied in order to answer the focus/research question.

FIGURE 3.1. Gowin's **V** showing epistemological elements that are involved in the construction or description of new knowledge.

The **V** is a name derived from the shape of the diagram. A **V** diagram is a structured, visual means of relating the methodological aspects of an activity to its underlying conceptual aspects. It focuses on the salient role of concepts in learning and retention. The components of the **V** diagram are shown in Figure 3.1.

Notice that the **V** diagram has a theoretical/conceptual (thinking) left side and a methodological (doing) right side. Both sides *actively interact* with each other through the use of the focus or research question(s) that directly relate to events and/or objects at the point of the **V** to be observed.

A telling question, or a focus/research question, is a verbal form of meaning that indicates or signifies an *uncertainty* in an event or object of interest to the questioner. A Telling Question is more of an umbrella type of inquiry. A Telling Question also raises uncertainty as it tells us that events can be studied in a new and important way. The uncertainty comes when you have to change your mind's thinking about patterns in events you assume have been regular in the past. Telling questions tell you to do something new, to start a *quest* for understanding the world in a different way. Questions initiate uncertainty. An inquiry begins a quest for certainty.

The **V** heuristic is developed to enable students to understand the structure of knowledge (e.g., isolated facts, relational networks, hierarchies, and combinations) and processes of knowledge construction (Gowin, 1981; Novak & Gowin, 1984). The fundamental assumption is that knowledge is not absolute, but it is dependent upon the concepts, theories, and methodologies by which we view the world. The philosophical basis of the **V** diagram makes concepts, and propositions composed of concepts, the central elements in the structure of knowledge and the construction of meaning.

The theoretical/conceptual side includes *philosophy, theory*, and *principles/conceptual systems* (which include developing a concept map), and *concepts*, all of which are related to each other and to the *events* and/or *objects*, and the methodological side of the **V**. When thinking about a question, or planning, studying, or interpreting an event, the thinking process does not occur in isolation. The path that researchers take to look at a particular investigation is influenced by their conceptual view of the research process. Their philosophies, theories, and perspectives lead them to ask certain questions, to design a particular event that they think will provide answers, and to interpret the data in a particular way. The left side of the **V** contains important components that are often neglected in research investigations. This portion of the **V** forces the researchers to be more explicit about the role that their *world view* plays in their research by requiring them to think about the *philosophies, theories, principles*, and *concepts* that are guiding their inquiry.

The methodological side includes *value claims, knowledge claims, transformations*, and *records*. These components form the activities of research. These records (facts) of events and/or objects are made by various types of data collecting instruments (e.g., log entries, journals, data from automated telescopes, video tapes to capture related events or objects, interviews, field notes, questionnaires, measurements of time, length, weight, height, temperature, and related documents). When planning a research investigation, it is important to think about what types of instruments you will use to record the events. The facts will then be transformed into data and organized by tables, graphs, charts, figures, and dialogues. These tabulated results enable you to make knowledge and value claims.

Knowledge claims are answers to the focus or research questions; claims to knowledge in the context that produced them. Typically, researchers focus on knowledge claims (the results of the study and what the results mean) without considering the value claims (the worth of the study) associated with the research investigation either before or after its completion. The value claim incorporates the researcher's views about knowledge. Knowledge is a human construct and knowledge-generating research cannot escape judgments of its worth. "What good is it?" "What uses does it have?" "Why is it important?" "For whom is it intended?" "What did it cost?" "What benefits does it provide?"

To go beyond knowing, we need understanding. The V diagram aids the researcher in focusing ideas, rearranging and revisiting these arrangements before, during, and after a study. Once a study is completed and interpretations of the arrayed components of the V are analyzed, an understanding of the knowledge derived from critical analysis is achieved. While this understanding of knowledge and its value seldom result in absolute resolution, it does provide the stimulus for future possibilities involving critical and imaginative thinking. Upon completion, the V serves as a template from which to write the report or paper.

While there is no set way to read a V diagram (either from left to right or right to left, top to bottom, or anywhere in between), it is advisable to begin with the events at the point of the V to the focus or research question(s) above. The reason for such a progression is that the *event* is paramount in determining the focus or research question(s) for the inquiry and the subsequent interplay among the theoretical/conceptual and methodological elements.

Familiarize yourself with these terms: *event, object, concept,* and *fact.* These terms, as they apply to developing and using a V diagram, are defined as follows:

Event: *Anything that happens, can be made to happen, or is in the realm of possibility to happen.*

Events can be made to happen by humans or they can be naturally occurring events. Examples of events that are made to happen by humans include a play, a war, class schedules, a concert, and a school graduation. Examples of events caused by natural circumstances include an earthquake, thunder, snow, and a volcanic eruption.

Object: *Anything that exists and can be observed. A name for a stable event.*

Like an event, an object can be made by humans or can be a naturally occurring object. Examples of objects made by humans include: a desk, chair, building, expressway, sculpture, robots, and a book. Examples of objects that occur naturally include: a star, planet, a tree, and bird.

Concept: *A sign or symbol that points to a regularity in events or objects.*

Concepts are usually identified by words, but they may be numerical or symbolic (such as musical notations ♪, ♪, chemical notations H_2O, CO_2, or mathematical symbols $+$, $=$, $<$). For example, an inverted yellow triangle appearing at a roadway intersection shows the regularity with which we in the United States use a symbol that conveys the meaning to "yield the right of way" to oncoming traffic.

Fact: *A record of an event.*

A wonderful irony attends the attempts to settle arguments by a direct appeal to the facts of a case. What is so often thought to be clear and compelling turns out to be clear and confusing. A fact has multiple meanings. Alas, a fact is complex, not simple.

The *Webster's* dictionary gives six meanings of the word "fact."

1. reality, actuality;
2. something known to exist, or to have happened;
3. something known to be true;
4. something said to be true;
5. idiom. "after the fact." done, made, formulated after something has occurred; and
6. in fact, in truth, in deed.

Each of these separate meanings can be related to the **V** definition of "fact" as a record of an event(s). In the event metaphysics of this book, reality is taken to mean "event(s)," and "fact" then means the record of that event reality. Simple. Clear. Original. New. Powerful. Enlightening. Edifying. Educative.

Facts are *made* in the process of recording events. The idiom "after the fact" needs to be changed to "during the fact-making event." The assumption that facts are somehow "true" can only be clarified by the tedious process of specifying which meaning of truth you have in mind at the time. Alas, our somewhat shaky hold on reality is firmed up, somewhat, by clarifying the exact connection between event and record of the event. Stay with this clear definition of "fact," and important meanings can be negotiated successfully.

By now you are aware that the books and articles you read and the daily happenings in which you take part are composed of events, objects, facts, and related concepts and images. What specific event, object, concept, or fact comes to your mind at this point?

A **V** diagram is a tool that is used as a code-breaker to reveal ideas and facts of a given work or to apply ideas when planning, carrying out, and finalizing a work such as a research study or report. The purpose of the **V** is to simplify complexity without denying it. The **V** acknowledges that making new knowledge is dependent upon mindful inquiry that looks at multiple perspectives that may explain certain events. Its function is to better enable the understanding of what is known by conceptualizing (thinking) about what is known; asking penetrating questions of the chosen events; finding appropriate records that support factual answers to what was asked and what has happened; and determining the value of the efforts that transpire from process to product.

THE LEARNING V

The main idea of learning as an eventful process is the reorganization of meaning with the aid of a newly learned idea. The reorganization of grasped meaning involves a large number of varying actions of integrating and differentiating. This type of learning activity is displayed on the **V** in Figure 3.2.

The activities of Questioning on the conceptual left side of the **V** are related to the activities of Answering on the right side of the **V**. Notice that the *questioning side* contains word and word phrases that are intended to *disorganize and unsettle fixed or stable claims* on the right side of the **V**, and "questioning," "imagining," "speculating," "criticizing," "philosophizing," and "thinking" are all ways of separating things so recombining can occur. These actions pull things apart so they can be put back together in a different and more satisfactory way. It is precisely the lack of this kind of agitation which occurs in classrooms, that perpetuates question answering rather than question asking. **Answering** on the right side of the **V** works to *organize claims in a definite and stable way*. Much school practice consists of giving definite, almost concrete answers. The activities of "recording," "transforming," and "claiming" are ways of establishing answers. When the connection is made between a good question and its appropriate answer, we believe learning is possible.

Levels of Intellectual Space

We can begin anywhere on the **V** with experienced events, with concepts, with factual answers; before we have finished we will cross over many times and move up and down; engaging in many different activities in

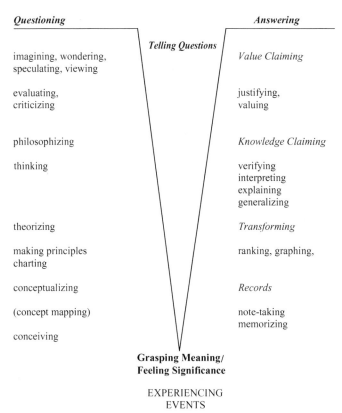

Questioning | Answering

Telling Questions

imagining, wondering,
speculating, viewing

Value Claiming

evaluating,
criticizing

justifying,
valuing

philosophizing

Knowledge Claiming

thinking

verifying
interpreting
explaining
generalizing

theorizing

Transforming

making principles
charting

ranking, graphing,

conceptualizing

Records

(concept mapping)

note-taking
memorizing

conceiving

**Grasping Meaning/
Feeling Significance**

EXPERIENCING
EVENTS

FIGURE 3.2. The Learning **V**.

order to complete our learning. Each side contributes something to the other; each level contributes something to what is above and below. It is this interplay between the left and right sides of the **V** that actively engages the mind to revisit previous knowledge, make judgments, discard, connect, verify, and make decisions about the structure of knowledge of a given event.

This notion of levels of intellectual space is not hierarchical but intended to aid the developer to make connections, question relationships, make determinations, and make evaluations during the process and at its completion. These levels of intellectual space can be represented metaphorically as an elevator in a department store that goes up and down stopping at floors containing different kinds of merchandise, the combination of which totals the entire store. Likewise, the elements on the **V** represent these floors: levels of intellectual space. Mindful and reflective inquiry is the cornerstone of this heuristic to aid the individual in changing the meaning of experience, making new knowledge, and getting smart through the use of the **V**.

The Left Side of the V

Conceiving. Conceiving an event works toward stabilizing that event; it gives a fix on the central tendency rather than variation. How one conceives an event is determined through one's prior knowledge and world experience to give order and coherence to an event. When conceiving an event, the commonalities associated with an event are made known.

Conceptualizing. This process brings together ideas in ways that show relationships among and between them. Being able to reveal and share these ideas can be done using concept maps. Concept maps are a visual representation of a person's thought processes and can be used to negotiate meaning by displaying arrangements and making known any misconceptions or faulty relationships that may be shown. It is a word diagram that is portrayed visually in a hierarchical fashion and represents concepts and their relationships. Concept maps are a way to visually display and share ideas with others in the research process.

Concept maps provide a starting point from which to determine what is already known about a given topic and what needs to be learned. For example, by making a concept map of a topic that is about to be studied, the researcher is able to determine: (1) the general knowledge with the topic; (2) how the topic is being perceived; and (3) if there are any misconceptions that need to be addressed before engaging in the research investigation.

Making Principles. The principle is a guide to the action of an event. Principles are conceived when the stability of an event and its stable characteristics are reconciled. These two activities of conceiving and making principles seem to be clear instances of learning because they indicate an active reorganization of meaning resulting in closure.

Theorizing. This activity relates concepts and principles so that they are coherent. We may invent new concepts and constructs to bridge to other concepts and principles.

Thinking. In a sense all of the activities on both sides of the V require thinking. Learning is not a matter of mindless association. Learning that results from thinking (in this special sense) engenders alternatives; it juggles possibilities; it shows how things could be otherwise. In the sense that we think with concepts, thinking presupposes conceiving.

Philosophizing. This activity is a persistent effort to think things through to assumptions, to presuppositions, or to clarify rational argument. The limits of arguments are pressed and assessed in the kind of philosophizing that seeks the general case, the uniform example, and the claim that requires "universalizability." The learning that results from philosophizing subsumes a wide range of concepts, examples, principles, and arguments. Philosophizing pushes us beyond the coherence of theory to the comprehensiveness of philosophy.

Criticizing. This activity brings cases together with criteria. The critic examines a case in the light of criteria relevant to the analysis, appraisal, and evaluation of that case. Clear cases and counter cases will test the aptness of criteria, and sometimes criteria change as a result. We judge cases, from criteria, and we derive criteria from cases. The reorganization of meaning that comes from the activities of criticizing, as one moves through cases and criteria, is high-level learning.

Imagining. The use of the imagination in philosophy is a working technique. We test clear cases by creating imaginary ones. Some books claim that philosophy itself begins in wonder. Speculating about the way things are and how they could be different – creating utopias and alternative patterns of meaning – seems clearly a part of the work of philosophy. It seems to be one way of learning as well. It is true of any discipline – art, history, mathematics – that philosophizing the subject matter reorganizes the content and thereby brings about new learning in students who study the philosophy. The reason is twofold: We add new knowledge (the philosophy), and the new knowledge restructures the meaning of prior knowledge. Scientific claims become nested in a philosophic context; we add a level of meaning and create additional intellectual space. Every subject has its philosophy; learning to a point of mastery requires us to learn the philosophy, too.

On the "answering" side of the **V**, we find many activities that firm up claims. The "questioning" side of the **V** has done its work to the point where we think we know what would count as a good answer. The task now is to establish the answer.

The Right Side of the V

Recording. A clear case of recording in the context of educating is notetaking. Students learn to take notes as a way to grasp meaning. Sometimes, however, they take notes only in the hope that later on, the notes will have meaning for them. Students have to choose to pay attention to grasp meaning. Students who are grasping meaning during a lecture take different notes from those who simply make a running record of the talk. Other forms of records include videotaping, journals of observations, stopwatches, and surveys.

Transforming. Changing facts into data is an act of reorganizing meaning. For example, when we simply make a table or draw a graph as a way to present facts, we are changing a complex pattern of meaning into one that is condensed, ordered, and simplified. These actions can readily be seen as possible acts of learning. When we make these transformations, we believe we can see something we did not see before.

Claiming. Making knowledge and value claims take us to the top of the **V**. In making knowledge claims we engage in acts of describing, generalizing, explaining, interpreting, verifying. Each and all of these acts reorganize meaning. Similarly, in making value claims we undertake actions of valuing, evaluating, and justifying. In establishing value claims we are, as it were, settling claims about the worth of something. These are marks of the closure of learning. In general, on the answering side of the **V**, we engage in activities that generate "objects" that seem to us quite solid, reliable, repeatable, and worthy – in a word – *objective*. When crossing over the arms of the **V** ceases to hold our interest because our questions have been answered, we may say we have *learned*. Learning as an event has occurred. We have successfully reorganized a piece of the world.

The Bottom of the V

Grasping Meaning. Grasped meanings are idiosyncratic and are obtained through self-proclamation, even if assisted by others. This learning, by grasping the meaning, is the responsibility of the individual and cannot be shared. Learning takes place after one has already grasped the meaning: It is the grasped meaning that one learns.

Feeling Significance. Feelings are very important to learning. They have a special significance when we consider learning in the context of educating. Some events stand out because they arouse our feelings. The experience of significant feelings in the context of educating gives students reasons to choose to learn. The learner, with the help of the teacher, faces the curriculum, shares meaning, grasps meaning, and feels the significance of the curriculum because the curriculum bodes forth criteria of excellence. Educative events are real events permitting an experience of value. Events can be compellingly felt when their significance is fully understood. Learning is its own intrinsic reward.

Experiencing Events. In order for events to be experienced, one needs to combine both the grasped meaning and the felt significance of the event that is happening or has occurred. It is this understanding that affects one's inner being and aids in resolving and making sense of the circumstances that are taking place (or have occurred) that enables one to contemplate the value of the experience. This change in the meaning of the experience combines the emotional and cognitive states and results in reorganizing our views by adding to our world knowledge.

The cognitive and emotive nature of the **V** combines knowledge, value, and learning in order to promote meaning.

4

Structuring Knowledge

*Principle 4. The **V** diagram is a way to show the structure of knowledge.*

The **V** diagram is a heuristic device used to analyze or formulate a research investigation within the context of the structure of knowledge in any academic discipline. In the field of Education, academic knowledge is named "subject matter." A teacher of English teaches the subject matter of English. The task of the teacher is to combine knowledge of an academic discipline with the knowledge used in practical activities of teaching. The teacher must be expertly knowledgeable in two separate fields – English, and the curriculum used to teach English. Becoming expert in the integration of these separate knowledge domains may take many years of study. The **V** diagram works to make knowledge claims readily accessible to the working teacher. It saves time and money. It increases comprehension and understanding. It simplifies complexity and increases the value of knowledge.

Structure of knowledge means that the elements or parts of knowledge are formed into a whole. Structure is just parts and their relations to each other. In Gowin's **V**, the elements and their relation to each other are arrayed around a **V** shape. The **V** shape accentuates the fact that all knowledge is about events. The **V** in the diagram points to happenings in reality. Knowledge is about something that human beings can experience in some way. Bringing abstract and theoretic knowledge into sharp connection with the realities it is about is not an easy task. Some highly specialized academic scholars believe that the task is beyond them. Most teachers understand knowledge structure differently with the help of the **V**.

WHAT IS THE KNOWLEDGE STRUCTURE?

The structure of knowledge may be characterized (in any field or exemplar of that field) by its:

- telling questions, key concepts, and conceptual systems;
- reliable and relevant methods and techniques of work;
- central products – the upshot or outcomes of inquiry;
- within-field and outside-the-field values;
- agents and audiences (the so-called "community of scholars"); and
- by the phenomena of interest the field deals with and the occasions that give rise to the quest for knowledge.

These characteristics of the structure of knowledge are difficult to grasp without scholarly study over time.

Knowledge is the result of inquiry represented in primary and secondary sources. Structured knowledge refers to these works of research and scholarship and to the parts and relations of the parts to each other.[1]

To illustrate the conceptual relationships that appear on the **V** diagram an analogy is made with a building "12-stories tall."

TWELVE-STORIES TALL

Imagine an intellectual building 12-stories tall. Within this building (structure) each storey (British spelling for "level") has its own story (a tale of the events and activities taking place on this level of meaning). On each floor there is intellectual activity. As you get off the elevator you see a lot of people working with ideas. Some are creating new ideas. Some are criticizing old ideas. Some are making new structures – boxes, cartons, closets, bathrooms, luxury suite areas, and variants of the maximum- and the minimum-sized constructions. Some pieces are marked for their beauty. Other constructions are noticeable for their utility. It is a busy place. On each floor all the workers are active with the ideas of that floor. When they are not going up and down the floors, some visit other floors for new ideas. Some never leave the floor they are working on; they just persist to exploit the creativity of that floor. Sometimes the freight elevator in the back is loaded up with stuff for other floors. Imagine that these stories represent intellectual space and events. These floors should not be viewed as being hierarchical, but rather on the same intellectual plane of knowledge and curiosity.

---

[1] D. Bob Gowin, *Educating* (Ithaca, NY: Cornell University Press, 1981), pp. 87–88; see also D. Bob Gowin, "The Structure of Knowledge," *Educational Theory* 20 (4), 319–328, 1970.

A simple sketch of this 12-storey building can be imagined as follows:

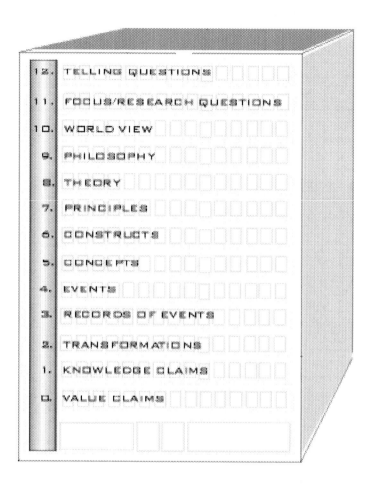

The main point here is about the structure of knowledge. All constructed knowledge has its own structure. Some of these structures are fragile or odd looking. Some buildings are startling in appearance. Some are easy on the eyes, pleasant places to work, and comfortable. The range of architecture is open, free, historic, and time consuming. The word "structure" means parts and relations between parts. Elevators and stairs are connectors, but so are phone and email. Their purpose is to stay connected and busy.

Twelve-Stories Tall suggests intellectual life and practical life are governed by activities of the mind working. Why is the mind's activity of creating and recognizing Telling Questions placed on the top floor of this fictional structure? Because it is the highest place where the mind's most powerful imagination is encouraged. We see much farther with the mind's questions than we do with the empirical answers we supply. A Telling Question opens up the freedom of the mind. Abstract questions can lead up and away from the sometimes dreary life of concrete reality. We become inspired, inspirited, we move off into free open space where anything could be possible. Alfred North Whitehead (1938) in *Modes of Thought* wrote about the "conceptual entertainment of unrealized possibilities." Ideas are both entertained by us and entertain us, and make us happy to be thinking. Unrealized possibilities have almost no limits to a vigorous, thinking mind. A question we ask ourselves is "So, what's possible now?"

Every period of growth in living opens up possibilities not before achievable. Achieving purposes that lead to educating add significant power for more educating, hence more growth. "Growth is a fact of life" wrote philosopher–educator John Dewey.

Telling Questions

The intellectual life of man consists almost wholly in his substitution of a conceptual order for the perceptual order in which his experience originally comes.

This statement is a conclusion philosopher William James makes after extensive analysis of the philosophic distinction between concept and percept, conception and perception.[2] James argues that the meaning of a concept can be stated only in terms of the percepts it stands for, and the consequences for the action that it suggests. The abstractions of claims to truth and knowledge are to be experientially described in terms of the relation of concepts to percepts of given events to which they lead when acted upon.

This statement about "the intellectual life of man" is a sweeping claim about humans' way of living connecting ideas to action and events. Is it true? Valuable? Not so? Mistaken? Just wrong?

As we question the claim, we see that we can convert the conclusion into a question. "Does the intellectual life substitute concepts for percepts?" This question is a Telling Question. It is a question that indicates a way to find an answer. Find an answer by connecting concepts and percepts and experiences of both. It is a question that "tells on" events of intellectual activity. A Telling Question differs from ordinary questions ("Do you know the way to San Jose?") because it presents a question and a hint or two about how to go about answering the question. The question tells you something about both events and methods of study of the selected events.

Where do we find Telling Questions? Look for answers that appear in the literature: Convert significant and conclusive answers into questions. Use

---

[2] William James, *Some Problems of Philosophy: A Beginning of a Introduction to Philosophy* (New York: Longmans, Green, and Co., 1911).

the same concepts found in the answers to pose the question. You want your new Telling Question to be about the same events as the answers were about.

In general, significant and conclusive knowledge claims are supplied by any field of study that has been pursued deliberately for a period of time. The work of inquiry, research, study is to supply answers to key questions. With enough time, any field stakes out a domain of interest within which key answers can be found.

Focus Questions/Research Questions

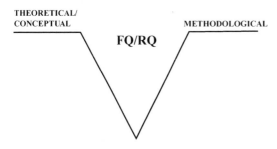

Two functions of *focus/research questions*: to sharpen the view and to magnify the view. To sharpen the view we limit the range of the view. We make our question(s) more precise. Precision is important to inquiry, and a question with well-defined concepts increases precision. Increased precision can also narrow the view too much.

Magnification enlarges the view. Magnification makes the details of the key events more clearly evident to inquiry. Like the enlargement of a photograph, the fine details clear up. Magnification can also distort the view by enlargement.

Focus questions increase precision and clarity. Sometimes increased precision narrows the view too much. Sometimes increased magnification distorts the view too much. The positive and negative aspects of Focus Questions are both important to inquiry. Examples of Focus Questions are found later on in this book.

World View – A point of view on the world

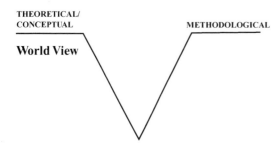

More important than almost anything else in one's maturing living is one's *world view*. The main reason is that a world view simplifies complexity. A world view is our response to troublesome choices. "Give me liberty, or give me death," patriot Patrick Henry's world view is famous. "The Lord is my shepherd" is a metaphor expressing a point of view toward daily living. "Life is short – eat dessert first" is a view toward daily dining. Also: "Live to eat and eat to live." "I can resist anything but temptation." These are short-hand *statements of beliefs you stand for*, and they are *conclusions more than invitations for questions*.

A point of view entails a place to stand. A platform. Your point of view depends on your platform viewpoint. Your world view can be anything you say it is. Its validity is a consequence of how that view treats you – well, or badly. A World View is a shorthand declaration of where you stand now. It serves as your declaration of independence, so to say. It is not really up for debate or for defensive argument. For such arguments you drop down to the floor beneath you (on Gowin's **V**) the supporting floor of Philosophy.

A statement of your world view can serve as an opening for an engaging and lively conversation with a stranger on a train, or a new-found bar companion, or a vacationing guest.

Suppose you claim "Love your enemies, it will drive them crazy." This thought puts a nice spin on things. If you are beset with pesky attackers, then tell them your world view. The more they disagree with you, the more you love them.

A World View can present yourself as having a sly grin, as joyous, mirthful, a tip of the hat to this good morning. It can be more serious: written *Exliberis* inside your cherished books or what is written on your gravestone. It can be a very familiar family saying, a prayer at mealtime, a poem, a song, a dance, one nod, or warm handshake of recognition of another's world view. Our world view is that everyone lives with a world view. World views simplify complexities.

Philosophy

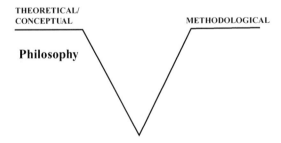

THEORETICAL/
CONCEPTUAL   METHODOLOGICAL

Philosophy

Philosophy takes simple things and makes them complex; and, takes complex matters and makes them keenly simple. Philosophy takes nothing for granted, whereas a world view takes itself for granted. The wonder of a satisfying world view is that you do not have to think about it. It was a joker with a mischievous world view who said "Be Philosophical, don't think about it."

Philosophy is Rodin's the *Thinker*. Right elbow on left knee, Rodin shapes the statue this way. Rodin's *Thinker* must have been a younger person, pondering maybe where he left his clothes.

Thinking – real-hard-serious-deep-ponderous-thinking – thinking can confuse us. Thinking is difficult, puzzling, and open-ended. A World View is settled and secure; a philosophy unsettles and makes us feel less secure (but maybe more excited) with the new options thinking proposes.

Alfred Whitehead stated:[3] "Simplicity this side of complexity is simplistic, worth nothing; but simplicity the other side of complexity is worth everything." "Seek simplicity and distrust it."

Theory

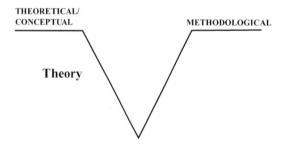

THEORETICAL/
CONCEPTUAL   METHODOLOGICAL

Theory

A good *theory* is one of the best aids you can have. A good theory organizes a lot of ideas. A good theory simplifies complexity. A good theory stimulates imagination. A good theory opens up all sorts of new possibilities; it can be a wild and wonderful playground for ideas. A good theory is a place one can construct various questions. A theory is a map. A good theory is a most valuable piece of knowledge. It is a guide to many new places. A theory spawns many questions. A theory is a guide to methodology, which, in turn, is a way of knowing.

Most of all, *a good theory gives you answers that explain.* Theory explains by citing both causes and reasons. "Why questions" are given answers by theories. Why? Why not? A good theory answers "why" questions by saying "because." Did you ever notice children playing games with each other? One asks "Why?" and the other, who does not know the correct

[3] Alfred North Whitehead. In W. H. Auden and L. Kronenberger (Eds.), *The Viking Book of Aphorisms* (New York: Penguin Books, 1966).

explanation, says "Because" or "Why not?" The children are trying to explain the world they experience. A good theory explains a lot about our experiences in this universe.

What constitutes theoretical thinking? Theoretical thinking occurs when the realm of the imagination expands on conscious reality. Can reality be different? In imagination, yes, it can. Theoretical thinking can be wild and wooly, can go against the grain, and can project possibilities beyond accepted boundaries. What seems possible in theory may be hard to believe if the believer stays too close to what is taking place. The theorists must imagine some connections back to reality. In the place where future events are imagined, stimulating connections to present circumstances and events must also be imagined. It's a place to anchor ideas for further testing.

A special meaning of a good theory is that a theory is theoretical. It is not a description of practical reality. It is not a display of the productive arts. It is full of ideas, concepts, conjectures, forward-looking notions. A theory encompasses possibilities. We say "in theory this should work." Sometimes it works, sometimes it does not work, and we invent a new theory.

A dictionary gives this definition of "theory."[4]

Systematically organized knowledge, applicable to a wide variety of circumstances; especially a system of assumptions, accepted principles, and rules of procedure, devised to analyze or predict, or otherwise to explain the nature or behavior of a set of specified phenomena.

This definition is a good overview of elements of theory. Notice how many epistemic elements arrayed around Gowin's **V** are included in this one dictionary definition. Note: *system, organized, knowledge, assumptions, principles, procedure, explain,* and *specific phenomena* (events).

A large watershed lies between the *theory* side of the **V** and the *method* side of the **V**. In accepted research practice, a major guide to research lies in the difference between "theory-directed research" and "method-driven research."

Theory is not an experimental method for finding out something. Theory is not a description of a practice, or of the practical. The Greek word "theoria" translates as "spectator." One wag said that a "theorist is a bemused spectator of the passing parade." Theory is the thinking side of research. Research guided by well-thought out ideas is better than method-driven research. Theory-guided research is more efficient in time spent, and money spent, than merely gathering data under some methodological procedure. Piles of facts and data need theory to explain what they mean for research. *Theories explain facts and data.*

---

4 William Morris (Ed.), *The American Heritage Dictionary of the English Language* (Boston: American Heritage Publishing Co., Inc., and Houghton Mifflin Company, 1975), p. 1335.

The book, *Educating*,[5] is an example of a Theory of Educating. It is not a theory of what is happening now in schools. Schooling is a practice of a school system. The school system is organized to keep the school system running. Sometimes we find educative events do happen in schools, but schools are not organized and guided by a theory of educating. Some day the *Art of Educating with V Diagrams* will have a major role in guiding schooling events. We know educators who care about educating realize that the school system needs to be governed by concepts of educating.

Principles

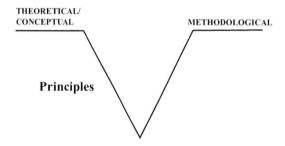

THEORETICAL/
CONCEPTUAL   METHODOLOGICAL

Principles

Principles are conceptual guides to action in events. An action is a behavior with meaning. Principles are written statements of regularities in events. These written statements are abstracted and derived from many prior claims about regularities in event. Knowledge claims from hundreds of research efforts can be abstracted into *principles*. Principles combine knowledge claims and value claims. These powerful meaning statements help us to perceive events as stable, reliable, surefooted, valuable, and understandable. Meaningful statements we name *principles* are made (constructed by humans) for the sake of some end, some purpose, some function.

Principles are knowledge claims shaped for valued human uses. For example, heating a pot of water causes the water to get hot, maybe boil (a scientific claim), and is useful in brewing an aromatic cup of tea (a principle guiding the use of a knowledge claim). "Heat causes water to boil" is a scientific knowledge claim. In this form, this claim is not a principle, but it is a knowledge claim based on repeated trials, laboratory projects, practical tests. To convert this knowledge claim into a principle we need to specify how this claim works or functions in ordinary living. It is that we are heating water because we desire to make a cup of tea. The claim of regularity has a perceivable function, or use, or end, or value, or importance in future events.

[5] cf Gowin, 1981.

A *principle of educating* is that it is a process that changes the meaning of experience and the experience of meaning. *Educating works to simplify complexity* without denying it. Thus, our principle of acting in educating is to simplify complexity. For Gowin's **V**, the assumption (not empirical claim) is that a small number (of anything) is *simple* compared to a much larger number (of anything) that is *complexity*. A small number of good ideas is better than a carload of facts that are uninterpreted. Implied here is the notion that getting at the key conceptual understanding in any human action is highly valuable. The brain is a powerful supplier of images and ideas; the mind simplifies these spot energies to act. Acting, doing, is an immediate rush . . . once the trigger is pulled, nothing can stop the events. On Your Mark, Get Set, Go . . . is a principle (as opposed to on your mark, go, get set – where go is where you lunge forward toward the finish line).

Constructs

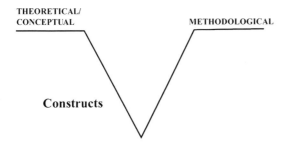

Constructs are conceptual creations that connect sets of concepts. Unlike concepts, constructs do not specify regularities in events. In genetics, for example, Mendel used the construct of "factors" that later gave way to "gene." These ideas did not have an operational meaning. As gene has now changed in some biochemical studies of genetics to "polypeptide" (one gene, one polypeptide is the central dogma today), the status of the word has shifted from that of a fertile construct to a definite concept.

The unexamined life is full of constructs. An example is the Dow–Jones Average. Dow–Jones Average is a made up number. This average is a number made up of hundreds of numbers of events called trades in a stock exchange. In general, an average, as the average number of children in an American family, is a made-up number, a secondary index to primary events. No real family has 2.7 children.

Other examples include, the FBI, OSS, Body Politic, Democracy, and Education. These names, and a newspaper full of constructs, are place holders for conceptual structures. Constructs are valuable short-cuts to complex intelligence.

In this work, the two major constructs are the **V** diagram and concept maps. Both are abstractions from experience that we use to make knowledge-making events happen.

Concepts

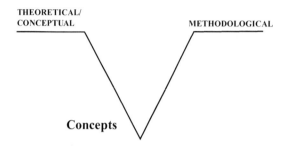

People think with *concepts*. Concepts are one step above perceived experience. Experiences come to us largely through our senses – our eyes, ears, sense of touch, taste, our vestibular balance sense. These various avenues produce what philosophers name as "sense data." Another name philosophers use is "percept." Percepts are products of our immediate experience. Concepts are a product of our mediated experience. Concept and percept, conception and perception are words making an important distinction in philosophy.

A concept is an idea. Concepts fill our minds. Our language (whichever one it is that we are using at the time) is a vehicle carrying concepts. Often, a concept is carried by one word; for example children use the word "Mama" or "Papa," or "Mom" or "Dad" to signify the regularities in the child's experience of their mother and father. A short word can be a concept that carries a large amount of meaning. As children grow, they learn to use languages full of concepts. Concepts expand greatly their grasp of their experiences. Conceptual growth is key for educators. Fostering conceptual growth may be one of the most important events of educating.

We define concept as a name (e.g., label, sign, word, or signifier) for a regularity in events or objects. The word "wind" is a name for an event of some kind of regular motion of the air. The word "chair" names an object, a thing we sit on. Concepts name events and objects of our experience.

Chair may also name the person who is in charge of a gathering of people, the "chairman" or "chairperson." The same word can name different objects or events, and this fact shows us that a word meaning may change. Meanings can be ambiguous, vague, or misleading as well as singular, clear, and illuminating. All language is always both misleading and illuminating. Language is yeasty; it grows.

Events

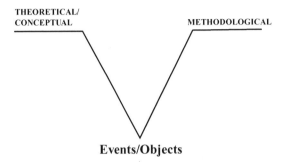

THEORETICAL/
CONCEPTUAL   METHODOLOGICAL

Events/Objects

Events are composed of happenings. They can be described as anything that happens, can be made to happen, or are in the realm of possibility to happen. Events are real. In philosophy, studies of reality are put in the category of metaphysics. In Aristotle's writings the section on metaphysics was just the section that followed physics. The term "meta" meant "after" or "beyond" in Greek language Aristotle used. Aristotle's famous metaphysical claim was that reality is a plurality of substance(s). Objects are substances. Objects are real. Objects are physical, have heft, can be lifted, sorted, stored and housed in other physical places. In deep contrast, in Gowin's **V**, the words, events, and objects are at the "happening" place at the point of the **V**. Any object exists as an event. All things are events of short, brief duration (a piece of ice) or long – ages and ages – duration (a glacier). In Gowin's metaphysics, events are the main reality, not objects. Reality is a plurality of events. An event metaphysics deals with events, processes, happenings, waves of energy. Events are the foundations of a Constructivist point of view.

These events can be made to happen by humans such as an athletic contest, an art exhibit, a musical concert, a meeting, and so forth. Events can also be naturally occurring events such as lightning, a rain storm, a volcanic eruption, or an extra solar planet (e.g., HD209458). In the teaching and learning process, we also have educative events that consist of social constructions formed by people.

At the point of the **V** are the circumstances that encompass the events that are being observed. These events directly relate to the focus/research question(s) that are formulated. These events are monitored by the records (instruments selected) of the facts that are taking place over a period of time.

Records of Events

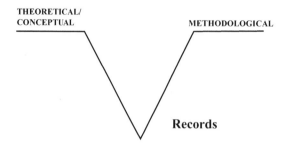

THEORETICAL/
CONCEPTUAL   METHODOLOGICAL

Records

Records are instruments that serve to monitor what is happening in the events being studied. Types of instruments include cameras of all sorts for photographing events directly, videotapings, sense data measurements (pulse – Galileo used his heart beat to time the pendulum swings), body temperature recordings such as thermometers, timing instruments of all sorts (clocks, watches), magnifying tools such as zoom lenses, surveying tools such as transits, telescopes, sextants, laboratory notes (especially important in chemical laboratory research) (sometimes chemists' sense of smell is the perfect recording device noted in lab journals), diaries, lie detectors, direct palpating as in physical examinations in medical research and therapy, sensitive listening devices for earthquake research, audiotapings (the music field is rich with recordings of sounds), personal interviews, shared observing in fields of action such as frontline war, coaches observing in sports (in general observations), and daily automatic recordings of stock market trades.

A major source of creative intelligence in science comes from those inquiries that focus on techniques of study of immediate events. The lab technician who invents a better way to make records of events is a hero, of sorts – some have won the Nobel Prize. It is very important that the records accurately reflect what is taking place during the events that are being monitored.

Reliable instruments need to be selected to record the facts that will occur from the events of keen interest. The records selected should be such that they provide facts of the event from different points of view. These records should be judged to be reliable indicators by a panel of experts (e.g., scholars, teachers, technicians, professors, and researchers).

During the process of recording events that lead to data collection ask yourself, "What is happening?" "Does what's happening make sense?" "If not, why not?" Upon completion of the recording and data collection analyze your data. Think about what happened as a result of recording events. The test is always between the events you chose to make happen and the recordings you used to grasp the event(s).

You can make mistakes here that will undermine everything you do higher up the right side of this **V**. There can be a disconnect between the questions you asked and the records you made. Find a way to make sense of the event. Use your theory's best concepts to explain what's happening. Moreover, what *key concepts* emerge from the *facts*? What do we mean by these concepts? How do we define them? Tie the key concept(s) to the particular part of the record of the event you call a fact. By identifying this key concept as exhibiting *regularity* to the event(s) being studied is to define the concept you are reporting.

In our work, electronic messages between teachers and students are kept in computer files. These transmissions are records of pedagogical events. If there were to become a science of pedagogy, it would find its primary facts in these electronic records. We believe educational research would take a great leap forward in validity given the reliability of these pedagogical facts.

The value of the knowledge you are constructing will be worthless if the events, records, and concepts are not connected to each other.

Transformations

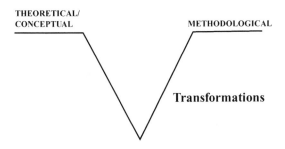

THEORETICAL/
CONCEPTUAL   METHODOLOGICAL

Transformations

Once your facts have been collected and analyzed you are ready to *make factual judgments*. Now comes the interesting moment in which you think and try to make sense of what has happened. During this phase, *you are gathering thoughts as well as data*. There are different skills needed for concept analysis, concept improvement, and concept definition than are needed for fact gathering. The skills needed for concept creation are much more philosophical than methodological. Philosophy has been defined (since Socrates) as *definition*. Getting at the meanings of terms is the work of definition. In contrast, using statistical procedures is data analysis; it is not concept analysis.

Compose a set of statements about the records in some form. This factual judgment can be a paragraph or a paradigm sketch that summarizes the judgments that have arisen from the facts. Depending on the data, you may wish to rank, correlate, rate, assign numbers to events according to a rule, analyze, synthesize, or use any system that you think reveals what has taken place during this investigation. Be sure that the results are portrayed clearly. These factual judgments are represented as *transformations*.

Knowledge Claims

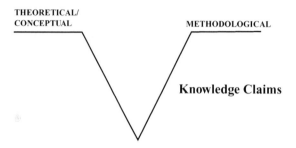

Knowledge claims are answers to the question(s) that you asked and appear in the middle of the **V**. Thinking and interpreting your findings lead to making assertions based on the questions that were asked. There needs to be a direct answer to each question that was asked at the beginning of the study. Each knowledge claim needs to be explained clearly with reasons for substantiating the interpretations you are making. During this process, focus and research questions, events, concepts, records, and transformations need to be revisited. Facts and ideas need to be reconciled based on the instruments used and the interpretations made of the results.

An important aspect that may arise from the stated knowledge claims is the *formulation of a new focus or research question(s)*. Whether this additional question arises from "Laying the **V**" on a research report, or comes about as the impetus for another study, this kind of thinking evokes a direction that builds upon what has been found to what can further be known and understood.

Value Claims

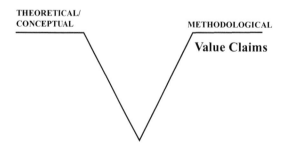

An important aspect of any investigation is the worth that is derived from the initial intent and the final evaluation. *Value claims* are statements based on the knowledge claims that declare the worth or value of the inquiry. Does your research have practical implications to the area you studied? Do your research findings help you to have a better grasp of the topic? Will someone else reading your research report learn from your work? Could your research be done in a much less costly manner?

Value claims are answers to value questions (Gowin, 1981; Gowin & Green, 1980). We believe only five value questions are enough to span the field of value claims.

1. *Instrumental Value Question.* Is X good for Y? For example, "Are concept maps good for theoretical thinking?"
2. *Intrinsic Value Question.* Is X good in itself? For example, "Is science just good enough in itself?"
3. *Comparative Value Question.* Is X better than Y? For example, "Is science better than philosophy?"
4. *Decision Value Question.* Is X right? Ought we choose X? For example, "Ought you to choose **V** Diagrams?" "Is **V** analysis of all research products right?"
5. *Ideal Value Question.* Is X as good as it can be, or can it be made much better ideally? For example, "Is Gowin's **V** as good as it could be? "Can we make it better?"

It is important that we do not overtly simplify value claims. Most events of human interest have a variety of value claims that are relevant and compelling. Value conflicts are common. Clarification of value meanings is a good thing in itself! Use of the **V** is better than sole use of the scientific method because the **V** is more inclusive of a variety of values – a comparative value claim. Indeed, many scientists believe that facts are different from values, and that value claims have no right place in science. That value claims are not desirable in science are value claims about science! Fortunately, the famous fact/value argument is no longer a main issue in the way we construct knowledge. In order to better understand how knowledge is constructed, it is important to view value claims as crucial to the advancement of any discipline.

This chapter has "complexified" the **V**. We have extended discussions of the many aspects of the structure of knowledge. We have given many examples and viewpoints to help explain the **V**. Your best grasp of these new ideas can only come from your use of these ideas in your practice.

5

Minding Events and Making a V

*Principle 5. A **V** represents knowledge of an educative event formed by human agents interacting in a social setting where the reality of the social constructions vary in complex ways. The **V** simplifies this complexity.*

A lot of thinking is required to make a **V**. It is not easy. The **V** forces you to look at events. It forces you to think, to pay attention to happenings not totally under your control. Minding educative events is like minding the children, or minding the store. The mind is active connecting past knowledge to present events. Surprises occur. Plans change. It takes knowledge to figure out what's going on. We use our knowledge of past events to help interpret new events.

Minding past knowledge takes time, a lot of time – months and years. Typically a four-year college degree is required for individuals who desire to become teachers. Unfortunately, the typical supply of undergraduate knowledge is not presented with **V** diagrams in mind. Teachers in action use whatever knowledge they can find to present new educative events. Their first requirement is to figure out what they already know. Next, they need to lay the **V** on this prior knowledge; again, not an easy task.

The **V** is a thinking tool that requires more than just a "make it and take it" form of preparation. It is a tool that requires the mind to draw upon past experiences and world knowledge in order to think new thoughts about our existing knowledge with a given problem or situation. When preparing a **V** it takes teachers, researchers, students, and anyone using it into a zone that takes time, effort, and decision making. Perhaps Michael Smith, a teacher, amply describes the process of using the **V** to simplify complexity by making an analogy with preparing a meal:

The **V** is a lot of work. I realized it takes a lot of thought and effort to put your ideas into the various categories of the **V**. Having said this though, I can see that just like preparing a good meal takes time, the effort is worth it. The **V** helps you think through the entire process of the topic or subject. This process results in thinking about the topic and subject in a lot of different ways, and this makes the learning process a lot more interesting and applicable.

Thinking about a problem or situation in different ways is exactly the intent of using a **V** diagram, but it is a mistake to believe that this is an easy process. There are several considerations that need to be confronted if the process is to evolve into a meaningful experience for the **V** user. Our high school and postsecondary undergraduate and graduate students (including preservice and inservice teachers) tell us of the complications that arise when first faced with making a **V**. The following are several excerpts that appear in student journals that offer considerations that may prepare you when making your own **V**.

R.L.: I'm not sure that I totally understand what is required under some of the headings (*theory, philosophy,* and *world view* specifically).

H.Q.: This is the hardest thing that I have ever done in my life. I am getting confused with some of the terminology, but the activity is fun. It does help organizing and storing information. I feel that after some practice, I will be in the swing of things.

M.B.: I found that when I took the various levels of the **V** diagram and broke down their meaning to a definition that made sense to me, then it made the process of understanding what to do a lot better.

J.N.: I have been working on my **V** diagram for the whole of the weekend. It has not been easy to tie the knots together, but it is interesting.

J.P.: Okay, so the **V** diagram blew me away. I enjoyed the concept and could see where it was leading. It is a fantastic plan for teachers who are also students. As soon as I got the hang of the **V**, my mind instantly started working on questions. Questions like 'Are students performing at their maximum capacity on standardized testing?' Needless to say, I hate it when I start to think outside of the box like that because these are questions that make people go 'Hmmm . . . ??' I instantly started placing this question into the **V** diagram and began to doodle over the components of the **V**, world view, philosophy, and mostly the value of this question. "How could this question benefit teachers and educators across the board?" The lesson plan **V**s were great. I will probably adopt this method instead of the 4MAT method that I learned in a workshop a couple of years ago. I can still see each category and aspect in the **V**, however, it seems to involve more thinking than the 4MAT.

V.T.: What I liked the best was the one page visual of the entire project. I wish I would have had this when I was doing my paper for research class. The trouble I had with the diagram was the difference between the world view, the principles, and the theory.

D.H.:   I am struggling to understand the V diagram. I understand the
        doing side, but the thinking side throws me. I think in a very
        concrete way and struggle with the abstract. I was glad to work
        with someone to do the **V** diagram.

Reading these excerpts gives an indication of these persons' thoughts
when considering how to "tackle" the **V**. At first it seems formidable, but
like any tool it is intended to simplify work, not add to the complexity
of the task. Thinking is work and requires concentration, effort, and decision making. These comments indicate the problem areas that need to
be considered, most of which revolve around the theoretical/conceptual
left side (thinking side) of the **V**, particularly world view, philosophy, and
theory. This is not an uncommon concern since this "thinking" aspect of
the elements arrayed on the **V** are not commonly part of the formal school
curriculum.

So then, a primary consideration to keep in mind when first confronted
with a **V** is to make sense of the terminology (refer to Chapters 3 and 4).
Heed the suggestion of M.B. by trying to make sense of the terms in a
language that you understand. The thinking side of the **V** seems to present
the most challenge and therefore needs to be considered by the **V** developer.
Of special note is the world view, philosophy, and theory components that
make-up this theoretical/conceptual side of the **V**. Students have told us
that this is difficult because they are not required to do much of this kind
of "thinking" in their formal school experience. Instead, most of their time
is devoted to completing tasks (such as those demanded on the right side
of the **V**) and answering questions asked by others (e.g., teachers and
questions in published materials including worksheets). However, with
practice and effort they report that it takes a good deal of rethinking about
what it means to educate and become self-educated to make this connection
with this side of the **V**.

How does the **V** change the meaning of these students experience? Let's
read what some have recorded in their journals:

T.M.:   This [**V**] is something I have never experienced before, therefore
        thanks for the new horizon.
L.V.:   The **V** makes you think about the big picture – concepts, global
        perspectives, etc. This is good for me as a special-ed teacher. I
        have to constantly think about what details to eliminate, since
        there is no way can my kids get everything. Planning with a **V**
        makes the important concepts evident.
J.H.:   I am always asking my students what can I do to help them
        understand new material and if the learning activities are of
        interest. One student informed me she would like for us to make
        connections with past concepts to the ones we are learning now.

She said it is easy for her to forget what she has learned in the past when I continuously introduce new knowledge. I understand exactly how she feels; however, I am under so much pressure to make sure I expose them to every concept that will be on state exams. I am sure the **V** diagram will meet her needs, as well as others and still allow me to move on with instruction.

P.O.: I have been looking for a tool for organizing research projects for a long time. I am glad that I now know about **V** diagrams. I think it is a powerful tool for research work.

M.B.: The action research plan helped me see the **V** diagram in a clearer light.

W.B.: I was recently called by a fellow student in the class and asked for assistance in laying the **V** over their lesson plan. I thought this is a great occasion to work with my fellow student and by so doing I could learn how to further develop my own understanding of the process. We talked about terms and the order of consideration of the terms. We started with rearticulating his learning objectives into research/focus questions. We followed this activity by considering the event that could potentially meet the objectives of the focus questions and then considered concepts and records together. We moved right along until we arrived at the terms of philosophy, principles, and constructs. Hold it, wait a minute . . . 'What's this all about?' The teacher needed to consider and think about, 'Why this lesson?' and 'Do the chosen records achieve these objectives with and in accord with some of the strategies we have learned about lesson planning and reading/learning strategies?' The course work for the lesson plan was organized to label and identify human body parts using cards, posters, chalkboard notes, and verbalization of the terms before the whole class. 'Are these word cards like graphic organizers?' I asked. 'Do the students make the flashcards and label a facsimile of a human body?' 'Do they sing the terms like, "the headbone is connected to the . . . ?" ' 'Are there any grouping activities where different groups learn different parts of the body and then present to the rest of the class to make a whole body?' 'Do you use any visual aids besides text based examples?' We had great discussions about different activities to do. We also had a chance simply to discuss the strategies we've learned in the course across content areas and age groupings. This mattered.

K.B.: What a great way to get all your thoughts together before you begin a project. After you get through the "tough" part of filling out the **V**, then you have all the information you will need right in front of you.

Below are excerpts that appear in the journal and in the threaded discussions of students in our research class:

I.D.:   The V diagrams make an individual (teacher or student) think through the whole process of responding to the focus question or what's being done. I think as it ties in with the concept map; it helps analyze and clarify the points to be researched. The interactive **V** diagram is more advantageous to the student. The student gets immediate feedback.

K.A.:   I found the concept of the **V** diagram a very difficult concept to grasp at first. However with time and usage it became a tool that I have found myself using more than I thought I would. It allows the user the ability to put an article into a logical framework so as to better understand not only the methodology but also if the results really match the question asked. The vee is a helpful tool in evaluating articles for research purposes. I had reviewed several articles. After selecting the five that I wanted to rereview, I read them again while completing the vee assignment. I noticed that I had read it the second time with greater eye for detail and focused on the important elements of the research.

S.B.:   This is the second time that I have used the **V** in one of your classes. Applying it to possible dissertation ideas helped to clarify the arduous process. This was especially true in relation to the Principles that I used to help to guide my research. It also assisted in understanding other student's projects as well. Initially I found the **V** diagram very new, very different, and very difficult. After working with the concept I now find myself analyzing any research article I read by use of the **V**. I feel it is a very good pedagogical tool for reviewing, analyzing and understanding research. I was really quite surprised how using the **V** diagram and Q-5 methods helped to highlight problems within a study that I would not have noticed before.

S.M.:   Initially, the vee is a bit difficult. But it actually makes you think, work through the "stuffing" and get to the main points in a study quickly. It can be a very useful analytical tool and saves time. I find myself analyzing all the studies I read, and all my labs using the parameters set forth by the vee, and I find it extremely valuable in helping me to analyze the worth of a study. I was able to go through several studies and decide which ones would be useful to me in my area of research by just "thinking with the vee." Though it took me a while to fully grasp this concept, I can now appreciate it fully because it makes a lot of difference in the number of articles I can work through now in a given time.

The comments indicate that social constructions can make the **V** more manageable and understandable. When social constructions work together, ideas can be shared and meaning can be negotiated with the terms and the events that need to be considered. "Laying the **V**" on a research document clarifies its use and purpose (see Chapter 7). The *lesson plan* **V** provokes a more thoughtful venue to actively involve students in a lesson, while promoting self-reflection of the "why" and "what" to do when planning lessons and assignments (see Chapter 6). Also, the *research strategy* (see Chapter 8) aids in clarifying the terms and provides a framework for using the **V** in research investigations.

MEANINGFUL LEARNING

The art of educating minds requires that we, and the students we teach, learn in a meaningful way rather than one that relies on rote learning or memorization. Meaningful learning occurs when new concepts and propositions are nonarbitrarily and substantively related (anchored) to existing ideas in cognitive structure (Ausubel, 1968). This is in contrast to rote memorization where new information is not associated with existing concepts in cognitive structure and result in little or no interaction between information that is newly acquired and information that is already stored. In meaningful learning the materials are not *already* meaningful but only *potentially* meaningful. The object of meaningful learning is to convert potential meaning into actual meaning.

Learners learn meanings they have grasped. Meaning is the stuff of learning. In meaningful learning, one set of meanings the learner has already learned is used to connect to the new set of meanings the learner has first grasped. Learners make this connection in a free, open, voluntary way, and, in the best cases, with awareness of the need to "learn the connection on their own." Learning is what the learner is doing.

"Anchors" for Meaningful Learning

In Ausubel's learning theory, "anchors" are mental models in a cognitive framework. These "anchors" are only postulated to exist in Ausubel's view of cognitive frameworks. There is no way the learner can externalize the cognitive framework and put it on a piece of paper. The **V** diagram and concept maps are ways an active learner can "externalize an anchor." Once a learner makes a **V** diagram of what he or she already knows, that learner has "externalized an anchor." In our approach, **V** diagrams do serve to anchor knowledge, that is, to serve as a way to hold knowledge on the point of the events of making new knowledge.

Three conditions are necessary for meaningful learning to occur:

- The learner must have *relevant prior knowledge* to serve as an anchor with new information to be learned.
- Materials need to be selected that have *potential meaning* for the learner.
- The learner needs to have a *predisposition* to learn this new information.

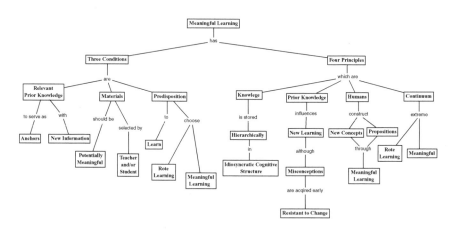

The concept map shows these three conditions and their relationship. In order for meaningful learning to occur, there needs to be relevant prior knowledge to serve as an anchor to which to relate to new information. Materials should be potentially meaningful in the sense that the learner has the requisite prior knowledge, experience, and reading abilities to make sense and establish connections with the new material. These materials can be self-selected by the learner and/or by the teacher who has taken relevant factors that are matched to the learner's interest, prior knowledge, experience, and reading abilities. The key for meaningful learning to occur is that the learner has a predisposition to learn this new material. This notion determines whether the new information will be learned either through rote learning or in a meaningful fashion.

Principles of Meaningful Learning

The basis for active learning is described by Ausubel's (1963) theory of cognitive learning. Ausubel's principles of nonarbitrary assimilation of knowledge through concept differentiation and concept integration have become fundamental principles for Meaningful Learning Theory. This Meaningful Learning Theory is based on these four principles:

1. Knowledge is stored hierarchically in idiosyncratic cognitive structures;
2. Prior knowledge influences new learning, although misconceptions are acquired early and are resistant to change;

3. Humans construct new concepts and propositions through meaningful learning; and
4. Meaningful learning is at one end of the continuum with rote learning at the other.

Learning and retention consist of such variables as the availability of
relevant anchoring ideas in cognitive structure, their stability and clarity,
and their discriminability from the learning material (Ausubel, Robbins, &
Blake, 1957). Meaningful learning occurs when new concepts and propositions are nonarbitrarily and substantively related (anchored) to existing
ideas in cognitive structure (Ausubel, 1968). This "anchoring" may transpire according to the degree of meaningfulness that icons appearing in
narrative and expository discourse, along with sounds and images in electronic discourse and media, have with an individual's cognitive structure.
Icons, such as those that appear in the form of illustrations appearing in a
text, may be seen by learners as representing a part of their world knowledge or experience, and are more vivid than others evoking images of past
experience with the event being portrayed.

An automobile owner's manual is an example of potentially meaningful
material. We may take little notice of this manual until a situation arises
that requires immediate attention. Granted that this owner's manual, like
a driver's manual, is often reviewed with teenagers or by new drivers
encountering their first experience with operating an automobile, however,
these materials become meaningful when a person has a predisposition to
learn. This occurrence is not unlike reading and learning how to apply
cardiopulmonary resuscitation (CPR), or reading a play and later seeing
it performed on stage, or learning about "friction" and applying it in an
experiment.

This owner's manual becomes a ready reference to explain the meaning of an indicator light that may appear on the instrument panel, or
a procedural reference such as how to change a flat tire at an inoppor-
tune moment. Our prior knowledge and experience with the workings
of an automobile vary. Some are very knowledgeable and can decipher
the indicator lights, and make the needed adjustments and repairs. Others
of us have limited prior knowledge or experience with the workings of
an automobile and rely upon others to make adjustments and repairs.
However, as automobile owners, we realize the potential that the manual has to enlighten us. We may have even a greater disposition to learn
about certain procedures that the manual contains when we are faced
with a situation such as the occurrence of a flat tire that needs to be
changed.

The **V** diagram deals with events that makeup the learning of new information with our world of experience. It is a tool that educates the mind
in a way that stimulates thinking and rethinking of ideas in indeterminate
arrays.

Events are units of experience (circumstances that surround the happenings that lead to its creation). As with any event (e.g., a war, a sculpture, a poem, a volcanic eruption, or a scientific experiment) all have a beginning, a middle, and an end. There are two considerations when beginning to make a V diagram. Either we make records of these events (as experimenters do) or we study records of the events already made (as historians do, or as students do in most of their formal school experience, or as we do in our daily societal curriculum).

Making a V – Changing a Flat Tire

Let's take a "clear" example of how to make a V diagram that more than likely is part of our societal curriculum (daily life experience): changing a flat tire. Although we may have never had to change a flat tire personally, it is something that we are probably aware of since it is a part of our automobile that needs to be considered for its operation. This example can take the form of either a record already made (as in the case of a manual that describes how to change a flat tire) or it can be part of an experiment to determine the best procedure for changing a flat tire given different circumstances that could be conducted in an automotive technology class.

For the sake of demonstration let us follow this example that is one that is somewhat typical. In this situation the need is to change a flat tire in a remote location and a cell phone is not available to call a friend, the automobile club, or a towing service. Although we may not think in the form of a V when engaging in this event, this event can be analyzed by its components.

First let's analyze what takes place in such an instance. You are driving along this remote road and you hear the "thumping" sound of a tire losing its air pressure.

1. You pull off to the side of road. Try to find a level surface rather than a slope.
2. You apply the parking brake and place the transmission in park (if automatic) or first gear or reverse.
3. Remove the spare tire, jack, and tire iron (lug wrench).
4. If there is a hub cap, pry it off with the sharp end of the tire iron.
5. Loosen each lug nut by turning the tire iron counterclockwise.
6. Place the jack under the position indicated by the automobile owner's manual. This position is usually the reinforced section of the car's body.
7. Depending on the type of jack, you may either need to pump the tire iron to raise the jack or turn the tire iron and crank it. Raise the jack until it contacts the car's frame and continue expanding the jack.

8. Once the tire is completely off of the ground, remove the wheel lugs completely and then the tire.
9. Lift the spare tire and align the holes with the axle hub and slide the tire onto the wheel studs.
10. Screw the lug nuts back on by hand until they are snug. Then lower the car back to the surface using the jack. Tighten each lug nut with the tire iron.
11. Put the flat tire in the trunk along with the jack and tire iron (and hub cap if there is one).

Now, let's represent this event on a **V** diagram.

Changing A Flat Tire:
An Example of a Clear Case

CONCEPTUAL/THEORETICAL
(Thinking)

METHODOLOGICAL
(Doing)

FOCUS/RESEARCH: QUESTIONS

WORLD VIEW:

Automobiles are necessary for transportation.

PHILOSOPHY:

Inflated tires are important for automobile travel.

THEORY:

Air pressure in automobile tires prevents flat tires.

PRINCIPLES:

Maintaining air pressure and tire tread awareness lessens the chances for a flat tire. Knowing the procedures for changing a flat tire lessens dependence on others.

CONSTRUCTS:

A clear case.

CONCEPTS:

Flat tire, jack, tire iron (lug wrench), spare tire.

FQ1 What are the procedures for changing a flat tire on an automobile?

VALUE CLAIMS:

Knowing how to change a flat tire is valuable in unexpected circumstances.

KNOWLEDGE CLAIMS:

There are a series of steps to follow when changing a flat tire.

TRANSFORMATIONS:

Applying the procedures to remove and replace a flat tire with an inflated spare tire.

RECORDS:

Mental and physical operations involved in changing a flat tire based on procedures. Changing a flat tire and replacing it with an inflated spare tire.

EVENTS AND/OR OBJECTS:

An automobile with a flat tire. An owner's manual describing the procedures for changing a flat tire. Given: spare tire, tire iron (lug wrench), jack.

Event: In this instance, a tire on an automobile has lost its air pressure resulting in a flat tire.

An immediate question arises in the circumstance described above of driving on a remote road that leads to a focus question for this event:

Focus Question: "What are the procedures for changing a flat tire?"

This focus question leads us to do something, to act, on this event. We need to consult some source to find out how to change this tire. A ready reference, in most cases, is the automobile owner's manual and the section of procedures for changing a flat tire. This owner's manual becomes part of the *event*, as do the implements necessary to change this tire: tire iron (lug wrench) and jack. An inflated spare tire also becomes a necessary item in this event.

In reading the procedures for changing a flat tire I need to be aware of certain concepts that need to be understood and kept in mind before, during, and when finalizing the tire removal and replacement: flat tire, jack, tire iron (lug wrench), and spare tire. At this point I may not know why the tire went flat, but I do know that flat means that the tire is almost level with the ground and is not round. Since I don't possess a gadget to inflate the tire that is currently available in automotive stores, I need to replace this tire if I am to continue my journey on this remote and desolate road. The description and the illustration in the owner's manual of a tire iron (lug wrench) and jack aids my understanding of these concepts.

By following these procedures, records are made that monitor what is transpiring in the events of changing a flat tire.

Records: Mental and physical operations involved in changing a flat tire based on procedures. Changing a flat tire and replacing it with an inflated spare tire.

These records, both mental and physical, enable me to better understand the process of changing a flat tire if it happens again or if asked by someone else how to change a flat tire. Going through the process of using these implements in changing a flat tire with a spare tire prepares me in future events of this sort and also increases my conceptual understanding of what is required when changing a tire. Depending upon my prior knowledge and experience with this event, the degree of educational value is correspondingly increased.

The thinking left-side of the **V** diagram can be represented. A *world view* is stated as "Automobiles are necessary for transportation." There are others that you can make. A *philosophy* is given: "Inflated tires are important for automobile transportation." Others can be stated. A *theory* about air pressure, and its effect on preventing flat tires, is stated. Other related theories can be stated, some of which may be more complex. The *concepts* needed to understand the focus question and the events are listed: flat tire, jack, tire iron (lug wrench), and spare tire.

The right-side of the **V** diagram is represented by the *records* given above, and the *transformations* that occurred: applying the procedures to remove and replace a flat tire with an inflated spare tire. To answer the focus question that was asked, the *knowledge claim* stated that "there are a series of steps to follow when changing a flat tire." These steps were consecutive and needed to be followed in a sequential order for the tire to be removed safely and replaced in a secure manner. The *value claim* of such a procedure was given as: "Knowing how to change a flat tire is valuable in unexpected circumstances." Flat tires happen unexpectedly, for the most part, and when and where this event occurs is not likely to be predicted with accuracy. Therefore, one must rely on knowing the procedures and being able mentally and physically for changing a flat tire if and when the situation presents itself.

If we were to rephrase the focus question into a research question, it would change the appearance of the example **V** diagram. For example, using the same event and asking the *research question*, "How do three people change a tire that has gone flat on an automobile?" The *events, records, transformations,* and *knowledge claims* are immediately altered. Without providing the three persons with procedures (e.g., an automobile owner's manual), and observing what procedures, implements, and order they engage in we can determine which of the three may have a better procedure than the one we followed or if they can change the tire without a given set of procedures. We can ask each if they have ever changed a flat tire and/or if they are familiar with the procedures for doing so to get a baseline. Our records can take the form of a videotape of the process each person uses to change a flat tire. *Transformation* of the data can be analyzed from the videotape, and the steps of each person's sequence used to change a flat tire listed on a chart. Making sense of how each person deals with the event depends on such variables as prior knowledge, actual experience of changing a flat tire, physical capabilities, and mental operations needed to sequence the stages. Of course, there are other factors to be considered within this operation of the event such as: Are the lug nuts "frozen" or tightened to a level that may require a certain amount of strength to loosen? Are the persons participating in this event limited to the implements that are a normal part of the automobile's cargo? Or, can they use a pneumatic wrench to remove and tighten the lug nuts?

This "clear" example may incur more complexity depending on the event and the circumstances that surround the question being asked. The degree of complexity can be simplified by the concepts that need to be known and understood, together with the kinds of records that are needed to make sense of what is happening in the event. For example, one may ask how can you discern the "mental operations" under *records* that a person is using during the process of first encountering a flat tire, removing it, and then replacing it with a spare tire. One way is to ask the person to "think aloud" as she goes through the process of completing the event. This narrative is recorded on the videotape and a transcript can be made for analysis of the mental operations that were used to physically change the flat tire.

Observing the event (records) over the years has changed the construction of an automobile's frame so that now it has a reinforced section to place the jack, and a crank for turning the jack so that it requires less expenditure of energy to raise the tire off the ground. This has replaced the "pumping" action needed previously with the jack handle that necessitated more effort and physical strength.

It is important to keep in mind that when trying to make sense of what is happening in an event with the instruments used to collect "the facts" that there are other factors to consider. Dewey (1933) reminds us that our observations of an event should not be solely to test an idea or find an explanatory meaning, but should also involve locating a problem or a relevant question.

As you begin to learn about the question or even create one, and thereby guide the formation of a **V**, remember that the more manipulations you do enables you to better understand its uses that are, in essence, your thoughts, perspectives, and curiosity. Originality is a vested interest into a question that focuses on an investigation of a problem or situation, and informs and makes known something that was previously unknown or not understood:

All thinking . . . contains a phase of originality. Originality does not mean or imply that the student's conclusion varies from the conclusion of others, much less it is a radically novel conclusion. . . . Originality means personal interest in the question, personal initiative in turning over the suggestion furnished by others, and sincerity in following them out to a tested conclusion." (Dewey, 1933, p. 258)

The notion of originality allows us to derive personal meaning from the experience whether you are a teacher, student, researcher, or one who is interested in learning more about the structure of knowledge of a particular topic of interest.

6

Learning and Teaching the V

*Principle 6. The **V** diagram clarifies ambiguities and makes new events happen.*

Teaching attempts to cultivate thought through shared meaning with the learner. The notion of this shared meaning is to arrive at reasoned judgments that can be agreed upon as either being accurate or making sense. However, while this fact or idea may meet a requisite requirement, it may be a stepping-stone to greater knowledge and meaning making once digested. Using the **V** to plan a lesson enables the teacher to think more deeply about the lesson for the learner that goes beyond mere "knowing" "understanding" and "application." The **V** becomes an enabler for the teacher to construct a lesson that takes into consideration the various components arrayed on the **V** that lends itself to ensuring that careful planning has occurred. Likewise the **V** provides a structure for the learner to think about these components to stimulate creative thought that provides for manipulation of these thoughts during the course of the resolution.

Assemblage: A Prelude to Learning

A primary notion anticipating learning is *assemblage* consisting of exploring new ways of thinking without abandoning one's own experiences in the process (Whitehead, 1938). Before learning begins, we need to assemble materials in a very special manner. Assemblage denies systematic ways to arrive at predetermined outcomes at the expense of understanding and refutes repetition of the known. Instead assemblage demands sorting, manipulating, contrasting, comparing, trying-out, failing, and mindful thinking that is multidimensional in scope and includes the affective domain. The notion of assemblage is that each of us (students, educators, administrators, researchers, engineers, mathematicians, artists, poets, writers, and scientists) starts with ideas predicated on our own prior knowledge and world experience rather than starting with a formulaic, systematic procedure when asking questions, solving problems, and delving into research investigations.

Our message for teachers, administrators, and policy makers is to allow students to focus more on *assembling* information by having them gather original sources, read and view other related source materials, compare and contrast points of view, analyze causes and effects, activate their own experiences, and provide opportunities for them to "show" what they can do. Having students make concept maps to reveal and share their thinking, develop **V** diagrams with a variety of source materials, and providing them with case-based situations to analyze, discuss, and write reports are some ways to teach students to use their minds as critical thinkers, stimulate their imagination, and decrease their reliance on memorized facts as a sign of school achievement and success. All of these events happen before learning. These kinds of events enable students to grasp meanings and "get the point" that lead to knowing, learning, understanding, and applying newly acquired facts and ideas to novel situations. This process of clarifying complex ideas and deriving meaning with understanding approximates our idea of "elucidating experience" that we insist upon for learning and teaching.

When using the **V**, students compose their own questions that they want answered based on the events they will examine. It is during this process of resolution of a topic with the **V** that students are more mindful with the events and pursue and test their thoughts along the way.

PROCEDURES FOR LEARNING/TEACHING **V** DIAGRAMMING

The ability to use a **V** diagram to learn about a topic under study or to use it to formulate and teach a lesson is important for both the teacher and the learner. The process enables the resolution of ideas that may at first seem complex and then simplifying them by learning about their construction and application. Below is an example that can be used in a science class to introduce **V** diagramming with students. Notice during the sequence that follows that different research questions demand different events and analyses. Of course, this same procedure can be used with any content area by adapting the procedures to accommodate a specific topic of a lesson.

An Example using a Laboratory Event

1. Select a laboratory or field *event* (or *object*) that is relativity simple to observe and for which one or more focus questions can be readily identified. Alternatively, a research paper with similar features can be used after all students (and the teacher) have read it carefully.

   An Example: Under Pressure. Boiling Water

2. Begin with a discussion of the event or objects being observed. Be sure that what is identified *is* the *event(s)* or *object(s)* for which *records* are made. Surprisingly, this is difficult.

   Event: Heat source, metal thermometer, distilled water, Pyrex beaker, ring stand, and clamp to hold thermometer.
   Records: time, temperature, and observations.

3. Identify and write out the best statement of the focus/research question(s). Again, be sure that the focus/research question(s) relate to the events or objects studied and the *records* to be made.

   Research Question: "What happens to the temperature of ice water when we add heat?"

4. Discuss how the questions serve to focus our attention on the specific features of the events or objects and *require* that certain kinds of records be obtained if the questions are to be answered. Illustrate how a different question about the same events or objects would require different records to be made (or require a different degree of precision).

   Different Research Question: "How does the appearance of water change as it changes from ice to steam?"
   Different Research Question: "Is the boiling point of water the same everywhere?"

5. Discuss the source of our questions, or our choice of *object(s)* or *event(s)* to be observed. Help students to see that, in general, our relevant concepts, principles or theories guide us in choosing what to observe and what questions to ask.

   Concepts: solid, gas, liquid (distilled water), and physical changes
   Principles: Pressure and the temperature affect boiling.
   Theories: Heat changes the properties of water.

6. Discuss the validity and reliability of the records. Are they *facts* (i.e., valid, reliable records)? Do these concepts, principles and theories that relate to our record making devices assure their validity and reliability? Are there better ways to gather more valid records? Time is both a valid and reliable measure. Temperature is a reliable measure, but uses an arbitrary zero rather than an absolute zero as its base measurement. Observation is a valid measure, but needs corroboration to be reliable. *A table can be created to organize the data.* Included in the table is location, elevation, air pressure, and boiling point. A Fahrenheit (°F) thermometer can be converted to Celsius (°C) using the relation $C = (F - 32)(5/9)$.

7. Discuss how we can transform our records to answer our questions. Are certain graphs, tables, or statistics useful transformations?

A table representing the data can be constructed to include: Location, elevation (meters), barometric pressure (mm Hg), liquid, boiling point (°C), average boiling point (°C), with number of trials.

8. Discuss how our concepts, principles and theories guide our record transformations. The structure of any graph or table, or the choice of certain statistics, should be influenced by our guiding principles.

9. Discuss the construction of *knowledge claims*. Help students to see that different questions could lead to gathering different records and performing different record transformations. The result may be a whole new set of *knowledge claims* about the source events or objects.

   In our example, what would happen if we investigated the relationship between temperature and time in water that is being heated in an open beaker?

   Would our representation change from a table to a graph: temperature versus time?

10. Discuss value claims. There are *value* statements such as X is *better than* Y, or X is good, or we *should seek* to achieve X. Note that *value claims* could derive from our knowledge claims, but they are not the same as *knowledge claims*.

11. Show how *concepts, principles*, and *theory* are used to shape our *knowledge claims* and may influence our *value claims*.

12. Explore ways to improve a given inquiry by examining which element in the **V** seems to be the "weakest link" in our chain of reasoning (i.e., in the construction of our knowledge and value claims).

13. Help students see that we operate with a *constructivist* epistemology to construct *claims* about how we see the world working, and not an empiricist or positivist epistemology that *proves* some *truth* about how the world works.

14. Help students see that a *world view* is what motivates or guides the investigator in what he/she chooses to try to understand, and controls the energy with which he/she pursues the inquiry. Scientists care about value and pursue better ways to explain rationally how the world works. Astrologers, mystics, creationists, and others do not engage in the same constructivist enterprise.

15. Compare, contrast and discuss **V** diagrams made by different students for the same events or objects. Discuss how the variety helps to illustrate the constructed nature of knowledge. For example, in the case of the Research Question that asks: "Is the boiling point of water the same everywhere?" Is there a general statement that can be made concerning the boiling point of water at different elevations? What about barometric pressures? These questions add to the knowledge with the concept of "boiling water."

Learning and teaching the **V** with an example from your content area aids students in clarifying the components that need to be considered when delving into a topic. Engaging in the thinking and doing process prepares students to examine new information with a critical eye and informs them of not only the complexity that new information may present, but also with a tool to simplify these complexities by learning about its structure in ways that are meaningful rather than through rote memorization. Comparing and contrasting **V** diagrams made by different students from the same events or objects promotes discussion and illustrates how knowledge is constructed.

The more we are able to critically examine a topic given the time and effort required to do so, the more intelligent will we become in solving problems and when dealing with situations. The final examination is not in the number of "right" answers to questions asked, but in the ways in which the knowledge that makes up our intelligence is *applied* when we are asked to deal with the complexities of life.

LESSON PLANNING Vs

Planning lessons are an important requirement for a teacher. While supplementary teaching aids accompany most textbooks prepared for students, nothing takes the place of the teacher for determining the kinds of lessons that are needed to introduce, reinforce, and lead to meaningful learning and understanding of key facts and ideas associated with a topic of study. *In order to have thinking students we need to have thinking teachers.* Teachers who plan their own lessons are better prepared to "teach" their students than are those who rely on others who prepare "ready-made" materials for them to use with their students.

Teacher Lesson Plan V and Student Study Plan

The **V** diagram is a tool that a teacher can use to plan a lesson that encompasses both conceptual (thinking) and methodological (doing) components for actively engaging the student while simultaneously creating a mindful learning environment. The teacher stimulates students in the *event* portion of the **V** with the materials and adjunct aids that will be used to activate students' schema with a given topic of study. Prereading strategies such as thematic organizers, graphic organizers, anticipation guides, reading visual aids guides, previews, can be part of this schema activation process.

In the example that follows, Bekki Pickney, a special education teacher, used the **V** to create a lesson with her students (see Figure 6.1).

In this instance, the focus question is stated asking the students to compare and contrast their lifestyles with those of Count Dracula. The events describe what the students will do in order to find information about Count

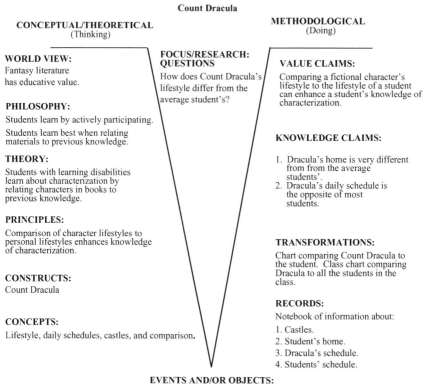

FIGURE 6.1. Lesson plan designed for students with learning disabilities.

Dracula from which to compare and contrast their individual lifestyles. The teacher anticipates the concepts that will be used by her students as they undertake this assignment. The expectations that students will have written in their notebook are listed under *records*. She has a philosophy that guides her in formulating this lesson and a theory about how students with learning disabilities can learn about characters that appear in books by relating them to individual world knowledge and experience. Transformations of the information gathered in the records will consist of charts. Using the data obtained from the records both an individual chart of each student's lifestyle and schedule and another comparing and contrasting the class as a whole will be constructed.

She expects students to answer the Focus/Research Question by the statements listed under knowledge claims. Further, she intends for this lesson to instill the principle that "comparison of character lifestyles to personal lifestyles enhances knowledge of characterization." If this occurs, as a result of the learning outcome derived from the knowledge claims, this principle, in this lesson, coincides with the theory she is testing. The value claim states what she intends as the worth of having her students undertake this lesson.

This **V** clearly provides the learner with the scope and the processes that will be undertaken when engaging in this lesson. Also shown are the thought processes that this teacher used to formulate the lesson in order for her students to delve into a reading, relate the circumstances of the character to their own lives (societal curriculum), and actively engage in meaningful learning.

A sample **V** diagram shown in Figure 6.2 portrays how a student might approach this lesson.

In this example lesson a student-completed **V** diagram is shown. Stage 1 asks a Focus Question and under *events* describes what to do in order to answer the question. Listed also are the concepts, records, theory, philosophy, principles, and how the information will be represented under transformations. The teacher is able to view this student's **V** diagram at this point to ensure that the Focus Question and the events are related. Also within this stage the teacher can view the student's entries and make any suggestions before proceeding. Stage 2 completes the **V** diagram in listing the answers to the Focus Question and the value of doing this lesson.

In this *Teacher Lesson Plan **V** and Student Study Plan* the four commonplaces of educating are in evidence as is the student's societal influence.

Teaching: Meaning is shared with the students by providing materials and circumstances that they can relate both their prior knowledge and experience (Dracula movies, stories about Dracula) with the lesson.

Curriculum: The events describe the print materials that will be used by the students and the requirements necessary for completing the lesson. The events, facts, and concepts that comprise this lesson promotes the educating process that will enable the learners to become self-educated in learning about the life style characteristics of a fictional character through analogies with themselves and other class members.

Learner: Students actively engage in the lesson by reading and comparing and contrasting their own life styles with that of Dracula. They are asked to draw and/or construct a model of a castle where he might live, and to make analogies between Dracula (a fictional character) and themselves. Students are able to compare and contrast their individual life style with other members of the class.

Governance: The ways in which the teacher exercises governance in this lesson are noted by the requirements that are expected of the students listed in the events. Students impose their own governance in this lesson by being permitted to convert the teacher's question on the **V** and tweak the events to meet their individual question in pursuing a resolution. Some may choose to access other texts or use the Internet to find out more information about Dracula and vampires. Students take charge of their own learning.

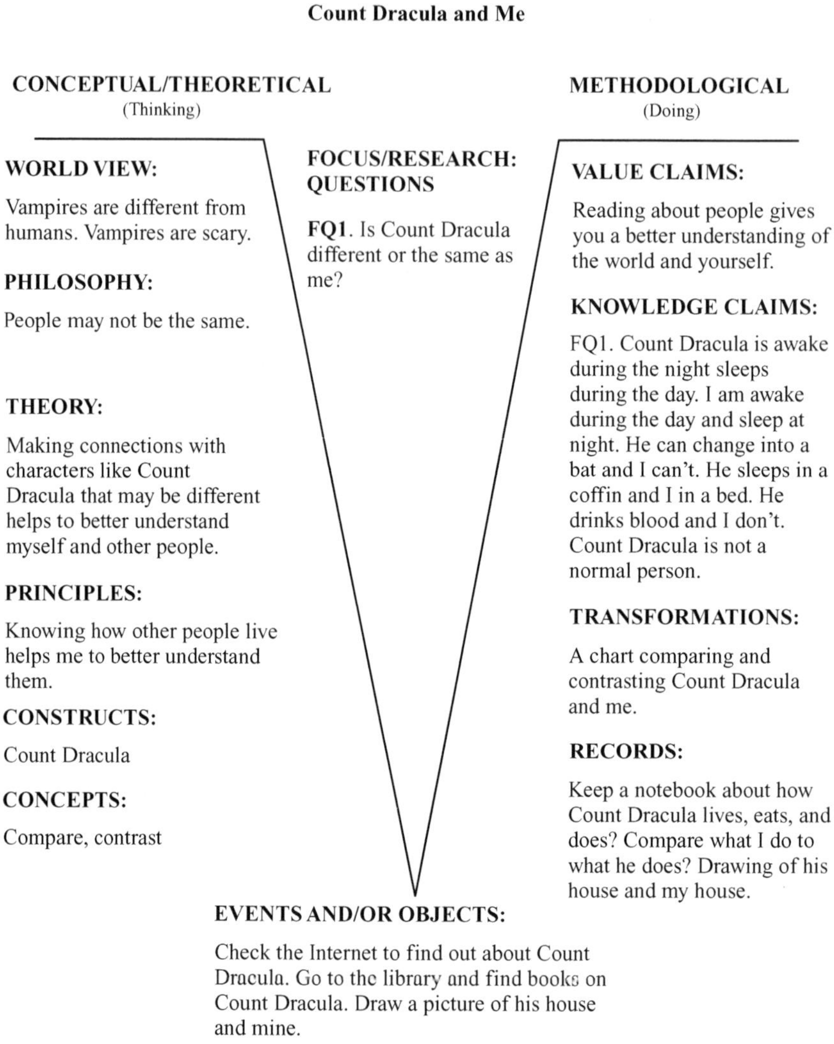

Count Dracula and Me

CONCEPTUAL/THEORETICAL   METHODOLOGICAL
(Thinking)   (Doing)

WORLD VIEW: **FOCUS/RESEARCH:**   **VALUE CLAIMS:**
                                   QUESTIONS
Vampires are different from   Reading about people gives
humans. Vampires are scary.   **FQ1**. Is Count Dracula   you a better understanding of
                                   different or the same as   the world and yourself.
PHILOSOPHY: me?
                                                              KNOWLEDGE CLAIMS:
People may not be the same.
                                                              FQ1. Count Dracula is awake
                                                              during the night sleeps
THEORY: during the day. I am awake
                                                              during the day and sleep at
Making connections with   night. He can change into a
characters like Count   bat and I can't. He sleeps in a
Dracula that may be different   coffin and I in a bed. He
helps to better understand   drinks blood and I don't.
myself and other people.   Count Dracula is not a
                                                              normal person.
PRINCIPLES:
                                                              TRANSFORMATIONS:
Knowing how other people live
helps me to better understand   A chart comparing and
them.   contrasting Count Dracula
                                                              and me.
CONSTRUCTS:
                                                              RECORDS:
Count Dracula
                                                              Keep a notebook about how
CONCEPTS: Count Dracula lives, eats, and
                                                              does? Compare what I do to
Compare, contrast   what he does? Drawing of his
                                                              house and my house.
                EVENTS AND/OR OBJECTS:

                Check the Internet to find out about Count
                Dracula. Go to the library and find books on
                Count Dracula. Draw a picture of his house
                and mine.

FIGURE 6.2. An example student **V** diagram of the Count Dracula lesson.

During the course of completing a lesson or assignment students may become risk takers and pursue paths that may not have been anticipated by the teacher. By formulating their own study plan based on questions of interest and curiosity that correspond to the teacher's lesson plan **V**, students are able to make connections with what they know and have experienced both in and out of school and the new information that they will be studying. Their ideas are revealed when the teacher examines the left side of their **V** diagram, thereby providing the teacher with a tool by which to evaluate and monitor their progress with the left side of their **V**.

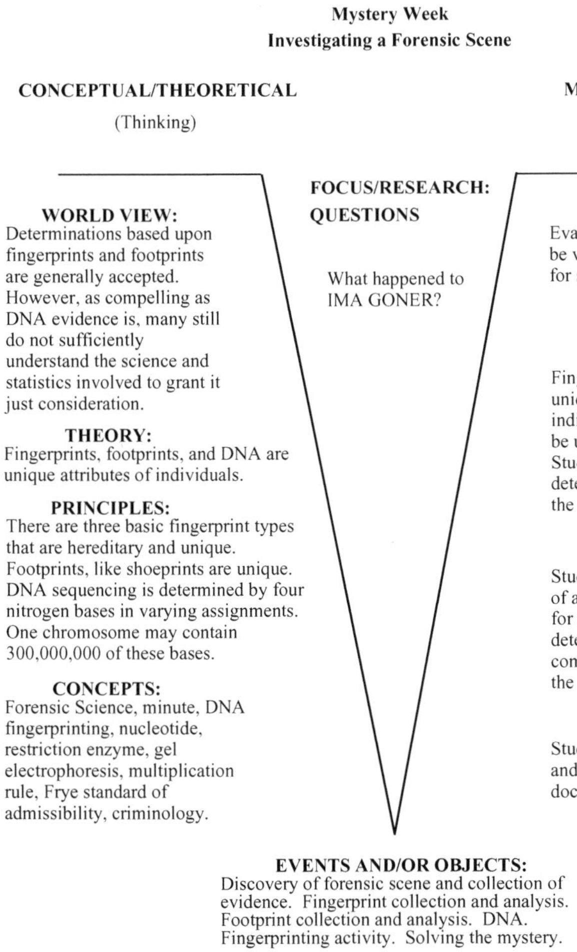

Mystery Week
Investigating a Forensic Scene

CONCEPTUAL/THEORETICAL

(Thinking)

METHODOLOGICAL

(Doing)

FOCUS/RESEARCH: QUESTIONS

What happened to IMA GONER?

WORLD VIEW:
Determinations based upon fingerprints and footprints are generally accepted. However, as compelling as DNA evidence is, many still do not sufficiently understand the science and statistics involved to grant it just consideration.

THEORY:
Fingerprints, footprints, and DNA are unique attributes of individuals.

PRINCIPLES:
There are three basic fingerprint types that are hereditary and unique. Footprints, like shoeprints are unique. DNA sequencing is determined by four nitrogen bases in varying assignments. One chromosome may contain 300,000,000 of these bases.

CONCEPTS:
Forensic Science, minute, DNA fingerprinting, nucleotide, restriction enzyme, gel electrophoresis, multiplication rule, Frye standard of admissibility, criminology.

VALUE CLAIMS:
Evaluations of forensic evidence can be valuable in making determinations for solving crimes.

KNOWLEDGE CLAIMS:
Fingerprints and footprints are unique and can be matched to individuals. DNA fingerprinting can be used to identify an individual. Students will make some definitive determinations based on analysis of the evidence.

TRANSFORMATIONS:
Students record information, method of analysis, and outcomes on a chart for evaluation. Identifying the person, determining fragment length, and comparing it with the one found at the scene.

RECORDS:
Students keep Detective Notebooks and science laboratory journals for documenting results.

EVENTS AND/OR OBJECTS:
Discovery of forensic scene and collection of evidence. Fingerprint collection and analysis. Footprint collection and analysis. DNA. Fingerprinting activity. Solving the mystery.

FIGURE 6.3. Lesson plan **V** for Mystery Week.

Converting Lesson Plans to V Action Plans

Engaging students with the **V** enables them to better understand a topic of study. There are instances where teachers use the **V** as a *learning tool* whereby students formulate their own questions to match the focus of the lesson and the events of the topic to be studied. Students are then able to use the **V** to penetrate the topic in more depth.

An example is Elizabeth Word's lesson plan **V** shown in Figure 6.3. In this lesson students participate in a variety of forensic events that require knowledge of conceptual analyses, documentation of the events, and a coherent plan that actively engages students and takes them through a process of representing their data and making knowledge claims.

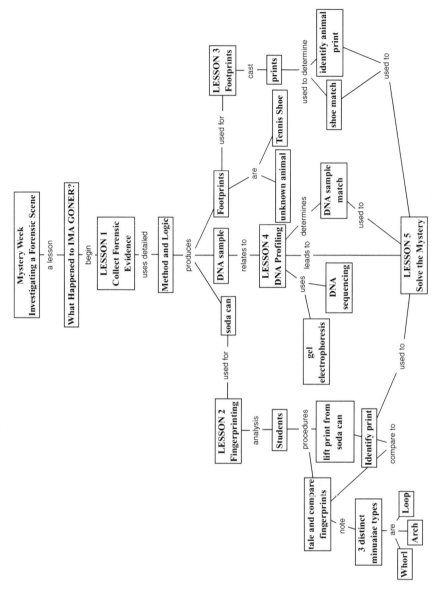

FIGURE 6.4. A concept map showing the construct portion of the V diagram for the Mystery Week lesson.

Her concept map of the lesson, listed under *constructs*, is shown in Figure 6.4.

A clearly designed lesson is shown in this five step lesson that guides the students in learning about forensic science in a meaningful way.

Using the **V** as a lesson plan enables the teacher to reflect upon those facts and ideas that are necessary for her students to better know and understand. The key to planning is selecting materials and creating problems or situations that have the potential to add to a learner's knowledge of the topic not only in assembling facts but also ideas that can be applied to "real-world" settings.

The same thoughtful processes that the teacher uses in creating the lesson plan **V** are internalized by the learners as they engage in the events, understand the related concepts, and make new knowledge happen by the records they use to monitor the events. Manipulation of the information derived from the records is then transformed into a "readable" display that is referred to when making the knowledge claims. The value of the lesson anticipated by the teacher is compared to the students' perceived value of the lesson. An example of a student **V** that could be initiated from "Investigating a Forensic Scene" is shown in Figure 6.5.

An Example of Negotiating Meaning

This **V**, shown in Figure 6.5, is an example whereby meaning between the teacher and the student is negotiated. Notice that the focus question contains the word "clues" as a primary focal point for study, however, this word does not appear under *Concepts*. This student's omission of this word provides the teacher with a place to mediate the discussion process and clarify other concept words listed such as: Why is the word "logic" listed? Should other words related to "clues" be listed under *concepts*? Words such as "soda can," "tennis shoe," and "examine," would be elicited based on the framework of the overall lesson plan.

The student is then able to proceed with the first phase of the Forensic study. Once completed the next lesson on *fingerprinting* follows. Each succeeding phase in this lesson series provides a multiple set of related **V** diagrams: a "Parade of **V**s."

PARADE OF Vs

A second **V** of Lesson 2, *fingerprinting*, would then follow this first **V**. Extending the use of **V**s to include Lesson 3: *footprints*, and Lesson 4: *DNA Profiling*, result in a "parade" of **V**s (see Figure 6.6). When these **V**s are placed sequentially beside each other a progression is visually displayed of the processes that a student or group of students undertook in reaching their final **V** that culminates in a synthesis of Lesson 5: the solving of the mystery.

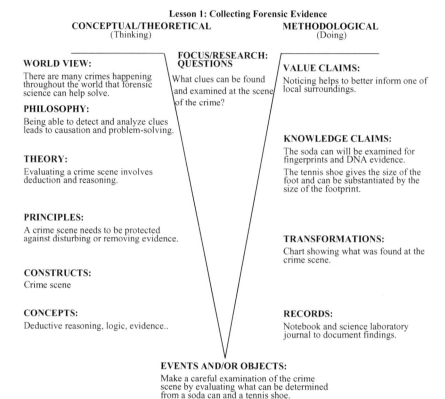

Lesson 1: Collecting Forensic Evidence

CONCEPTUAL/THEORETICAL   METHODOLOGICAL
(Thinking)   (Doing)

FOCUS/RESEARCH:

WORLD VIEW: **QUESTIONS**
There are many crimes happening   What clues can be found   **VALUE CLAIMS:**
throughout the world that forensic   and examined at the scene   Noticing helps to better inform one of
science can help solve.   of the crime?   local surroundings.

PHILOSOPHY:
Being able to detect and analyze clues
leads to causation and problem-solving.

                                                                          KNOWLEDGE CLAIMS:
                                                                          The soda can will be examined for
THEORY: fingerprints and DNA evidence.
Evaluating a crime scene involves   The tennis shoe gives the size of the
deduction and reasoning.   foot and can be substantiated by the
                                                                          size of the footprint.

PRINCIPLES:
A crime scene needs to be protected
against disturbing or removing evidence.   **TRANSFORMATIONS:**
                                                                          Chart showing what was found at the
                                                                          crime scene.

CONSTRUCTS:
Crime scene

CONCEPTS: **RECORDS:**
Deductive reasoning, logic, evidence..   Notebook and science laboratory
                                                                          journal to document findings.

EVENTS AND/OR OBJECTS:
Make a careful examination of the crime
scene by evaluating what can be determined
from a soda can and a tennis shoe.

FIGURE 6.5. A **V** diagram of Lesson 1: Collecting Forensic Evidence.

A "Parade of **V**s" shows the path that a research investigation or a lesson is taking as it evolves. It enables the comparison of these **V**s to be shared and discussed among peers, teachers, or mentors. This side-by-side judgment illustrates that knowledge construction is a continuous process wherein new knowledge contributes new concepts, principles, and theories (or modifications in existing ones) and thus influences further inquiries.

Comparing and contrasting the results of each **V** leads to further discussion of the events, records, and knowledge claims associated with the questions that were asked that ensued during this examination of forensic evidence. It is foreseen that students using the **V** become more engaged, thoughtful, and imaginative with the theory of deductive reasoning and its role in determining the relevant from irrelevant clues and analysis resulting from this lesson.

An Example of using a V with Fantasy Literature

Allison Rinner developed this **V** as a six-week lesson on "fantasy literature." Her events consist of a variety of readings, literature concepts, class

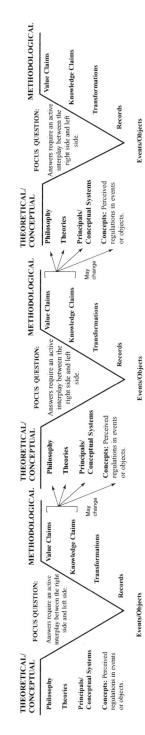

FIGURE 6.6. An example of a "Parade of Vs."

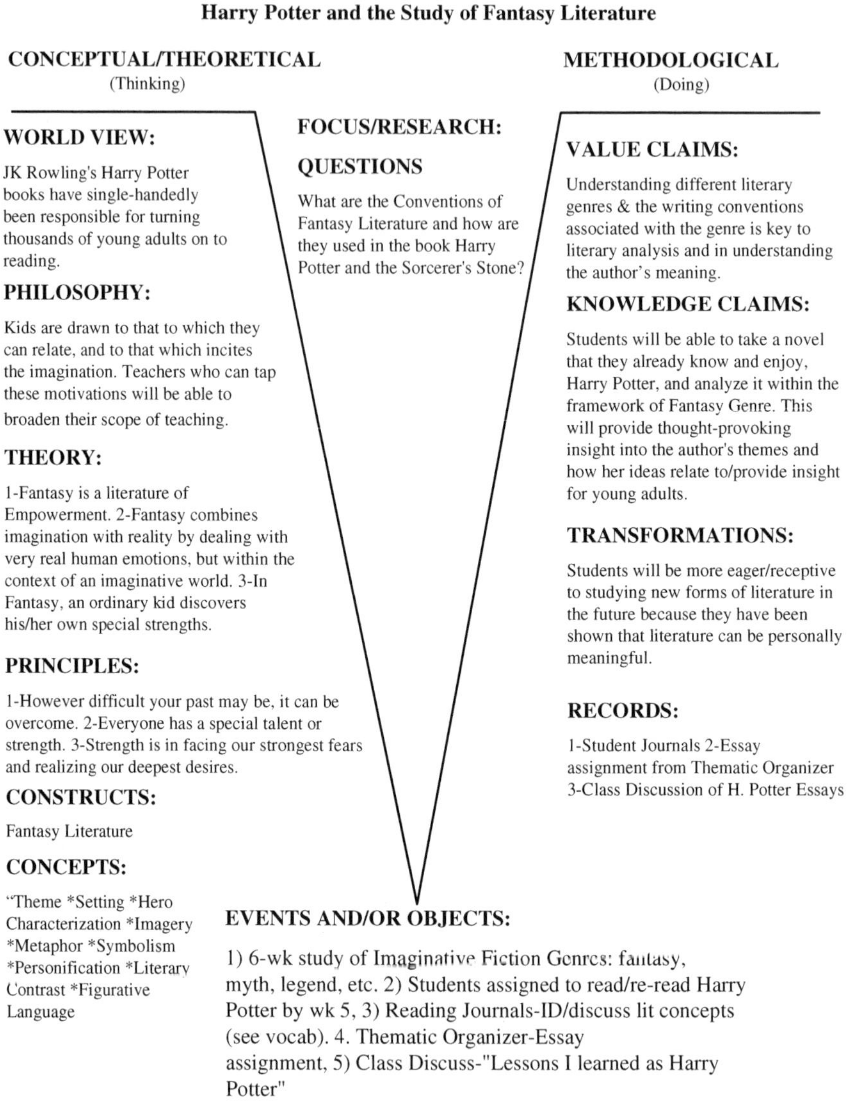

Harry Potter and the Study of Fantasy Literature

CONCEPTUAL/THEORETICAL   METHODOLOGICAL
(Thinking)   (Doing)

WORLD VIEW:

JK Rowling's Harry Potter
books have single-handedly
been responsible for turning
thousands of young adults on to
reading.

PHILOSOPHY:

Kids are drawn to that to which they
can relate, and to that which incites
the imagination. Teachers who can tap
these motivations will be able to
broaden their scope of teaching.

THEORY:

1-Fantasy is a literature of
Empowerment. 2-Fantasy combines
imagination with reality by dealing with
very real human emotions, but within the
context of an imaginative world. 3-In
Fantasy, an ordinary kid discovers
his/her own special strengths.

PRINCIPLES:

1-However difficult your past may be, it can be
overcome. 2-Everyone has a special talent or
strength. 3-Strength is in facing our strongest fears
and realizing our deepest desires.

CONSTRUCTS:

Fantasy Literature

CONCEPTS:

"Theme *Setting *Hero
Characterization *Imagery
*Metaphor *Symbolism
*Personification *Literary
Contrast *Figurative
Language

FOCUS/RESEARCH:

QUESTIONS

What are the Conventions of
Fantasy Literature and how are
they used in the book Harry
Potter and the Sorcerer's Stone?

VALUE CLAIMS:

Understanding different literary
genres & the writing conventions
associated with the genre is key to
literary analysis and in understanding
the author's meaning.

KNOWLEDGE CLAIMS:

Students will be able to take a novel
that they already know and enjoy,
Harry Potter, and analyze it within the
framework of Fantasy Genre. This
will provide thought-provoking
insight into the author's themes and
how her ideas relate to/provide insight
for young adults.

TRANSFORMATIONS:

Students will be more eager/receptive
to studying new forms of literature in
the future because they have been
shown that literature can be personally
meaningful.

RECORDS:

1-Student Journals 2-Essay
assignment from Thematic Organizer
3-Class Discussion of H. Potter Essays

EVENTS AND/OR OBJECTS:

1) 6-wk study of Imaginative Fiction Genres: fantasy,
myth, legend, etc. 2) Students assigned to read/re-read Harry
Potter by wk 5, 3) Reading Journals-ID/discuss lit concepts
(see vocab). 4. Thematic Organizer-Essay
assignment, 5) Class Discuss-"Lessons I learned as Harry
Potter"

FIGURE 6.7. Harry Potter and the study of Fantasy literature.

discussions, and the use of a thematic organizer (a teacher-developed adjunct aid, see Alvarez, 1983; Alvarez & Risko, 2002, 1989; Risko & Alvarez,
1986). The **V** shown in Figure 6.7 focuses on the *Harry Potter* book series.

Her value claim states the worth of engaging students with such a lesson
over a period of time. Her **V** displays her reasoning for teaching fantasy
literature, the results of which convey these notions of having literature
take on the dimensions of personal meaning for her students.

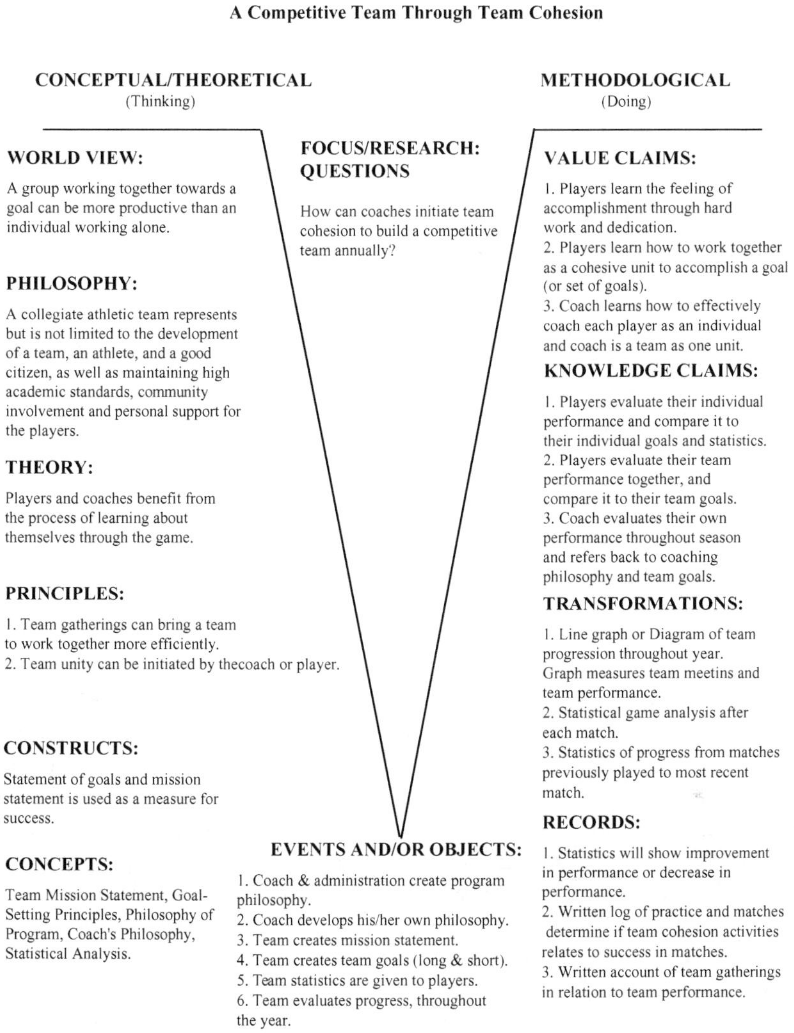

A Competitive Team Through Team Cohesion

CONCEPTUAL/THEORETICAL
(Thinking)

METHODOLOGICAL
(Doing)

FOCUS/RESEARCH: QUESTIONS

How can coaches initiate team cohesion to build a competitive team annually?

WORLD VIEW:

A group working together towards a goal can be more productive than an individual working alone.

PHILOSOPHY:

A collegiate athletic team represents but is not limited to the development of a team, an athlete, and a good citizen, as well as maintaining high academic standards, community involvement and personal support for the players.

THEORY:

Players and coaches benefit from the process of learning about themselves through the game.

PRINCIPLES:

1. Team gatherings can bring a team to work together more efficiently.
2. Team unity can be initiated by the coach or player.

CONSTRUCTS:

Statement of goals and mission statement is used as a measure for success.

CONCEPTS:

Team Mission Statement, Goal-Setting Principles, Philosophy of Program, Coach's Philosophy, Statistical Analysis.

VALUE CLAIMS:

1. Players learn the feeling of accomplishment through hard work and dedication.
2. Players learn how to work together as a cohesive unit to accomplish a goal (or set of goals).
3. Coach learns how to effectively coach each player as an individual and coach is a team as one unit.

KNOWLEDGE CLAIMS:

1. Players evaluate their individual performance and compare it to their individual goals and statistics.
2. Players evaluate their team performance together, and compare it to their team goals.
3. Coach evaluates their own performance throughout season and refers back to coaching philosophy and team goals.

TRANSFORMATIONS:

1. Line graph or Diagram of team progression throughout year. Graph measures team meetins and team performance.
2. Statistical game analysis after each match.
3. Statistics of progress from matches previously played to most recent match.

RECORDS:

1. Statistics will show improvement in performance or decrease in performance.
2. Written log of practice and matches determine if team cohesion activities relates to success in matches.
3. Written account of team gatherings in relation to team performance.

EVENTS AND/OR OBJECTS:

1. Coach & administration create program philosophy.
2. Coach develops his/her own philosophy.
3. Team creates mission statement.
4. Team creates team goals (long & short).
5. Team statistics are given to players.
6. Team evaluates progress, throughout the year.

FIGURE 6.8. Teaching plan for coaching "team cohesion."

A Coach Uses the V

Another use of the **V** diagram is shown as a teaching plan designed to teach "team cohesion" by Jennifer Adeva, a women's volleyball coach (see Figure 6.8).

Coach Adeva reveals her thought processes in developing the **V** in her journal entry. Notice in her reflections the way she approaches the process of dealing with the elements that comprise the **V**.

After completing the Vee Diagram on building a successful team through team cohesion, I realized the subject was more difficult than I had imagined. I had a very hard time coming up with a focus question for this subject. As I was completing the events/objects, world view, philosophy, and theory, I was rewording my focus question. The subject I dealt with an aspect of coaching that I consider one of my weaknesses. I believed dealt with a lot of xs & os" versus building team cohesion. This topic interested me after I took the present team I am coaching now bowling. After doing an activity that had nothing to do with volleyball, they actually played very well the next day. I thought team cohesion was more working through practice and games together rather than activities spent outside of the sport.

Constructing this Vee Diagram really made me get a better perspective on coaching and the necessary tools to become successful. I followed the steps in doing the Vee Diagram from the manual as opposed to jumping around each topic. When I brainstormed by looking at each topic in no particular order it was virtually impossible to complete the Vee. After completing the events and objects portion, I went up the right side and down the left side of the Vee, this seemed to help me put my ideas together easier. I think the Vee Diagram can be used as a tool for coaches and players at the beginning of a season to build team unity.

Clearly the **V** stimulates thought and action through conscious and strategic planning as described in this entry. Coach Adeva's rethinking with incorporating the topic "building team cohesion" revealed a weakness she perceived in her coaching and led to a reformulation of approaching the affective domain of coaching and combining it with the cognitive domain for a more complete portrayal of the coaching profession.

Action **V** diagrams are putting into practice the tool by which a person is able to engage in intellectual gymnastics that causes minds to "hurt" and ideas to "flourish." The degree to which the teacher permits students to formulate their own questions that correspond with the events being studied determines the degree of innovative ideas that emerge from the topic under study. Asking students to formulate their own questions at first is an unsettling experience: Students are not typically asked to form questions; instead, they are usually given the questions to predetermined answers or outcomes. Our experience indicates that many students are at first frustrated at having to think about questions to events that they must garner. This process requires careful crafting of the question that matches the events that are being studied. However, this process enables students to better conceive the needed relationship and initiates the path of inquiry to be taken in order to clarify what is needed in this undertaking.

V Diagram and Concept Map of V

Sharia Kharif developed a lesson **V** diagram for a literature assignment on Shakespeare's *Othello*. Her focus questions are more general to indicate that she wishes her students to develop their own focus questions with more specificity depending on the paths they take during the events portion of the assignment (see Figure 6.9).

"Othello...thou hath slain me..."

CONCEPTUAL/THEORETICAL (Thinking)		METHODOLOGICAL (Doing)

WORLD VIEW:

Great Literature can be educative.

PHILOSOPHY:

Students often see no relation between Shakespeare and modern media.

THEORY:

Different genres...similar stories

PRINCIPLES:

Once students are stimulated, they gain greater levels of understanding.

CONSTRUCTS:

Shakespeare's Othello

CONCEPTS:

Relevant themes, character relationships, event, relevance to modern entertainment.

FOCUS/RESEARCH: QUESTIONS

FQ What is Shakespeare talking about?
FQ Are his themes relevant today?

VALUE CLAIMS:

Once students recognize similarities in genres, they will begin to relate modern media with the old.

KNOWLEDGE CLAIMS:

Answers to what are themes?
Are they relevant?

TRANSFORMATIONS:

Venn Diagrams

Student reenactments

RECORDS:

Student journals; quizzes gauging text understanding; student essays

EVENTS AND/OR OBJECTS:

(1) Introduction of Shakespeare's *Othello*
(2) Students receive reading study guide for Act I
(3) Students record themes and events from each act,
including 3 questions per act that they think should be answered in class
(4) Introduce " The Lion King" and repeat journal process. Students answer:
Does it work? Why or why not? Similarities?
(5) Construct Venn Diagram displaying relationship between materials
(6) Students write essay on one theme consistent with both materials.

FIGURE 6.9. A **V** diagram for Shakespeare's *Othello*.

Her concept map of the **V** diagram reveals how the ideas are related to each other (see Figure 6.10). Ideas appearing on her **V** diagram show ideas and their relationship and provide the viewer with a visual representation of her thought processes when she designed the lesson for this topic.

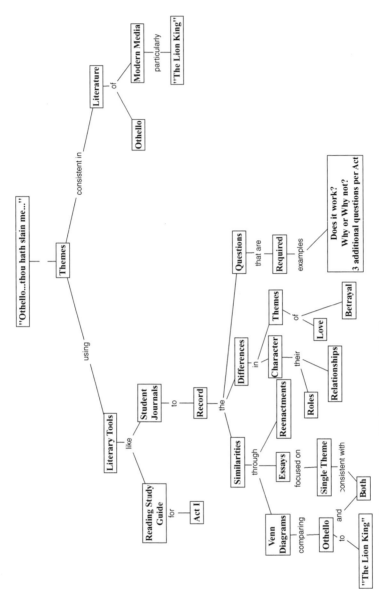

FIGURE 6.10. Concept map of **V** diagram on *Othello*.

Hierarchical concept maps enable students, teachers, and researchers to reveal their ideas with a theme or target concept under study. Software programs such as Inspiration 6.0 or CMap[1] can be used to construct concept maps. In our project, students use the concept mapping portion that is housed on our password protected Exploring Minds Network.[2]

A Lesson Plan V for First Graders

Susan Rogers developed a **V** for a lesson with her first grade students (see Figure 6.11). Her lesson challenges students to examine how the work they see others perform directly relates to their own lives.

Notice the events that will involve the students, the concepts that will be learned, and the records that will evolve from the students' experience with the lesson. Students make judgments between goods and services, they visit and see workers in their community, and are able to develop personal meaning with the jobs of these workers and their own life.

Lesson Plan **V**s inform teacher practice. They serve as both teaching and learning tools that enable this engaging process to occur due to the thoughtful and methodological procedures that are undertaken in its development. Planning an event is the most important part of any teaching or research process. Without careful and methodological planning the effort expended on a specific event results in shoddy outcomes and ambiguous findings. In order to prepare a lesson, it is important that innovative activities are an integral part of the teaching and learning process and those paths of inquiry toward resolution are varied. This enables learners to exercise their curiosity and actively engages them in meaningful learning outcomes.

CREATING MEANING OUT OF EVENTS OF HUMAN EXPERIENCE

Learning and teaching the **V** enables meaning to be shared with lessons that actively engage students in the process. To educate is to change the meaning of human experience. After a person has undergone an intentional educative event, the meaning of experience has changed for that person. The change in meaning will range from the trivial to the profound. The durability will also vary.

Teaching, Learning, and Meaning

We understand the creation of meaning out of human experience when we understand that something (A) can come to stand for something new (B).

---

[1] CMap was developed at the University of West Florida and can be used without cost for educational projects. http://www.coginst.uwf.edu/CmapV2/Download.html.

[2] Exploring Minds was developed at the Center of Excellence in Information Systems, Tennessee State University. http://exploringminds.tsuniv.edu.

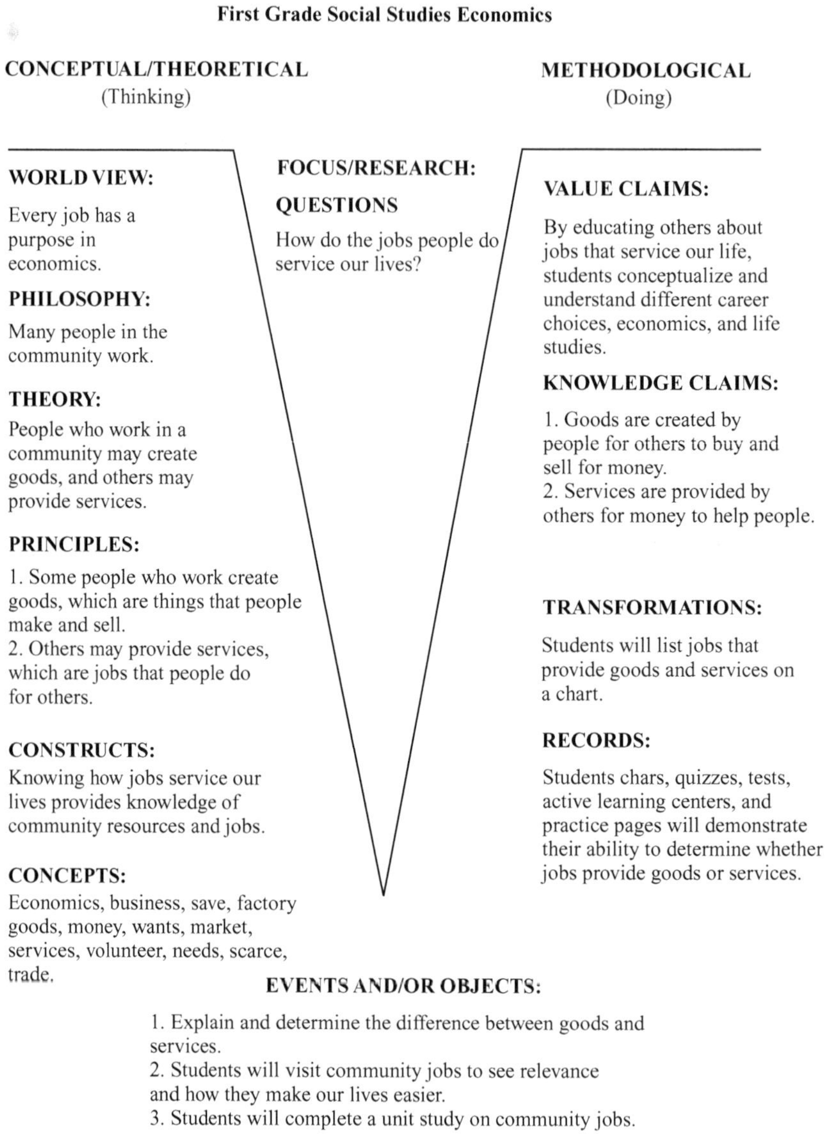

First Grade Social Studies Economics

CONCEPTUAL/THEORETICAL	METHODOLOGICAL
(Thinking)	(Doing)

WORLD VIEW:

Every job has a purpose in economics.

PHILOSOPHY:

Many people in the community work.

THEORY:

People who work in a community may create goods, and others may provide services.

PRINCIPLES:

1. Some people who work create goods, which are things that people make and sell.
2. Others may provide services, which are jobs that people do for others.

CONSTRUCTS:

Knowing how jobs service our lives provides knowledge of community resources and jobs.

CONCEPTS:

Economics, business, save, factory goods, money, wants, market, services, volunteer, needs, scarce, trade.

FOCUS/RESEARCH: QUESTIONS

How do the jobs people do service our lives?

VALUE CLAIMS:

By educating others about jobs that service our life, students conceptualize and understand different career choices, economics, and life studies.

KNOWLEDGE CLAIMS:

1. Goods are created by people for others to buy and sell for money.
2. Services are provided by others for money to help people.

TRANSFORMATIONS:

Students will list jobs that provide goods and services on a chart.

RECORDS:

Students chars, quizzes, tests, active learning centers, and practice pages will demonstrate their ability to determine whether jobs provide goods or services.

EVENTS AND/OR OBJECTS:

1. Explain and determine the difference between goods and services.
2. Students will visit community jobs to see relevance and how they make our lives easier.
3. Students will complete a unit study on community jobs.

FIGURE 6.11. First grade **V** lesson plan

The footprint in the sand is taken as a sign that a person probably walked there; the footprint that is present is a sign of the person who is absent. The footprint is a record of an event. If the ocean washes over the footprint, that record is destroyed; there is no remaining basis for a sign of those past events. We say that smoke is a sign of fire, and sometimes it is. We say that dark clouds are a sign of rain, and sometimes the rains do come. When we take something that is in present time (the footprint) to be a sign of something else, we are making inferences. We are also making meaning. When we say that "A is a sign of B" or that "A stands for B," we are also saying that "A" means "B." The footprint stands for or means a person. The smoke means that fire is likely; the clouds mean rain.

When meanings are constructed, we come into possession of our world. Meanings connect things. It is this feature that gives certain events their educational value. The construction of meanings connects the present to the past – the footprint to a person. They connect the present to the future – the clouds to the likelihood of rain. They connect events to causes both present and future. They also connect facts to principles and hope to memory. In these kinds of events, arising out of the construction of meanings, we discern our coming into possession not only of our powers, but also of the world we live in. Educational value arises out of the construction of meanings that tie things together and thus create our world.

Educational Value

Education is a process through which we come into possession of our powers for the exercise of intellect, emotion, imagination, judgment, and action. It is also a process by which we come to self-understanding, including the capacity to "change our minds." If any object, program, or pattern of instruction has educational value, then its value resides in its utility for educating. That is to say, its educational value is its utility for helping us come into possession of our powers. To say that one educational program or object is educationally better than another is to say that it has more educational value. It contributes more to our coming into possession of our powers as human beings.

What is in the lesson, its contrivance, its placement in a sequence, the method of approaching it – all of this may be predetermined. However, the educational worth of what is learned can never be predetermined because it must remain always an open question as to what the learner will *do*. What is being taught may be predetermined; but what is learned and whether what is learned has educational worth, must remain always an open question, since it depends upon what the learner *does*. The study of "effects" is destined always to avoid the measure of educational worth because what needs examination is not what the *lesson* does, but what the *learner* does.

We think there is probably an inverse relation between our capacity to preplan what the learner will learn and our capacity to measure the educational worth of what is learned by measuring our preplanned objectives. In other words, we can control for *what* is learned in any lesson (i.e., curriculum, text, pedagogy, and school) only to the extent that we can control what the learner *does* with the lesson. The educational worth of the lesson resides, however, not in the lesson itself – whatever its design – but in the *combination* of the lesson and what the learner does with it. The possibility of educational worth, like the possibility of education itself, rests upon the fact that meanings are social constructions that, on the one hand allow us to exercise the powers of inference, self-understanding and thoughtful action, and, on the other hand, tie things together in the world we inhabit.

To teach is to try deliberately to change the meaning of students' experience; and students must grasp the meaning. They must "get the point," before deliberate learning can occur. Within the context of educating, educational value is evident in those moments when grasping the meaning and feeling the significance of that meaning come together. When cognition is educative, then it is never separable from emotion. When cognition occurs without emotion, then it is always cognition that does not matter. It is learning and knowing that is not truly educative.

Part Two

Summary

The **V** is a symbol that serves as an anchor for conceptualizing the elements on the theoretical/conceptual and the methodological sides, together with the Focus/Research Questions and events in the middle. Maturing of the **V** in the mind of the user grows with continued use by clarifying conceptually the elements arrayed, and by providing a reference point for resolving confusion. The **V** reveals a new look at the *facts* and enables the user to see events as ways that the related *concepts* point to a *regularity of events* – the anchoring point.

The **V** diagram is a tool that deliberately manipulates cognitive structure so as to spur inquisitiveness through mind-bending channels that lead to more introspective thought and analysis. A "Parade of **V**s" enables this process to occur by providing conceptual clarity in its repeated use by serving to anchor ideas, and to stabilize and clarify meanings. This repeated use of the **V** with a related topic provides the user with more knowledge brought about through discriminability of new information induced by increasing the clarity and stability offered by the V, and can lead to an individual being able to become better acquainted with other points of view contrary to those previously held.

The components arranged on the **V** diagram are not isolates nor are they hierarchical arrangements. Instead, they represent levels of intellectual space that aid in the thinking, formulation, question asking, event making, and reflecting on a work or happening in order to enrich our knowledge and understanding with a given event.

Grasping meaning entails understanding its structure by having the learner make connections from what he or she already knows or has experienced to the new knowledge that is being attached. We come into the possession of our world when our meanings connect the present to the past, and connect the present to the future. Grasping the meaning is fundamental to the educative process. It is a major plank in the theory of educating espoused in this book. Grasping the meaning is an act that we must do for ourselves, even though we require extensive help from others. *A powerful moment in educating occurs when grasping the meaning and feeling the significance come together.* When human feelings merge into meaning, we achieve a way to make sense of experience.

These elements arrayed on the **V** are intended to create a thinking environment that goes beyond conventional thinking when it comes to analyzing a work, planning a research investigation, or thinking about ways to implement a lesson in order to derive the most meaning of the learners engaged in the educational event. The intent of the **V** is to take the creator beyond the realm of superficiality and into the depths of the structure of knowledge. Although a complex process, it becomes an illuminating endeavor when one's ideas are sifted and recombined to better understand what perhaps was misconceived or not previously known.

Seldom are students exposed to this kind of indepth examination of the structure of knowledge that encompasses a given topic or domain. If learning is to become meaningful and eventful, time to learn needs to become a priority that will continue beyond the required years of formal education.

Making a **V** diagram enables better understanding and use of its components and enables one to learn new information in a meaningful manner. The starting point for making a **V** is always educative events and each of the four commonplaces of educating: teaching, curriculum, learner, and social governance – each of which carries equal weight. This Theory of Educating is to hold these concerns together so all can serve a proper role in improving our intelligence about educating our minds.

In order for understanding to be achieved, all components arrayed on the **V** are to be completed. Until then, the **V** is a work in progress.

Human understanding is also a work in progress, only pieces of which are sometimes elegantly achieved. Educating adds to human understanding the capacity to acquire capacity and that leads to higher levels of understanding. Philosopher Michael Scriven (1976) believed human understanding to be the greatest human achievement. The **V** contributes to this value.

When making a **V**, there are basic requirements. First, identify the event. Second, find a way to make a record of the event. Third, find a way to make sense of the event: "What's going on here?" "Is someone teaching?" "Is some person learning?" "Is some claim of knowledge being asserted"? "Is the process governed by humane and reasonable rules so that it is likely that a person might sensibly grasp the meaning of the material the teacher presents?" These are easy questions for experienced educators to ask. What is not so easy is to realize that embedded in them are key concepts: of teaching, of learning, of knowledge, of governance. Fourth, once the information has been gathered, and the concepts you think with have been defined, try to make some order out of the facts. Make tables, draw graphs, and assign numbers to events according to a rule (e.g., rank, rate, and correlate). Analyze and synthesize. In short, compose a set of statements about the record in some form, be it a paragraph or a paradigm sketch that consists of a set of summary judgments of the facts. Notice that in the category of facts are included these items in relation: the event itself (which either is made to happen or just happens), the record of the event, and the factual (including moral) judgments based on the record. Fifth, make knowledge claims by thinking about the concept of educating: teaching, learning, curriculum, and governance. We now ask a variety of new questions about the meaning of the data we have gathered, the claims we have made. We can go back and redefine some of our key concepts. We are engaging in rethinking the concepts rather than rehashing the data.

These five basic requirements are not intended to be followed through a fixed chronological sequence. Moreover, thinking can take place before and after each step, and as a result one can begin by clarifying the concepts or by ordering the facts, and so forth. Concepts of education and concept analysis are the substance and method of the philosophy of education. Philosophizing is a method of work.

The **V** stimulates the thinking and learning process by endeavoring to take what is known and advances making new events happen. In essence, the **V** produces event makers: individuals who negotiate the task by relating what they know to the new, and reach resolution through understanding.

ANALYZING, EVALUATING, AND CONDUCTING RESEARCH

7

Evaluating V Diagrams

*Principle 7. The **V** Diagram of the structure of knowledge provides a basis for evaluating. The developer of a diagram judges worth by criteria of congruence–correspondence, coherence–conceptual clarity, the question–event connection, and the fit between questions asked and answers given.*

Evaluating anything needs some working concept of value. Evaluating a scientific research publication requires a concept of the value of Science. In general, scientists value Science as a way to get at the truth about reality. They can undertake theoretical and experimental manipulations of nature to get at what is not known. The theoretical papers of Einstein in 1905 upset several sets of scientific beliefs (the photoelectric effect, for example). His work over a lifetime changed modern physics because his ideas were verified. Verification requires many tests of many aspects of scientific claims by many different minds working at many different places. Over time the Truth (or the many truths) is expressed by the communities of scientists working out their agreements about the value of scientific claims.

Philosophy of Science presents two theories of Truth: Correspondence and Coherence. Historically, the correspondence view is attributed to Aristotle and the coherence view to his mentor, Plato. The views of these two great philosophers have been widely debated, challenged, revised, changed, and, often, dismissed by working scientists. In our critical analysis of over 3,000 works of science, we have adopted and adapted a view of scientific value useful in **V** diagram analysis. The Value claims component of the **V** diagram requires any **V** diagram-maker to spell out their view of value on each **V** diagram they are constructing.

Two other philosophic views of truth are the Pragmatic and the Consensus gentium. American pragmatist William James said, in two words, truth is "what works," an engineer's ideas of making things work out. The consensus view holds that "everybody knows better than anybody," and that truth is what people can really agree about as a value.

In our work with **V** diagrams we use some features of all of the four views. Facts are records of events. Events happen, or are made to happen, and a record, or many different records, can be made of events. *The connection between the reality of events and the records of events as they are happening* is our version of the correspondence view of truth. Coherence of meaning of all components of the **V** diagram is a high standard for intellectual work. A pragmatic view is found in Action Research. And the consensus of three top experts in any field adds to the criteria of excellence in that field. The poet's claim that "truth is beauty, beauty truth" is a pointed comment on the art of educating.

An Example – DNA

One human cell carries 1,847 strands of DNA. How do scientists know that this claim is true? Carl Vintner said it was so. He found that out in his work on the human genome, an attempt to make a map of all the genes in the human organism. Did he have a bias? He worked for the government, and he had arguments with government authority for their slowness and their secrecy; he was controversial, but the authority in Science rests not with Governments nor virtuoso individuals.

The famous twin virtuosos of DNA, James Watson and Francis Crick, made their fantastic claim in 800 words connecting ACTP proteins (no numbers, no statistics, no photographs). Their 800 or so conceptually rich words pass the Coherence test of truth. As it turned out they needed to apologize to Dr. Rosalind Franklin who made the first photograph of the double helix. Her photographs pass the Correspondence test. Her pictures match reality, protein for protein. Moreover, Watson and Crick were very grateful for her keen laboratory work. They worked the conceptual side of the **V**; she focused on the methodological side of the **V**. The greatest piece of scientific genius of the twentieth century is not in the field of physics (with relativity theory, quantum mechanics coming in second and third) but in the field of biology. DNA is life creating life. All living creatures will be the better off in the twenty-first century because of scientific knowledge of DNA. Do not forget the mathematics of Alan Turing (a left side of the **V** conceptual–coherent claim) that gives rise to the computer mechanics inventions of the middle of the twentieth century. We rank them fourth.

A **V** diagram of the knowledge claims about DNA can also pass the Coherence Test of Truth. All the elements required by the **V** structure can be shown to hang together nicely. The events of the regularities of protein molecules are named *Conceptualized* (DNA), the events can be recorded in photographs, and so the Facts are apparent. The neat connections of concepts–events–facts are in place. The elaborations up and down the **V** can be connected satisfactorily. Both the Foundationists and the Constructivists in philosophy of science can be pleased.

Evaluating **V** diagrams can use both coherence and correspondence tests of truth. A method to analyze the degree of "structure" and "knowledge" of a given work is to apply the Q-5 technique to probe its contents.

THE Q-5 TECHNIQUE OF EVALUATING

The Q-5 technique is a series of questions that help to evaluate the degree of conceptual and factual makeup that forms a particular document.

Five key questions asked and answered about any given set of knowledge claims can give us a shorthand technique to grasp the knowledge's structure and worth. Q-5 is an excellent way to begin one's effort to understand any work.

The Q-5 functions as a code-breaker. It is a quick way to break into the often daunting boiler-plate-like knowledge claims of published research. A Q-5 brief scan can save time and effort in one's review of the literature.

To crack the code by getting at knowledge structure is very liberating, and cracking the code is a great step forward in one's learning.

The Q-5 Technique As Code Breaker

Q-5 functions as a *code breaker* when analyzing documents and research reports. Q-5 provides five questions we can ask of any piece of knowledge.

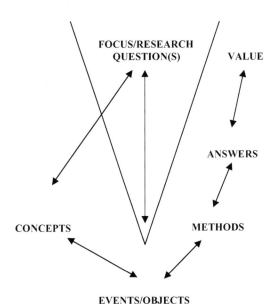

FIGURE 7.1. The Q-5 technique as code breaker

1. Questions. *What is the question?* What events is the question about? This starting question develops in the **V** to the concern there is with the *Telling Question (Focus, Research Questions)* as central to the **V** analysis. The idea of a starting point of questions sets the whole in motion. Questions themselves require keen evaluating. Students need to be alert to what is often missing. Read directly looking for the explicit or implied questions the author must have asked in order to supply the answers (knowledge claims) found in the published articles and books academics use. Question asking is central to inquiry. New learning can begin with genuine interests and questions students have in their prior knowledge and world experience. What is the telling question of the work? What does it tell on, or is about? (event/object): The phenomena or reality of the event or object. This is a very important aspect of the work. *The question needs to be answered by the event that is taking place.* A lack of compatibility between the question and the event makes the work suspect.

2. Concepts. *What are the key concepts in the question asking?* This question expands into the whole left side of the **V** with its concern with conceptual structure. Ranking concepts needed for concept mapping is a difficult task of evaluating ideas. It takes courage to tell others which ideas you put in first place, and which ideas are the lesser. It takes courage to evaluate. Questions are formed by connecting concepts. All questions contain concepts. Any piece of research is framed by a structure of concepts. These sets of concepts indicate the thinking required for the inquiry to continue. The conceptual structure shapes and guides (gives meaning to) the ways one seeks answers. The importance of theory as a guide to selecting and using methods is crucial. A strong theory impels questions and methods. What are the key concepts? What concepts are needed to ask the question? Concept mapping technique fits here to show the hierarchical representation of these ideas (see Alvarez in Pauk, 1989, pp. 212–219; Gowin, 1981; Novak, 1998; Novak and Gowin, 1984). Chapter 8 describes the procedures for making a concept map.

3. Methods. *How (by what methods) are the questions answered?* Are records-of-events evident? This question expands into the whole right side of the **V**, especially the lower right with its close ties to events and objects and ways of making records of these events. Methods are modes of inquiry. They are the ways used to construct answers (knowledge claims). Methods are "how" questions: "How do we find out something?" "How do we proceed?" "How do we make facts?" "How do we transform facts into data?" Methods are so important to inquiry that they often overwhelm other parts of inquiry. "What methods were used to answer the telling question?" "What methods are useful in answering the question or questions?" "How am I going to find out what's happening?"

4. Answers. What answers are presented? Do they match the concepts in the questions? This question expands into the top levels, knowledge claims and the key functions of claims – interpretations, generalizations, explanations. Inquiry closes when facts, data, and knowledge claims are completed. These claims are often named "conclusions." It is as if nothing more needs to be done. The important role of knowledge claims is to supply a fertile source for new inquiry questions. "What are the major knowledge claims of the work?" "What answers are produced?" "What new questions can be asked?" These questions are often overlooked or omitted entirely. Research articles often include a section titled "Implications." Sometimes these implications are presented as the new questions to ask in further research. In **V**-guided research we have a new way to tell when research is completed. It is when all parts of the **V** can be found in the research paper.

5. Value. So What? What is the upshot? The worth of the work. This question expands into value claims. What is the value? What value claims can be made given the knowledge claims presented? This sort of question is central to combat the frequent denial of scientists that no value claims are necessary because science is objective. Arguments for value-free knowledge are a foundation for Logical Positivism and Logical Empiricism. Pragmatism, however, often asks about the "cash value" of any idea, claim, and belief. "What use does Science have?" The Objectivists answer is that science seeks the truth. Objectivists believe truth is a knowledge claim not a value claim. Truth as verified knowledge is valuable in many ways in a democratic society (think of the legal system and its search for verified knowledge). It enables the user of the **V** to take a look at the coherence of the **V**, at the ways parts feed into other parts. "What value claims are made in the work?"

Cracking the code is an enabling step forward in one's own learning. Using the Q-5 technique can give the user the sense of the coherence and the quality of the document being analyzed. Coherence is one theory of truth.

EVALUATING DOCUMENTS

Documents that we evaluate have a structure, many different structures in fact. As products of human effort they take different forms to serve different purposes. By structure in this context we mean only the parts of the document in relation to other parts that together constitute the whole. Structure is simply parts-and-their-relations. In particular, we believe that evaluation documents have a philosophic structure, a structure of a special kind. That structure is a structure of *claims*. Through philosophic analysis we make this structure of claims explicit, and we reveal philosophical assumptions. When we come to understand the philosophic structure of evaluation documents, we come to understand the philosophical grounds for evaluation.

Conceptual Design Analysis

We present an example as a systematic method to use when analyzing the structure of claims found in documents. From the use of this method of analysis it should help in the analysis of completed studies and in the creation of new studies. Further, it should help to show the source and meaning of the *criteria of excellence* used in judging existing studies and in guiding the development of new studies. The method and its use on a clear case of evaluation of "The Sequencing of Human Chromosome 19," based on the Human Genome Project (HGP), are given.[1]

Evaluation is defined as the assessment of worth, the determination of merit, the appraisal of value. Value is the key concept in evaluation. Yet it is surprising how infrequently the concept of value is discussed in evaluation studies. The Q-5 technique can be used to begin the appraisal of any set of documented claims. It is a good way quickly to scan documents for future criticism. It is a method we use here to analyze and critique the structure of claims found in evaluation documents. Q-5 contains questions that can be asked of any evaluation study.

Within the Q-5 is a structure that shows the pattern of concepts to be considered to make sense of the evaluation. We refer to this method of analysis as a *conceptual design* to distinguish it from the usual concern of methodology that focuses on establishing matters of fact (e.g., data, variables, and measurements). This conceptual design analysis has the special intent of locating the criteria of excellence; that is, the value standards for value judgments.

By focusing on *value questions*, we also find ways of making sense of evaluation work. We believe only five value questions are enough to span the field of value claims.

1. *Instrumental Value Question.* Is X good for Y?
2. *Intrinsic Value Question.* Is X good in itself?
3. *Comparative Value Question.* Is X better than Y?
4. *Decision Value Question.* Is X right? Ought we choose X?
5. *Ideal Value Question.* Is X as good as it can be, or can it be made much better ideally?

When evaluating a document almost all of these value claims are taken into consideration.

---

[1] "The DNA sequence and biology of human Chromosome 19," *Nature, 428,* 529–535, April 2004.

Starting Points. Take some evaluation study that you are familiar with and put it in front of you. The clear case we use is an evaluation of Chromosome 19. The first step in the analysis is to decide to locate (or infer) the important question of the study and the main answer given in the study. The relation between questions asked and answers given is a key useful in unlocking the structure of any evaluation study. In some evaluations, no clear question is explicit. Answers are given as facts and data are presented to the reader to find the questions. The reader then has to realize that answers can be converted into questions.

An Example: The Sequencing of Human Chromosome 19

Applying the Q-5 technique to *The Sequencing of Human Chromosome 19*, a descriptive report.

What is the question? What events are the focus questions about?

FQ1. Do certain cancers arise from defects in DNA-Repair pathways?
FQ2. Will knowing the sequence-information of Chromosome 19 help us understand the damage caused by exposure to radiation and other environmental pollutants?

2. *What are the key concepts in the question-asking?*
Chromosome 19, gene density, genome-wide average, gene families, euchromatin, manual curation of gene loci, mendalian disorders, familial hypercholesterolaemia, insulin-resistant diabetes, tandemly arranged families, coding, and noncoding.

3. How *(by what methods) are the questions answered?* Are records-of-events evident?

Events made to happen by the researchers: A physical mapping of multiple DNA repair genes to the Chromosome 19 was conducted. Sequence was generated using a clone-by-clone shotgun sequencing strategy followed by finishing using a custom primer approach.

Records of the Event: Each clone was finished according to the agreed international standard for the human genome. Internal and external quality checks to estimate accuracy of finished sequencing. Compared Chromosome 19 sequence and previously existing physical and genetic maps. Compared recombination distances in the deCODE female, male and sex-averaged meiotic maps with physical distance as determined from the sequence assembly. Gene model transcripts. A comparative analysis was performed of finished human Chromosome 19 versus the draft mouse and *Takifugu* (fish) genomes. A homology map was developed.

Data Transformation: A table of interspersed repetitive elements of Chromosome 19. A figure of Chromosome 19 showing the meiotic distance versus sequence-based physical distance A figure of the Chromosome 19 landscape of human/mouse blocks of homology larger than 100 kb.

A figure showing recent segmental duplications on Chromosome 19. A figure showing the extreme density of Chromosome 19 relative to other human chromosomes. A table showing Chromosome 19 gene family clusters. 4. *What answers are presented?* Do they match the concepts in the questions? Answers to the questions asked:

FQ1. Studies of DNA-repair genes are yielding insights into the development of certain cancers, many of which appear to be caused by defects in DNA-repair pathways.

FQ2. Embedded in this sequence information are critical regulatory networks of genes tasked with controlling functions as repairing DNA damage caused by exposure to radiation and to other environmental pollutants.

5. *So What?* What is the upshot? The worth of the work. This question expands into value claims. What is the value? What value claims can be made given the knowledge claims presented?

The finished sequence of Chromosome 19 will facilitate the identification of additional genes contributing to single-gene disorders as well as complex traits.

The sharing of this sequence to the scientific community will enable physicians and researchers to better ascertain individual responses to medicines, which will lead to more effective individualized therapeutic strategies.

A revelation of this study, maintains the notion that ideas once thought to be irrelevant are, with the advancement of technology, knowledge, and reasoning, an important contribution to understanding. A case in point is the value of noncoding regions once considered nonsense, are now proving to have powerful regulatory influence over the genes that they bracket.

Let us apply the value questions to this study.

1. *Instrumental Value Question.* Is X good for Y?
   Is the mapping of the Chromosome 19 good for something else?
   Is it good for future academic achievement?
   Is it good for the health and well-being of society?
2. *Intrinsic Value Question.* Is X good in itself?
   Is DNA good?
   Is it good in and of itself?
   What value does DNA have as life creating life?
   What value does this Chromosome 19 have as a single chromosome?
3. *Comparative Value Question.* Is X better than Y?
   Coding one chromosome is costly. Coding can be done for diseases such as insulin-dependent diabetes, myotonic dystrophy, migraines, and familial hypercholesterolemia (an inherited form

of elevated blood cholesterol that increases the risk of cardio-vascular disease). Does coding of Chromosome 19 outweigh future research endeavors with other genes?

In that it took 18 years of research to understand the complex interplay between our human health and the environment, is it worth the time and effort to continue future research in this area?

4. *Decision Value Question.* Is X right? Ought we choose X?

Ought we examine the causes of health disorders with regards to the kinds of pollutants emitted into our environment?

Is this new knowledge about Chromosome 19 enough to make lawmakers' change their decisions with environmental regulations?

5. *Ideal Value Question.* Is X as good as it can be, or can it be made much better ideally?

How can the results of this Chromosome 19 study become better in advancing health care?

Can the results of this study lead to new discoveries and uses in other genes?

This descriptive report also prompts other questions such as "What changes will knowing the sequence of Chromosome 19 make in decisions about human health and the environment?" "What is the link between DNA damage from radiation exposure and human cancer?" These questions serve to further advance the knowledge and use of this Chromosome 19.

"LAYING THE **V**"

By "Laying the **V**" on a study, we have a template, a guide, a form, a device that gives us knowledge about knowledge: metaknowledge, metaevaluation. We also preserve complexity while simplifying the way we represent the analysis of claims.

V Diagrams for Evaluation

A primary or secondary source document can be analyzed by the structure of knowledge of its composition. By "Laying the **V**" on a document of interest a determination can be made by analyzing its Telling Question (Focus/Research Question), the key concepts and conceptual systems that define the work, the methods and techniques of the work itself, the claims of the results, discussion, and values, and the coherence that is evidenced by taking the document apart and putting it back together again.

The soundness of the work is demonstrated by how well the *concepts, events*, and *records* tie together at the bottom of the **V**. If a discrepancy exists between any of these components then the results reported are suspect. Included within this analysis is the *telling question* that must be directly related to what is happening in the events.

Investigations Gone Awry

Investigations often go awry at the bottom of the **V**. Focusing on the relevant key events or objects or key concepts draws attention directly to these components. One of the most common flaws is the technical inadequacy in methodology that is part of the events and records.

- Details are not sufficiently described.
- How the data are to be collected is vague.
- The link between the research question(s) and the analysis of the event is unclear.
- The concepts are not clearly related to the events and the records.

An Example of Details Not Sufficiently Described and Vague Data Interpretation

Let's say we are reading a document that assessed different students in the same classroom using different textbooks by their test scores. The researcher gave three kinds of textbooks to the students over a period of weeks, and then gave them a test on the material in the first three chapters to determine whether or not the kind of textbook influenced their academic achievement. The researcher then applied some statistical test across students in this classroom setting to assess the relationship between different textbook types and test scores.

Are the details of the study sufficiently described in this example? No! Does the use of a statistical procedure remove bias from this methodology? No! Why? Because, in this example, the students in the class will be interacting with each other, talking about the new books they will be using, and will eventually be contributing and influencing each other's responses to the test, thereby, causing the results of the statistical test (e.g., correlations or p-values) to be inaccurate.

An Example of Selecting An Appropriate Method of Analysis.
Suppose we read a study in which a teacher wanted to see if her students in a 6th grade English class preferred the writings of Betsy Byars, Judy Blume, or Avi. "Laying the **V**" on this study shows under Events that the teacher selected 30 students who had read selected books by each author and asked the students which author they liked best. Since the data are put into categories (nominal data having students choose the author whose stories they like to read best) rather than data that have been normally distributed, we would expect to see an appropriate method of analysis such as Chi square rather than ANOVA.

An Example of a Confounded Design. Take an experimental study where the "Laying of the **V**" under events shows that the researcher has taken a class of students and randomly assigned them to two groups. The treatment group received an advance organizer that has been written to accompany an implicit science passage followed by the reading of an explicit science passage in order to determine if a concept such as "deductive reasoning" that appeared in each passage facilitated transfer of learning through the use of an advance organizer. The control group first read the explicit science passage; then they read the implicit science passage. The independent variable that was manipulated is the advance organizer developed to accompany the implicit science passage. The research experimental design is represented as:

> Group 1 (treatment): Advance organizer with implicit science passage; then explicit science passage.
> Group 2 (control): Explicit science passage; then implicit science passage.

The records, transformations, and results of this experiment are likely to be inaccurate given the confounded nature of the design. There is a strong possibility to suggest that the investigation has gone awry, and inaccurate records of the events have been gathered. The reason being that passage order has not been ascertained as a factor. It may be that the explicit passage serves as a preorganizer for the implicit passage or vice-versa. To avoid this uncertainty a better counter-balanced design can be developed that randomly assigns each of the members in Group 1 to Groups 1A and 1B and does the same with members in Group 2 forming Groups 2A and 2B. Represented as:

> Group 1 (treatment): Advance Organizer
> > Group 1A: Advance organizer with implicit science passage; then science passage.
> > Group 1B: Explicit science passage; then advance organizer with implicit science passage.
> Group 2 (control): No Advance Organizer
> > Group 2A: Explicit science passage; then implicit science passage
> > Group 2B: Implicit science passage; then explicit science passage.

When these two respective subgroups have been compared for passage order, and if there are no significant differences then the data can be collapsed and compared again with the combined Group 1 (1A + 1B) compared to Group 2 (2A + 2B). Given this design, the researcher is less likely to gather inaccurate records or fail to see the meaning of the records that are gathered. A flawed design and/or inadequate or inappropriate instruments used to collect the data play a major role in evaluating the educational and scientific worth of a document. Whether "Laying the **V**" on a document to be analyzed or planning a research investigation, determining the appropriateness of the records is a crucial consideration. In this example, we also see the lack of a robust conceptual theoretical context.

Misinterpreting Test Scores As Records of Learning. Another example illustrating a misjudgment in educational research is when an investigator fails to recognize that the test response marked by a student is a very limited record of what that student is thinking. The investigator may proceed to total the number of items marked "correctly," perform elegant statistical transformations on the test scores, and then produce claims about the "learning" effectiveness demonstrated by some group, procedure, or ability. In fact, no records of learning were made; no event of learning was observed. Whole sets of conceptual assumptions about the event of cognitive output that led to the student's marks on the test paper were simply ignored. Again, this common error in research illustrates a lack of conceptual concern. Using this framework of "Laying the **V**" for conceptual analysis can be undertaken to determine how well the component parts satisfy the total structure of knowledge of the work.

"Laying the **V**" on a document provides the reader (reviewer) with an in-depth analysis and lessens the chance of focusing on some of the findings and ignoring others that may be important. When reviewing research studies, there occurs, more than should be the case, misinterpretations or inaccurate reporting of the findings. This occurs, in part, because of a cursory rather than a careful evaluation of the study that focuses on the overall methodology, analyses, findings, and educational worth of the study itself. "Laying the **V**" on a document ensures that the content has been taken apart and then put back together, revealing the educational significance and worth of a given work.

Flashback: Comparing the Knowledge Claims with the Questions

Reading improvement and understanding results when students become eager critics as they carefully scrutinize and look for defects in published research papers. One major defect that appears often is when the concepts in the questions asked are not found in the answers given. An easy way to find if this discrepancy exists is to:

1. *Start with the knowledge claims.* These claims are stated near the end of the article. Go directly to the findings and/or conclusions and scan this part of the article looking for the knowledge claims.
2. *Rephrase* these knowledge claims and write them as questions.
3. Read to *compare* these questions you have written with the ones presented at the beginning of the article by the author. Check the *congruency* of the knowledge claims and the research or focus questions.

This analysis process makes the reader aware that good questions must be carefully crafted, and, with corresponding concepts, events, and records, lead to well-formulated answers or suppositions. It also helps the reader to better understand the degree and level of the structure of knowledge that this article conveys.

An Example of a Well-Developed Research Study

Let's look at an example that illustrates this situation. A **V** diagram used to analyze a doctoral research investigation titled "Forgotten Voices: Why We Left High School," conducted by Gladys Aileen Adams, appears in Figure 7.2. In this study the elements arrayed on the **V** enable us to identify the components of knowledge, clarify their relationships, and present them in a visually compact and clear way. The **V** diagram is used to analyze the structure of knowledge of this investigation and make determinations as to the degree of congruence and conceptual clarity of this study. It also enables us to compare the research question to the knowledge claims, and to make a value judgment of its merit.

If one were to go directly to reading the findings of this investigation and then rewrite the findings into questions, there would be a high degree of congruency with the research questions asked at the beginning of this study. It is important when "Laying the **V**" onto a report, article, document, and so forth, that an effort be made to see how the parts that make up the whole can be separated for scrutinization and then be reassembled to determine its worth and accuracy.

This document is analyzed by "Laying the **V**" on its contents. In so doing, the document is taken apart and then brought back together to its original state. The degree of complexity of the document is simplified by using the elements on the **V** to assess this work. In addition to the **V**, the use of the Q-5 technique is used to further analyze the document.

The Q-5 technique breaks the code by answering five questions of this research document:

1. *What is the question?*
   RQ1. Why were students aged 16 and older dropping out of high school before graduating?
   RQ2. What impact did the school environment have on these students?
   RQ3. Was the decision to withdraw influenced by family environment and/or peer relationships?
   RQ4. What significance did the students' academic records and attendance patterns have in their decision to drop out of school?
2. *What are the key concepts?* The key concept in this study is "drop-outs", since it tells on the research questions being asked. Other concepts

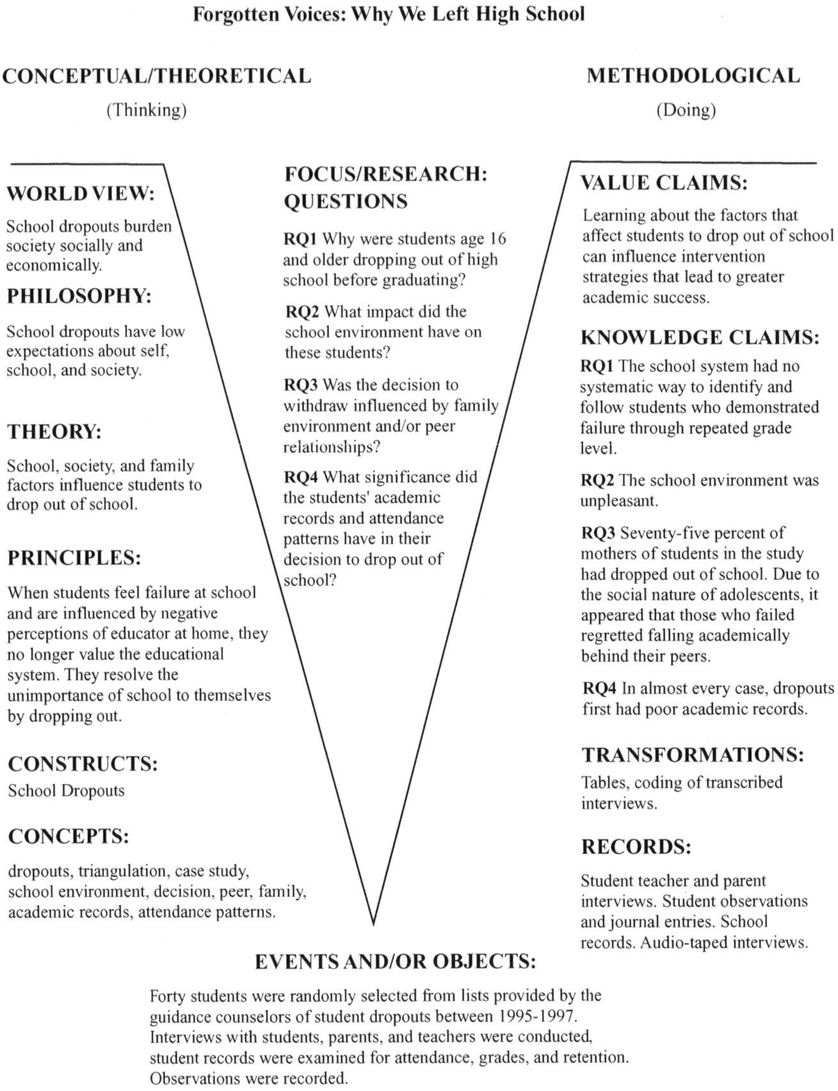

Forgotten Voices: Why We Left High School

CONCEPTUAL/THEORETICAL   METHODOLOGICAL
(Thinking)   (Doing)

WORLD VIEW:

School dropouts burden society socially and economically.

PHILOSOPHY:

School dropouts have low expectations about self, school, and society.

THEORY:

School, society, and family factors influence students to drop out of school.

PRINCIPLES:

When students feel failure at school and are influenced by negative perceptions of educator at home, they no longer value the educational system. They resolve the unimportance of school to themselves by dropping out.

CONSTRUCTS:

School Dropouts

CONCEPTS:

dropouts, triangulation, case study, school environment, decision, peer, family, academic records, attendance patterns.

FOCUS/RESEARCH: QUESTIONS

RQ1 Why were students age 16 and older dropping out of high school before graduating?

RQ2 What impact did the school environment have on these students?

RQ3 Was the decision to withdraw influenced by family environment and/or peer relationships?

RQ4 What significance did the students' academic records and attendance patterns have in their decision to drop out of school?

VALUE CLAIMS:

Learning about the factors that affect students to drop out of school can influence intervention strategies that lead to greater academic success.

KNOWLEDGE CLAIMS:

RQ1 The school system had no systematic way to identify and follow students who demonstrated failure through repeated grade level.

RQ2 The school environment was unpleasant.

RQ3 Seventy-five percent of mothers of students in the study had dropped out of school. Due to the social nature of adolescents, it appeared that those who failed regretted falling academically behind their peers.

RQ4 In almost every case, dropouts first had poor academic records.

TRANSFORMATIONS:

Tables, coding of transcribed interviews.

RECORDS:

Student teacher and parent interviews. Student observations and journal entries. School records. Audio-taped interviews.

EVENTS AND/OR OBJECTS:

Forty students were randomly selected from lists provided by the guidance counselors of student dropouts between 1995-1997. Interviews with students, parents, and teachers were conducted, student records were examined for attendance, grades, and retention. Observations were recorded.

FIGURE 7.2. Analyzing a research investigation.

are triangulation (the method used to collect and organize the data), and case study (the design of the study).

3. *What methods are used?*

Events made to happen by the researchers: Forty students were randomly selected from lists provided by the guidance counselors of student dropouts between 1995–1997.

Records of the Event: Interviews with students, parents, and teachers were conducted and student records were examined for attendance, grades, and retention. Observations were recorded.

Data Transformation: Transcribed interviews, created tables, and coded transcribed interviews.

4. *What answers are presented?* There were four questions asked and each was answered.

RQ1. The school system had no systematic way to identify and follow students who demonstrated failure through repeated grade level.

RQ2. The school environment was unpleasant.

RQ3. Family environment, particularly educational level and values of the mother, appeared to have significant impact on those who dropped out of school. Of the 40 participants, 30 had mothers who had also dropped out. Even though most parents interviewed expressed disappointment in the choice of their child to drop out, student interviews indicated that 75 percent of the dropouts were doing what they knew had been done by their mothers. Peers had a strong influence on the student's incentive to stay in school until the student fell behind in grade level and became separated from friends. Many dropouts expressed disappointment in not being with their peers once they fell behind and in not seeing their friends who were still in school after they dropped out.

RQ4. In almost every case, dropouts had poor academic records. Ninety-two percent of dropouts in this study were at least one grade level behind their peers with many at least two or more due to failure in elementary or middle school and some lacked credits earned in high school to graduate. Almost all had failed a grade before entering high school.

Each of these answers reflects deeper meaning in this particular study. Let's look at RQ2 and elaborate upon this finding. When reading the report detailed information is given that goes beyond stating that the "school environment was unpleasant." What is meant by "unpleasant?" In this report, "unpleasant" meant that school dropouts had negative opinions of their teachers (more than 67 percent). None of the students felt comfortable discussing their personal problems with their school counselor. Absenteeism was an indicator of not wanting to be in school (92.5 percent had high levels of absenteeism). Parents indicated that frequently they were unaware of attendance or academic problems until their child had a record of truancy and/or failure. Twenty-five percent of the participants were never involved in any extracurricular activities while in high school. These figures indicate the degree that students felt left out of the school environment.

5. *So What?* What is the value? Learning about the factors that affect students to drop out of school can influence intervention strategies that lead to greater academic success and retention. The value of this particular study influenced the decision makers, and an alternative school was designed using the findings of this investigation.

Value Questions:

1. *Instrumental Value Question.* Is X good for Y?
   Is it good to know why students are dropping out of school?
   Is this knowledge good for the community?
   Is it good for future academic achievement?
   Does knowing the factors that affect school dropouts promote student awareness?
2. *Intrinsic Value Question.* Is X good in itself?
   Is dropping out of school good?
3. *Comparative Value Question.* Is X better than Y?
   Is preventing school dropouts better than avoiding the issue?
   Do high school graduates fare better in wage earnings over a lifetime than do high school dropouts?
4. *Decision Value Question.* Is X right? Ought we choose X?
   Ought we examine the causes of high school dropouts and reform our curriculum?
   Is it right to let high school students at risk for dropping out of school fend for themselves?
5. *Ideal Value Question.* Is X as good as it can be, or can it be made much better ideally?
   How can the results of this study promote high school students to remain in school and graduate?
   Can the results of this study lead to new and different educational practices that make school a more accommodating learning environment for diverse student backgrounds, interests, and academic levels of achievement?

Using the Q-5 in conjunction with the value questions helps us to read and understand any research book or set of research papers by informing us as to the quality and worth of the work.

An Example of a Research Question Not Matching the Event

This example analyzes a hypothetical research report on how temperature and moisture stress affect seed germination. The V diagram represents on one page the question, key concepts of the study, methods used, the

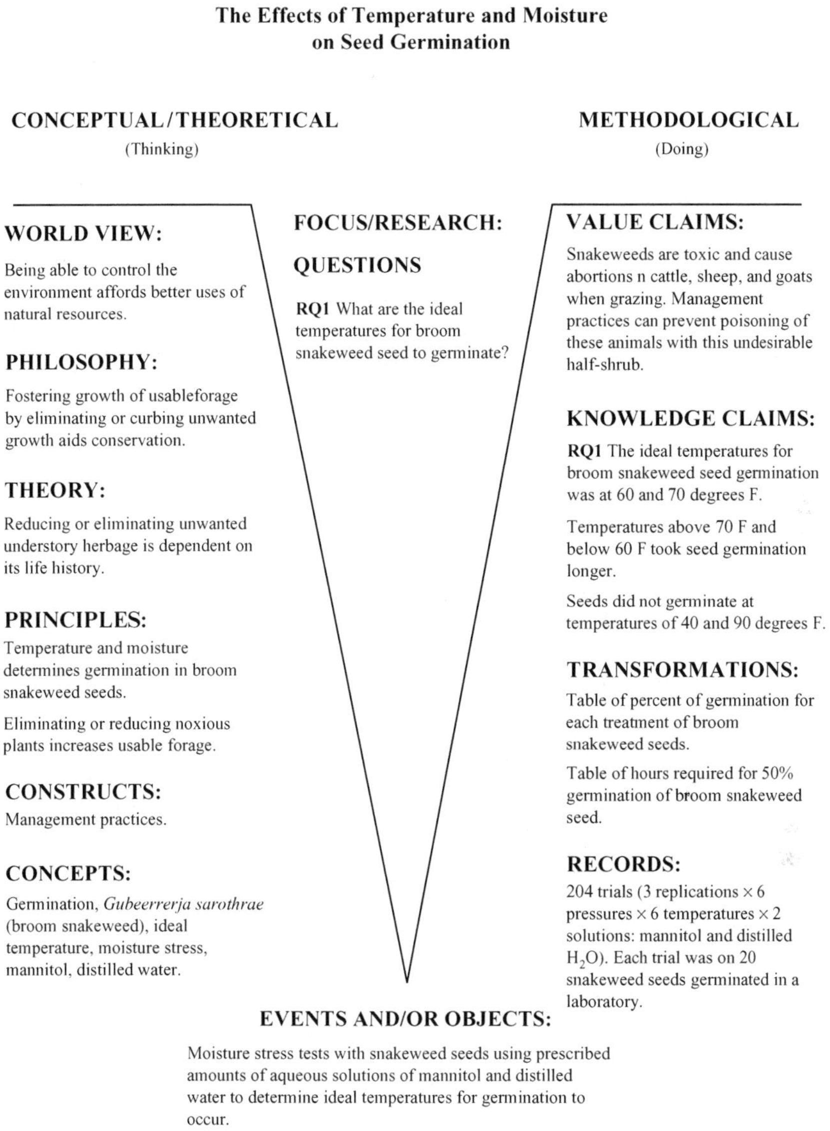

**The Effects of Temperature and Moisture
on Seed Germination**

CONCEPTUAL/THEORETICAL   METHODOLOGICAL

(Thinking)   (Doing)

WORLD VIEW:

Being able to control the
environment affords better uses of
natural resources.

FOCUS/RESEARCH:

QUESTIONS

RQ1 What are the ideal
temperatures for broom
snakeweed seed to germinate?

VALUE CLAIMS:

Snakeweeds are toxic and cause
abortions n cattle, sheep, and goats
when grazing. Management
practices can prevent poisoning of
these animals with this undesirable
half-shrub.

PHILOSOPHY:

Fostering growth of usableforage
by eliminating or curbing unwanted
growth aids conservation.

KNOWLEDGE CLAIMS:

RQ1 The ideal temperatures for
broom snakeweed seed germination
was at 60 and 70 degrees F.

THEORY:

Reducing or eliminating unwanted
understory herbage is dependent on
its life history.

Temperatures above 70 F and
below 60 F took seed germination
longer.

Seeds did not germinate at
temperatures of 40 and 90 degrees F.

PRINCIPLES:

Temperature and moisture
determines germination in broom
snakeweed seeds.

Eliminating or reducing noxious
plants increases usable forage.

TRANSFORMATIONS:

Table of percent of germination for
each treatment of broom
snakeweed seeds.

Table of hours required for 50%
germination of broom snakeweed
seed.

CONSTRUCTS:

Management practices.

CONCEPTS:

Germination, *Gubeerrerja sarothrae*
(broom snakeweed), ideal
temperature, moisture stress,
mannitol, distilled water.

RECORDS:

204 trials (3 replications × 6
pressures × 6 temperatures × 2
solutions: mannitol and distilled
H_2O). Each trial was on 20
snakeweed seeds germinated in a
laboratory.

EVENTS AND/OR OBJECTS:

Moisture stress tests with snakeweed seeds using prescribed
amounts of aqueous solutions of mannitol and distilled
water to determine ideal temperatures for germination to
occur.

FIGURE 7.3. **V** analysis on a research report.

answers derived from the investigation, and the value of doing such a
study (see Figure 7.3).

The research question and the knowledge claim in the **V** Diagram do
not mention "moisture," however, the Concepts, Events, and Records all
have "moisture" as a key concept under study. "Mannitol" is also included

as a concept, and the events, objects, and records indicate that some seeds were exposed to distilled water and others were exposed to a "mannitol" solution, but there is no research question and no knowledge claim that mentions "moisture" or "mannitol."

This example points out that research studies lack completeness when key elements of the V are not addressed. In this instance, a key concept mentioned in the title of the report, "moisture," is not part of the investigator's research question. As one reviewer remarked: "Is it appropriate to 'simplify complexity' by ignoring a key concept in the study's title (and presumably in its research questions)?" The use of concept maps would have made the researcher aware of the need to include the key concepts in the question and events. Concept maps should be explicit in V diagram analysis.

The value of such a study, while not stated in the report, does have potential worth in both cost and educational importance. The reason being that because of the toxicity of snakeweed, these weeds can cause abortions in cattle, sheep and goats when grazing. The value of knowing the temperatures that are ideal for snakeweed to germinate enables management to instill practices that can prevent poisoning of these animals with this undesirable half-shrub.

Consensus V Diagram Evaluations

Consensus gentium is used as a theory of truth. Poets have told us that, "Everybody knows better than anybody." Achieving shared meaning to the point of consensus takes a lot of good talk and a lot of time. Talking around the V diagram focuses discussions and thereby saves a lot of time.

V diagrams are effective in a variety of evaluative settings such as demonstrations, performances, laboratory or field events, or in any creative event that takes place.

Students were given an experimental research article to read and to analyze its contents by "Laying the V." They used the interactive V diagram (see Chapter 9) to conceptualize their understanding. Prior to their next class meeting the students were able to electronically submit their Vs to the professor. The professor made comments on each of the students' Vs and electronically returned them.

Discussions arose as to how the research questions were posed, if the events matched these questions, and if the concepts, events, and records combined to give an accurate portrayal of what transpired. They compared their world views, philosophy, theory, and principles. This helped in resolving how these components were used to formulate the research questions. The statistical analysis and the tabling of the data enabled the students to compare the record data to the aggregate arrangement of the data. They then compared the knowledge claims derived as a result of the study to the research questions to see if they were congruent. The value of the study stimulated discussion within these individuals and led to generalizations as to the educational worth of the study. Consensus was reached using the **V** to mediate the navigation process of the analyzed document.

Joseph Novak (1998) reports the use of **V** diagrams as an interview instrument. He asks his students to create a **V** with subjects on any topic they choose to select and also with any kind of a sample group of students they wish to interview.

The **V** is a very comprehensive evaluation tool and requires a commitment to constructivism in its use both as a learning tool and an evaluation tool (see Mintzes, Wandersee, & Novak, 1998). The use of concept maps and **V** diagrams satisfies many of the requirements for authentic assessment.

SCORING Vs

When **V** diagrams are used by students as an inquiry to a laboratory science experiment or as a heuristic to learn about events and objects in the subject disciplines of art, music, history, literature, mathematics, business education, technology, health education, and so forth, there may be times when the teacher may wish to score their **V** diagrams. Analyzing a document or a series of documents may also lend itself to scoring each one to determine their effectiveness.

Scoring **V** diagrams is an arbitrary process and the point system used should be determined by the scorer based on the type of material being analyzed or to emphasize acquisition of particular skills. The Focus/Research Question, events/objects, records, and concepts might receive more than two or three times the number of score points assigned to the others. Depending upon the weight of the criteria being judged, the point value will accordingly be adjusted. The degree of importance is determined by the scorer when deciding upon the significant aspects of the **V** to weight more or less. When more than one rater is used, interrater reliability can be determined. Table 7.1 shows a scoring procedure for **V** diagrams. A *V diagram scoring protocol* is shown in Appendix I.

The actual assessment for each **V** requires judgment. As the scoring criteria are modified or developed to suit a particular task or situation (e.g., analyzing a research report, determining the value of an assignment or project that requires the making of a **V**), it becomes relatively easy, consistent, and reasonably objective. It is important when scoring **V** diagrams that we are flexible and take into consideration other viewpoints that can be considered feasible.

By using the Q-5 technique we show both the complexity of research analysis, and the value of evaluation and critical appraisal of published research. The Q-5 technique is a method of analysis. Concept mapping is

TABLE 7.1. *Scoring V Diagrams.*

Focus/Research Question
0 = No focus or research question is identified.
1 = A question is identified, but does not focus upon the major event or objects OR the conceptual side of the V.
2 = A focus/research question is identified; includes concepts, but does not suggest objects or the major event OR the wrong objects and event are identified.
3 = A clear focus/research question is identified; includes concepts to be used and directly relates to the major event or object.

Events/Objects
0 = No events or objects are identified.
1 = The major event or the objects are identified, but are inconsistent with the focus/research question.
2 = The major event or the objects are identified, and are consistent with the focus/research question.

Concepts
0 = No concepts are identified.
1 = Concepts are identified but are unrelated to the focus/research question and/or the events/objects.
2 = Concepts are identified that are related to the focus/research question and/or the events/objects.

Records
0 = No records are identified.
1 = Records are identified, but are inconsistent with the focus/research question or the major event.
2 = Records are identified for the major event and are consistent with the focus/research question.

World View
0 = No world view is given.
1 = A world view is identified that relates to a well-stated focus/research question.

Philosophy
0 = No philosophy is given.
1 = A philosophy is identified that relates to a well-stated focus/research question

Theory
0 = No theory is given.
1 = A theory is identified, but does not relate to the conceptual side of the V or to the focus/research question and the events.
2 = A relevant theory is identified that relates the conceptual side of the V to the focus/research question and the events.

TABLE 7.1. *(continued)*

Principles
0 = No principles are identified.
1 = Principles are identified that are relevant to the theory.

Transformations
0 = No transformations are identified.
1 = Transformations are inconsistent with the intent of the focus/research question and the data collected from the records.
2 = Transformations are consistent with the intent of the focus/research question and the data collected from the records.

Knowledge Claims
0 = No knowledge claim is identified.
1 = Knowledge claims are inconsistent with the focus/research questions.
2 = Knowledge claims are derived from the records and transformations.
3 = Knowledge claims are consistent with the data collected in the records and represented in the transformations.
4 = Knowledge claim contains the components of 3, and leads to a new focus/research question.

Value Claims
0 = No value claim is identified.
1 = Value claim is identified that indicates the worth of the document.

---

a technique of this analysis method, and so is the use of the **V** diagram. By "Laying the **V**" on a study, we have a template, a guide, a form, a device that gives us knowledge about knowledge: metaknowledge and metaevaluation. We also preserve complexity while simplifying the way we represent the analysis of claims.

Criticism shows us the structure of claims. By raising questions to value claims we are better able to judge the worth of a document. The kind of questions asked determine the educational and practical worth of the document. They can stimulate new inquiries or spur interest in the ramifications that evolve from this new knowledge.

Evaluation documents present multiple claims. Of all claims, four are important: factual, valuational, conceptual, and methodological.

Factual claims are answers to questions about what exists as an object or event. Facts, that is, records of events, are the *facts of the case* and are important to establish descriptively. But they must be transformed into data, that is, given some order and significance. Data then are used to back knowledge claims.

Value claims are answers to questions about the existence of value. Simple claims of value are transformed into five fundamental forms of value claims.

Conceptual claims are answers to questions about the *meaning* of concepts. *The meaning of concepts is a function of their use in a context of inquiry and evaluation.* When constructing a concept map we make conceptual structures evident.

Methodological claims are answers to questions of *how* we establish other claims.

To know what multiple claims exist in the analysis of studies as well as in the creation of new studies is helpful. It is from an analysis of prior studies that we derive criteria of excellence. These criteria can be used to judge existing studies and to guide the development of new studies. The concept of value is fundamental to the practice of evaluation.

8

Researching Educating

*Principle 8. The **V** diagram mediates conceptual and methodological research design and practice.*

Researching educating begins in midstream. Some things are already known and some things raise questions. Think about the mess before you choose a method to clean it up. It may be that our ignorance is not what is so confounding as much as what we already know that isn't so. Beginning in midstream is beginning with events that are happening – events that in some sense you believe are events of educating.

Planning a study begins with making a **V**. It requires the selection of a conception and a research method or procedure that best constructs the answers to the question posed. Research is a systematic process of thinking and doing, collecting and analyzing information for some stated purpose. Various research conceptions and methods are used when conducting research: historical, causal-comparative, descriptive, experimental, correlational, qualitative, mixed qualitative and quantitative, and action research. Action research is a process that may encumber a research method with the latitude to modify the events and record making for finer discrimination of the knowledge-making taking place.

Action research is a paradigm that is grounded in the reality of classroom culture and under the control of teachers. Findings emanating from this type of research investigation inform teachers and guide their practice when formulating lessons and conducting future classroom research projects. They also enable students to become actively engaged in the research process. Action research is defined as the *acting* on an event, object, problem, or an idea, by an individual or group directly involved in gathering and studying the information for themselves, and using the results for the purpose of addressing specific problems within a classroom, school, program, organization, or community (Alvarez, 1995). This action research strategy is accomplished through a recursive cycle of (1) identifying an idea problem area; (2) studying it by gathering data; and (3) reflecting on the data in order to make teaching and learning decisions grounded in evidence.

The *research strategy* described in this chapter is a paper version of the interactive research strategy described in Chapter 9, and can be modified and applied to any procedures using the V diagram. The action research strategy described in Appendix II is intended for teachers and students doing action research projects.

WHAT IS AND IS NOT RESEARCH?

Many students from elementary school to college have mistakenly engaged in what they believe were research endeavors when in fact they were not. Research practices were mistakenly believed to occur because the students were asked to find information, make notes, and write a paper.

What Research Is Not

Finding information and making knowledge are different tasks. Information like that found in telephone directories, newspapers, and the Internet can be useful information, but as such it is not the same as the knowledge that is constructed by research efforts. The truth of Internet information is untested. Much information found in advertisements is also unreliable. Many sources of information are unreliable. Finding information of this unreliable quality is not doing research.

Often school assignments are given to students under the heading of "research." Students complete assignments by gathering information from dictionaries, libraries, and newspapers, and they think they are doing research. We note a huge difference between compiling information and making knowledge. A student going to the library and reading information on the Lewis and Clark Expedition is not doing research in the sense of making knowledge. To consult several sources and reading about a topic, doing a literature review, or finding established answers to questions is not research. Instead, this is more information gathering or the learning and doing of reference skills (Best & Kahn, 1989; Hopkins & Antes, 1990; Leedy & Ormrod, 2001). Library skills are those needed to search for information, and reference skills are those needed to search for knowledge (Allgood, Risko, Alvarez, & Fairbanks, 2000). Getting background information is one part of a more complex effort of constructing knowledge.

What Research Is

If the above descriptions are not research then what is research? Research is a systematic inquiry to solve problems and create knowledge. Listed below are Leedy's (2001) characteristics of formal research.

Research originates with a question or a problem.
Research requires a clear articulation of a goal.
Research follows a specific plan of procedure.
Research usually divides the principal problem into more manageable subproblems.
Research is guided by the specific research problem, question, or hypothesis.
Research accepts certain critical assumptions. These assumptions are underlying theories or ideas about how the world works.
Research requires the collection and interpretation of data in attempting to resolve the problem that initiated the research.
Research is, by its nature, cyclical; or more exactly, spiral or helical.

A COMPREHENSIVE THEORY GUIDING RESEARCH IN EDUCATION

For research in education to be meaningful there needs to be a comprehensive theory. The four commonplaces of educating, teaching, learning, curriculum, and governance plus the societal environment are spheres of influence that determine educational worth. Events in educational research are influenced by each of these commonplaces; they are difficult to isolate. This theory of educating, described in Chapter 1, guides the research process and is used to interpret its outcomes.

Inherent in these four commonplaces of educating plus one are two kinds of research: practical and theoretical. Both practical and theoretical research are used when planning and evaluating questions of interest that are investigated.

Practical

Research makes records of an event or a set of events. An event occurs or is *made* to happen by the researcher and some record of the event is made. A study is a record of an event. An event occurs or is made to happen by the researcher and some record of the event is made. A study of the record generates factual statements serviceable as evidence for inferences leading to generalizations, explanations, interpretations, predictions, and decisions. The research technique is the process of converting events into records and records into factual statements (including tables, charts, and other ways of showing relationships).

Theoretical

Research in the theoretical sense of reasoning is a matter of using concepts, conceptual systems, constructs, models, theories, etc. An event can be studied effectively if the researcher generates a telling question. Such questions require key concepts or generative ideas, which lead and guide the inquiry. Facts without concepts are blind and concepts without facts are empty. Research brings together conceptual systems and techniques. Appraisal of research is methodology.

The **V** is a tool that can help us understand and learn. Since knowledge is not discovered, but is constructed by people, it has a structure that can be analyzed. The **V** helps to identify the components of knowledge, clarify their relationships, and present them in a visually compact and clear way.

Focus/Research Question (Center)

A **V**'s shape is, literally, a "**V**." In the center of the **V** diagram is the question the researcher is asking. The development and phrasing of this question is of paramount importance for either analyzing a document or when planning a research investigation:

[T]he worth of any study is limited by the quality of the questions posed by the researcher. It is extremely important for consumers of research reports (and for applied researchers as well) to recognize this fact, because fancy statistics and complex design strategies tend to both impress and intimidate many people. We argue as vigorously as we can that it is the quality of the research question(s) that determines the maximum worth of any investigation.[1]

The **V** points to the event that the researcher designs to help answer the question. Clarifying these two components, the question and the event are the critical initial steps in any study. *Rigor occurs when the design of the research meets the question.*

It is important to note that there is active interplay between the left and right side of the **V**. They are not separate entities. The research question(s) and the events tie both sides of the **V** together.

Conceptual Design: Theoretical/Conceptual (Left Side)

No question is asked, or event designed, studied, or interpreted, in isolation. All research is influenced by the researchers' own views, the "conceptual goggles" through which the work is viewed. The researchers' philosophies, theories, and perspectives lead to asking certain questions, to designing a particular event that they think will provide answers, and to interpreting the data in a particular way. Thus, the left side of the **V** contains important, and often neglected, components of research. The **V** challenges researchers to be more explicit about and aware of the role that their world

---

[1] Schuyler W. Huck and William H. Cormier, *Reading Statistics and Research*, 2nd ed. (New York: HarperCollins, 1996), Preface.

view plays in their research by forcing them to really think about the philosophies, theories, principles, and concepts that are guiding their research. The components of the left side, therefore, interact with those of the right side.

Methodological (Right Side)

The right side of the V contains those components with which we likely are most familiar, the actual activities of research: making records (collecting the raw data), transforming the data into an analyzable form (e.g., statistics, graphs, charts, tables, and concept maps), and making claims from the results. As mentioned, these activities are influenced by components of the left side.

Many researchers focus on knowledge claims (what the results mean) without considering what value claims (the worth of the study) should be made about, or should be considered prior to, their research. The inclusion of this category on the right side of the V reflects the view of its creator about knowledge – that it is a human construct and that knowledge generating research cannot escape being asked: "What good is it?" and "Who cares?" Some researchers would like to avoid these questions, claiming that they are doing objective, basic research to which such queries don't apply. The V suggests that answers to these questions ought to be an important part of *any* research because they assist us in grasping the meaning of the research claims.

STAGES OF THE V DIAGRAM PROCESS

When planning a research study the V can be divided into two stages. Stage 1 consists of the Focus Questions/Research Questions, event(s)/object(s), concepts, records, theory, world view, philosophy, and value claims (prethoughts). Transformations are sometimes included in this stage in general terms to indicate how the data will be represented (see Figure 8.1, Stage 1).

In this *first stage* the focus/research questions and the events/objects are closely examined. The theoretical/conceptual side is directly related to the methodological side through the use of the focus or research question. Focus and research questions are influenced by the event(s) object(s) of an investigation. It is crucial that the Focus Questions/Research Questions and the event(s)/object(s) are compatible. This union is the basis for formulating a sound research investigation (see Figure 8.2).

The concepts, event(s)/object(s), and records work in conjunction with each other. The concepts are those that need to be operationally defined in the investigation or lesson. These concepts are directly related to the Focus Questions/Research Question, to the event(s)/object(s) being studied, and

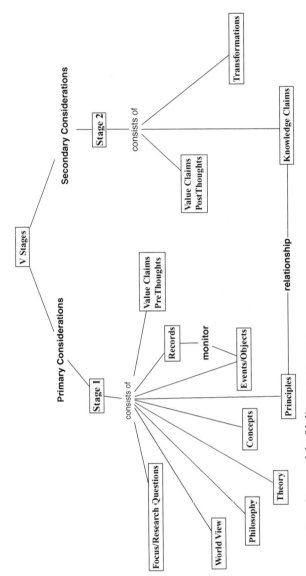

FIGURE 8.1. Stages of the **V** diagram process.

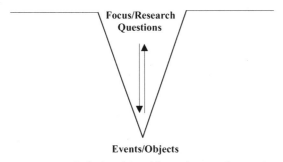

FIGURE 8.2. Relationship of focus/research questions and events/objects.

to the records (instruments) used to collect the facts emanating from the event(s) object(s) (see Figure 8.3).

The research task is to tie the key concepts to the telling questions about the phenomena of interest (the educative event) that are recorded in a systematic way by the techniques and methods of research. This epistemological **V** permits crossovers at different levels of abstraction but the crucial consideration is to maintain the **V** at the bottom (concepts, events, records).

In essence, completing the *first stage* of the **V** research process serves as the preliminary plan or research proposal that is tinkered with for final approval to begin the investigation.

The *second stage* in a **V** research study occurs after the data have been collected. It is during this stage that the data are analyzed and transformed. Knowledge claims are formulated from the data. Answers are then provided that directly relate to the questions that were asked in the first stage.

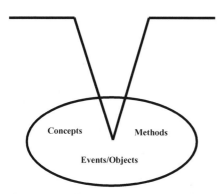

FIGURE 8.3. Connecting concepts, events, and records.

The value claims (postthoughts) are then revisited and compared to what was forecasted in stage one (prethoughts).

Steps in the V Research Process

Stage 1
First:

The first consideration is also the last. Begin by identifying some event that can be called an "educational event." Begin with a clear case of an educational episode. Then, find a case that serves as a counterexample to the first case selected. Next, look for and find truly puzzling cases. Finally, think up imaginary cases. With a supply of such examples, then the next step is to find a criterion that helps decide which cases are examples of educating and which cases are not. Experts help. The criteria for selecting an educative event are for three competent judges of educating to agree that the selected case is an event of educating. Doctoral students doing the most advanced research need three competent professors to agree; there is no better standard. When judged to be so, validity is established before reliability of the record, a reversal of standard research recommendations. What is the Telling Question of this event? What Focus Question(s)/ Research Question(s) are you trying to answer that directly relates to this event?
Second:

Determine a way to make a record of this episode. Examples of records include videotapes, journals, surveys, questionnaires, timing devices, examinations, and photographs. The record of the educative event must be reliable.
Third:

Think about your investigation using the left side of the **V**. This is the most time-consuming part of your effort for conceptualizing the research process. What is your world view? What is the philosophy that is guiding your inclination toward this research study? What theory are you advocating? What are the principles that can be related to your theory? What concepts need to be listed and defined that are related to the Focus/Research Question and the events? What value do you foresee as a result of undertaking this investigation?

   NOTION OF A CONCEPT MAP. 1. Concepts are signs or symbols (words, numbers, etc.) taken as pieces of language that point to regularities or commonalities in the phenomena of interest.
   2. We easily distinguish three elements in concepts:
      a. The Person-Sign Connection: concept-user (person).
      b. The Sign-Sign Connection: signs and symbols.
      c. The Sign-Event Connection: the regularities in the events that the sign-symbol points to (the referent).

3. Concepts are what we think with.
4. A concept map is a form of showing meanings and linkages between concepts.
5. Several styles of maps are possible. One style arranges concepts in an order of greater to lesser power; the more powerful concept "subsumes" the lesser ones. Concept maps make fundamental distinctions readily "visible." Concept maps locate ideas, give them a place, so that discussion can be clarified.
6. Three sources of concepts:
   a. Some concepts derive from other concepts (e.g., statistical inference from inference and knowledge structure from building structure).
   b. Some concepts derive from regularities of events (e.g., clouds mean rain and day follows night).
   c. Some concepts derive from personal meanings developed through experience as a way to make sense of human experience (e.g., an act of kindness, or a style of cooperation).
7. Concept improvement is a process of reducing ambiguity and vagueness and increasing precision of words and clarity of meaning.

MAKING A CONCEPT MAP. A hierarchical concept map is a visual representation of an individual's thought processes. It is a word diagram that is portrayed visually in a hierarchical fashion and represents concepts and their relationships (see Figure 8.4). A concept map shows the interrelationship between ideas, facts, and details. A hierarchical concept map progresses from most inclusive (general) ideas to least inclusive (specific) ones.

In this map, ideas are linked by labeled lines that contain either a word or word phrases to show their relationship. This is referred to as a *proposition*. Propositions are meaningful relationships between concepts and are expressed by a connecting line and linking word(s). Once a student has constructed a map, writing about the visual display is an easy task due to the labeling and linking of the ideas in the arrangement. Better comprehension gives greater meaning to a concept. Concept maps can be constructed to map a textual passage or to map ideas for written reports or oral presentations.[2]

---

[2] For a comprehensive description and examples of varied uses of concept maps see Joseph D. Novak and D. Bob Gowin, *Learning How to Learn* (New York, Cambridge University Press), 1984; Joseph D. Novak, *Learning, Creating, and Using Knowledge: Concept Maps as Facilitative Tools in Schools and Corporations*, (Mahwah, New Jersey: Lawrence Erlbaum Associates, 1998); Marino C. Alvarez in Walter Pauk, *How to Study in College*, 4th ed. (Boston, Houghton Mifflin Company, 1989), pp. 212–219.

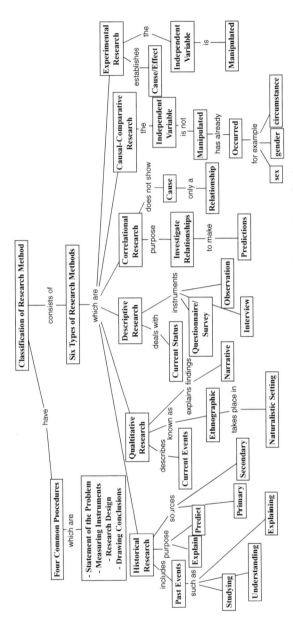

FIGURE 8.4. A hierarchical concept map displaying an overview of research methods.

The following steps are for developing a concept map when preparing a research investigation:

1. **Select** a topic and decide upon the most important idea to which all other concept words can be related. Put this key concept in the top center of your paper. Think about how other concept words can be related to this central idea. (Brainstorm your thoughts.) Make a listing of each of these concepts on a sheet of paper. (Electronic software programs are available to construct concept maps. Two of these are Inspiration 6.0 and a free program for educators, CMap, available at http://www.coginst.uwf.edu).

2. **Rank** these concept words hierarchically from most inclusive (general) to least inclusive (concrete and specific). Eliminate the ones that do not pertain to your key concept.

3. **Arrange** the concept words on your paper according to hierarchical structure and relationship. For example, arrange concepts that can be subsumed and/or related to each other. As you post each concept, simultaneously **link** each of the concept words by drawing lines showing the connections among and between the ideas. Label each line using a word or word phrase to explain the relationships. If an idea relates to others that have already been represented in another portion of the map, show the relationship of this idea by drawing a broken line to indicate cross-linkage. Once you complete your first effort take time to examine your arrangement. At this time, you may want to rearrange or redo your map. You also may add other concepts to the arrangement.

4. **Review** your concept map. Look again at your concept map. Can you add any other information to the map? Can you think of another way that this map can be developed?

5. **Write** a paragraph(s) describing the conceptual arrangement of the map. This is a relatively easy process since the map is now organized into coherent and unified threads evolving from a focus or theme.

Concept maps connecting questions and events are extremely helpful. Do not be afraid to construct a dozen or more concept maps at this point. Clarifying conceptual thinking is as difficult as it is significant for the progress of research.

Once this stage has been established, the *second stage* is carried out (refer to Figure 8.1, Stage 2). Collecting the data and monitoring the event(s)/object(s) under study are constant operations. It is this interplay that informs the researcher.

Stage 2
Fourth:

Make sense of the event. We ask ourselves, "What's going on?" "What's happening?" "Is some knowledge claim being asserted?" It is here that an important task is to tie the key concept to that particular part of the event that you wish to call a fact. The focus of this task is to use a concept that pervades one part of the complex event that exhibits regularity. It is important to define and clarify the concept being used. If this concept needs to be changed later because the facts do not fit then do so. This is the process of "concept improvement." To use facts to improve concepts is another significant change in standard research recommendations.

Fifth:

Make some order out of the facts once the concept you think with has been defined. Take the facts and arrange them to be represented in a table, graph, chart, and so forth. This may involve ranking, measuring, rating, correlating, relating, analyzing, and synthesizing. Compose a set of statements about the record in some form, be it a paragraph or a paradigm sketch, which consist of a set of summary judgments of the facts. These are factual judgments; the judgment part comes in when we give order to the facts, and thereby judge their merit according to some criterion of selection, order, or significance. Notice the category of facts includes items in relations: the event which is either made to happen or just happens, the record of the event, and the factual (including moral) judgments based on the record. It is easy to make mistakes at each of these three places, so we need reliability checks at each position.

Once the data have been recorded, the process of representing them in some form (e.g., chart, graph, figure, illustration, table, or map) is undertaken.

Sixth:

Display these facts by transforming them into an arrangement. A table, graph, chart, and diagram are examples of ways to represent your data. Select the display or a variety of displays that help to connect Focus Questions to relevant facts.

Seventh:

Answer the Focus/Research Questions you have asked in the knowledge claims. For every question asked there needs to be an answer or a response. Be sure to answer the question(s) directly.

Once meaning is made from the data obtained from the records then the knowledge claims are determined and tie directly to the Focus/Research Questions that were asked. Making this connection between the question and the answer is an important learning objective. Once the question has been answered then principles can be revisited to determine if the knowledge claims influence these principles.

Eighth:

Revisit your value claims (prethoughts). Decide on the worth of the findings and answers to your Focus/Research Questions. How do you perceive the value or worth of the outcomes? In what situations? Under what circumstances or conditions? What mistakes were made that need changing? Evaluating research is important for progress in research programs.

Principles are then compared to the theory in order to affirm, negate, or extend this theory that was tested. The value claims signify the worth of the outcomes and are important in deriving the practicality and application of the knowledge claims. The value claims are the conditions that aid in establishing what further exploration needs to be undertaken. Making knowledge leads to the formulation of new ideas and imagined possibilities for future study.

Q-5 Technique As a Process and Product of Self-Inquiry

The Q-5 technique asks five questions. It is a condensed version of a pattern of inquiry. It aids transitioning into formulating ideas onto a **V** diagram as described above. Planning, carrying out, and finalizing one's own research require the same processes as when analyzing the works of others (see Chapter 7).

1. What is the question? What is the Telling Question of the work? What does it tell on, or is it about? (event/object), *the phenomena or reality of the event or object*. This starting question develops in the **V** to the concern there is with Telling Questions and Focus Questions as central to the **V** analysis. The idea of a starting point of *questions* sets the whole in motion. Good questions require further study and development. Many times, however, authors do not write out their guiding questions. Students need to be alert to what is missing. What is the question about? What does the question reveal? (event/object). This is a very important aspect of the work. The question needs to be answered by the event that is taking place. It is vital for congruence to be accomplished between what is being asked and what is taking place in the events.

2. What are the key concepts? What are the key concepts? What concepts are needed to ask the question? This question expands into the whole left side of the **V** with its concern with conceptual structure. Concept-mapping technique fits here.

3. What methods are used? What methods are useful in answering the question or questions? How am I going to find out what's happening? This question expands into the whole right side of the **V**, especially the lower right with its close ties to events and objects and ways of making records of them.

4. What answers are presented? What are the major claims of the work? What answers are produced? This question expands into the top levels, knowledge claims, and the key functions of claims – interpretations, generalizations, and explanations.

5. So What? This question expands into value claims. Plus it enables the user of the **V** to take a look at the coherence of the **V**, at the ways parts feed into other parts.

Using the Q-5 gives the researcher the sense of the extent of coherence of the research investigation. Coherence is one theory of truth.

Examples of Levels of Complexity with the Same Topic Using Q-5

We present examples of applying stage 1 in the **V** research process using the Q-5 technique. The examples that follow ask three questions that involve the application of the Q-5 technique to the use of *readability formulas*. Readability formulas are often used to determine the ease or difficulty of a text. These readability formulas all take sentence length (number of sentences per 100 words) and either word length (number of syllables per 100 words) or percent of unfamiliar words to determine the approximate difficulty or ease of a text. To measure factors not measured by readability formulas, readability checklists are applied as an added indicator to inform the evaluator of the degree of complexity of a text. Notice in this graduated series how the question shapes the degree of complexity with a readability formula and leads to a more simplified understanding of the degree of reading ease or difficulty that a textbook presents to a learner.

We have a graduated series of examples using the Q-5 technique with the concept of "readability factors measured and not measured" when matching printed text to student reading abilities based on readability formulas.

Simple Example Using the Q-5

1. **The telling question:** "How do you determine the readability of a text?"
2. **The key concepts:** readability and text.
3. **Methods:** The Fry Readability Formula (1977), which measures word length and sentence length, will be applied to three social studies passages within a textbook starting somewhere near the beginning of the textbook, then selecting a passage near the middle of the textbook, and then applying the formula to a passage near the end of the textbook.
4. **Knowledge claims:** Using the criteria established by the Fry Readability Formula and the Fry Graph, the approximate level of difficulty for the social studies textbook will be determined given a standard error of measurement of plus or minus one grade.

5. **Value claims:** Knowing the approximate difficulty of a text enables the teacher to match reading materials to an individual's level of reading comprehension: independent or instructional.

Moderate Example Using Q-5

1. **The telling question:** "What factors are measured by a readability formula? "What factors are not measured by readability formulas?"
2. **The key concepts:** factors, measures, and readability formulas.
3. **Methods:** The Fry Readability Formula will be applied to three passages with a social studies textbook. A *readability checklist* that takes into account factors not measured by word length, sentence length, and / or percent of unfamiliar words will be applied to the same social studies textbook.
4. **Knowledge claims:** The degree of difficulty as measured by the Fry Readability Formula combined with the readability checklist will reveal the level of reading difficulty of this selected social studies text.
5. **Value claims:** Knowing the factors that are measured and not measured by a readability formula permits the teacher to become more aware of the ease or difficulty of a text when matching the text to the student than relying solely on the formula alone.

Complex Example Using Q-5

1. **The telling question:** "In which instances do matched materials enable the reader to better comprehend the concepts and facts of a themed unit?"
2. **The key concepts:** Instances, matched materials, comprehension, concepts, facts, and themed unit.
3. **Methods:** The Fry Readability Formula will be applied to determine the degree of passage and textbook difficulty. A readability checklist will be used to check factors not measured by readability formula(s). To determine students' prior knowledge, reading ability, and interest with the concepts and facts of the themed unit, an *informal reading inventory* will be given to each student, an *interest inventory* will be administered, and a pretest with concepts and facts will be given to determine students' prior knowledge with the topic to be studied, student reports and an examination will administered.
4. **Knowledge claims:** The degree to which matched reading materials enable learners to learn concepts and facts of a themed unit will be determined.
5. **Value claims:** Matching reading materials to students' abilities and interests require complex measures and decisions by the teacher. Matching reading materials to student abilities and interests with texts enables students to activate their prior knowledge, pique their

interest, and increase their comprehension with the target concepts and facts of a given themed unit.

We see in these examples that the kinds of questions determine how the events will be structured. Research is question-driven. So is human learning. Asking *any* question is perhaps the most important event in inquiry.

Using Q-5 to Plan a Golf Lesson

Next, we present an example and a counter example using the Q-5 technique in designing a study with golf instruction. An example of developing a **V** diagram for teaching a student the concept of "shot making" when hitting a draw.

An Example Using Q-5. **Illustration:** An example and counter example using the Q-5 technique with the concept "shot making" (see Figure 8.5).

1. **The telling question.** How can I improve my shot making in golf by learning how to hit a draw? *What does it tell on, or is about? (event).* Golf instructor teaching how to hit a draw shot (having the ball move left to right for a left-hander and right to left for a right-hander).
2. **The key concepts.** Shot making, draw shot. The concept "shot making" comes first and names the event. Shaping the flight of the golf ball so it goes left or right instead of straight is the main idea.

An Example Using Q-5

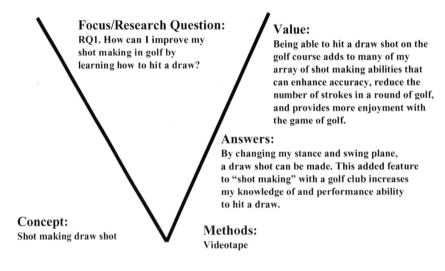

Focus/Research Question:
RQ1. How can I improve my shot making in golf by learning how to hit a draw?

Value:
Being able to hit a draw shot on the golf course adds to many of my array of shot making abilities that can enhance accuracy, reduce the number of strokes in a round of golf, and provides more enjoyment with the game of golf.

Answers:
By changing my stance and swing plane, a draw shot can be made. This added feature to "shot making" with a golf club increases my knowledge of and performance ability to hit a draw.

Concept:
Shot making draw shot

Methods:
Videotape

Events/Objects:
Golf instructor teaching how to hit a draw shot

FIGURE 8.5. An example of using Q-5 for shot making.

3. **Methods.** Learning how to hit a draw by the golf teacher and having it *recorded on videotape* for analysis. The videotaping of the event becomes the record from which to view and learn through analytic and physical practice. In this instance I am getting smart about hitting a draw by instruction, engaging in the activity, and viewing the procedure of the stance and swing plane on videotape.

4. **Knowledge claims.** By changing my alignment to a target to the right of the flagstick (maybe 10 or 15 degrees to the right), and closing the club face, and then hitting the ball to the right, a draw shot should result for a right-hander. The ball should fly from right to left in its path to the target. This added feature to "shot making" with a golf club increases my knowledge of and performance ability to hit a draw.

5. **Value claims.** Being able to hit a draw shot on the golf course adds to my array of shot making abilities that can enhance accuracy, reduce the number of strokes in a round of golf, and provide more enjoyment with the game of golf.

A Counter Example Using Q-5. This counterexample shows the inaccurate relationship between the components forming the bottom of the **V** (*concepts, events, methods*). See Figure 8.6.

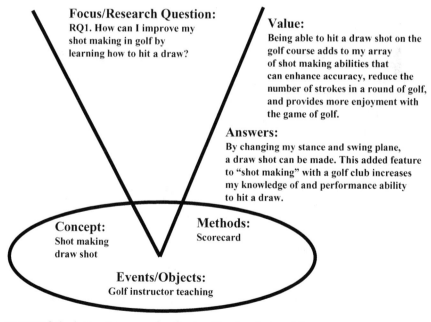

FIGURE 8.6. A counterexample of using Q-5 for shot making.

1. **The telling question.** How can I improve my shot making in golf by learning how to hit a draw? *What does it tell on, or is about? (event).* Golf instructor teaching how to hit a draw shot (having the ball move left to right for a left-hander and right to left for a right-hander).
2. **The key concepts.** Shot making and draw shot.
3. **Methods.** Learning how to hit a draw by the golf teacher and having the number of strokes *recorded on a scorecard.* In this instance, the use of a scorecard is **not** a record of shot making and is an inappropriate record of what is taking place in the event and does not correspond with the telling question being asked. A scorecard is a record used to count the number of strokes per golf hole. It is not a record that indicates whether or not progress has been made in the shot making ability of hitting a draw. How well the "shot making" ability to hit a draw shot on the golf course is an important consideration, however, in this instance, the scorecard is an artifact added to this particular event and is not a record of "shot making."
4. **Knowledge claims.** In this instance, the knowledge derived from the event and the method would be an inaccurate portrayal of what had occurred and therefore would not be a valid answer to the telling question.
5. **Value claims.** Likewise a claim as to the worth of the event would be misleading.

In this counterexample, there is a discrepancy between the *concepts* (shot making and draw) and the *event* with the method of the record being used to find out what was happening during and after the golf lesson.

An Example of Applying the Q-5 to a Study of Global Warming

To illustrate further, an example is given that shows the topic "global warming" and a way that it could be represented with the Q-5 technique. This use of the Q-5 technique is demonstrated to begin a study with the topic "global warming."

Illustration: An example using the Q-5 technique with a concept that has contrasting theories about "global warming." See Figure 8.7.

1. **The telling question (Focus/Research Questions).**
   RQ1. Can global warming be explained by correlating the amount of carbon dioxide and other greenhouse gases in the atmosphere brought about through the burning of coal, oil, and gas?
   RQ2. Can global warming be explained due to a relationship between solar luminosity and changes in the sun's magnetic activity? *What does it tell on, or is about? (event).* Reviewing the literature and data contrasting human activity and the natural effects on global warming.

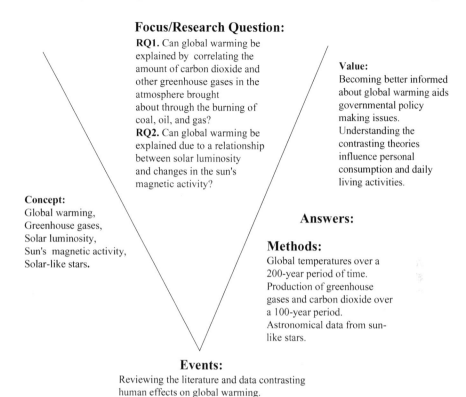

FIGURE 8.7. An example of using Q-5 for global warming.

2. **The key concepts.** Global warming, greenhouse gases, solar luminosity, sun's magnetic activity, and solar-like stars. The concept "global warming" comes first and names the event – the reality named by the concept.
3. **Methods.** Global temperatures over a 200-year period of time. Production of greenhouse gases and carbon dioxide over a 100-year period. Astronomical data from sun-like stars.
4. **Answers (knowledge claims).** In this instance, the investigation would need to be carried out to find answers to the questions posed.
5. **Value claims.** Becoming better informed about global warming aids governmental environmental policy-making issues. Understanding the contrasting theories aid personal consumption and daily living activities.

A concept map showing these contrasting theories of "global warming" appear in the constructs portion of the **V** diagram in Figure 8.8.

FIGURE 8.8. A concept map depicting the constructs of "global warming."

The Q-5 technique reveals the structure of knowledge by probing both the conceptual and methodological sides of the **V** diagram and making connections between the two sides. Ideas are analyzed and viewpoints discussed in ways that determine the quality of the work and/or the direction that the work will take.

Planning, carrying out, and finalizing a study with "global warming" could take the form of the **V** diagram shown in Figure 8.9. In this **V**, both theories are stated and the plan is initiated.

This **V** has been designed to carry out and finalize the event and the answers to the questions that are stated. This type of research would require study of related journal articles, sun-like star data such as those received through automatic photoelectric telescopes, tree rings, interviews with scientists in this area, and other fact-gathering information of global temperatures over a 200-year period, and the production of greenhouse gases over a 100-year period.

AN ON-SITE UNIVERSITY/SCHOOL DEMONSTRATION PROJECT

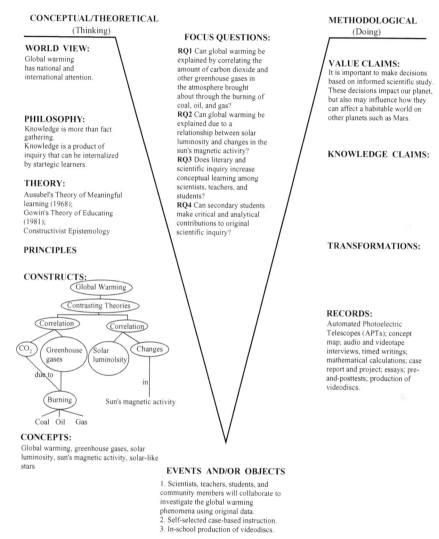

CONCEPTUAL/THEORETICAL
(Thinking)

FOCUS QUESTIONS:

METHODOLOGICAL
(Doing)

WORLD VIEW:
Global warming has national and international attention.

PHILOSOPHY:
Knowledge is more than fact gathering. Knowledge is a product of inquiry that can be internalized by startegic learners.

THEORY:
Ausubel's Theory of Meaningful learning (1968); Gowin's Theory of Educating (1981); Constructivist Epistemology

PRINCIPLES

CONSTRUCTS:

Global Warming

Contrasting Theories

Correlation — Correlation

CO_2 — Greenhouse gases / Solar luminolsity — Changes

due to — in

Burning — Sun's magnetic activity

Coal   Oil   Gas

CONCEPTS:
Global warming, greenhouse gases, solar luminosity, sun's magnetic activity, solar-like stars

RQ1 Can global warming be explained by correlating the amount of carbon dioxide and other greenhouse gases in the atmosphere brought about through the burning of coal, oil, and gas?
RQ2 Can global warming be explained due to a relationship between solar luminosity and changes in the sun's magnetic activity?
RQ3 Does literary and scientific inquiry increase conceptual learning among scientists, teachers, and students?
RQ4 Can secondary students make critical and analytical contributions to original scientific inquiry?

VALUE CLAIMS:
It is important to make decisions based on informed scientific study. These decisions impact our planet, but also may influence how they can affect a habitable world on other planets such as Mars.

KNOWLEDGE CLAIMS:

TRANSFORMATIONS:

RECORDS:
Automated Photoelectric Telescopes (APTs); concept map; audio and videotape interviews, timed writings; mathematical calculations; case report and project; essays; pre- and-posttests; production of videodiscs.

EVENTS AND/OR OBJECTS
1. Scientists, teachers, students, and community members will collaborate to investigate the global warming phenomena using original data.
2. Self-selected case-based instruction.
3. In-school production of videodiscs.

FIGURE 8.9. A **V** diagram of showing global warming.

High School Students Using the V Research Process

Bobby Hullan and Adelicia Graham were 10th graders when they engaged in a research project to investigate "Black Holes." Their high school astronomy teacher monitored their choice of topic and progress along with an astronomer. Their paper was presented at the American Educational

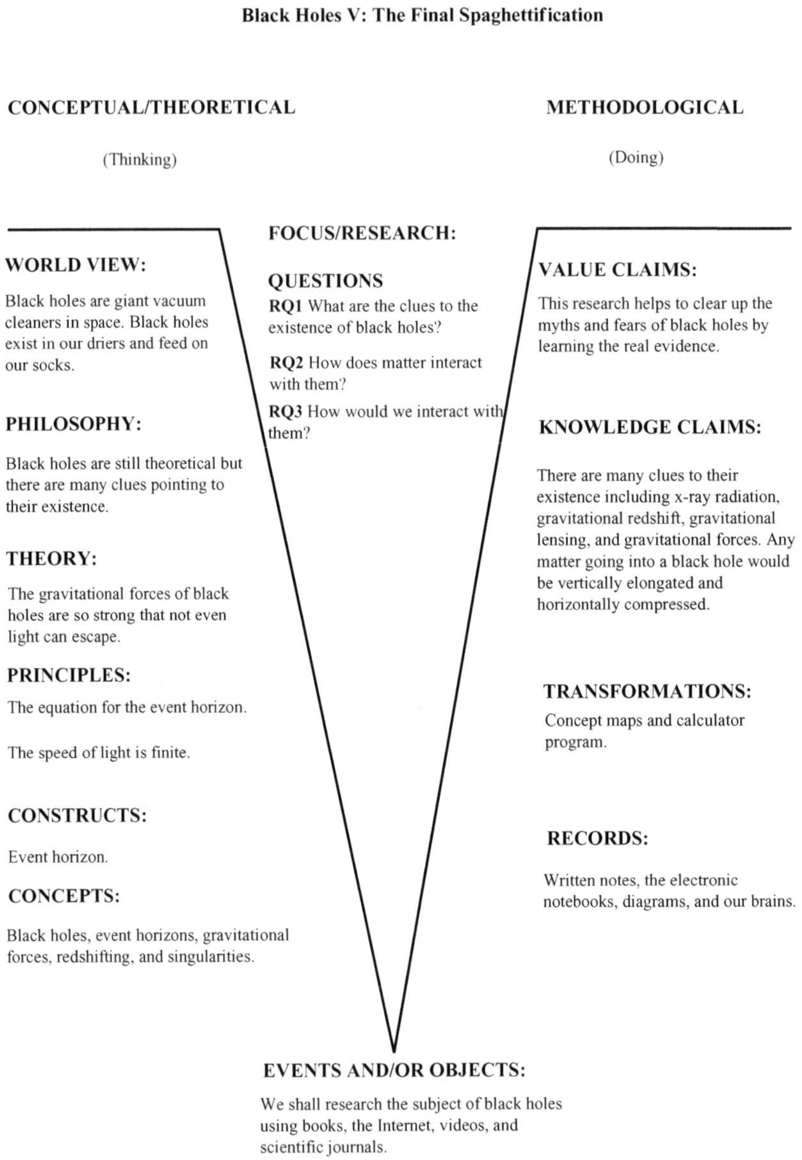

Black Holes V: The Final Spaghettification

CONCEPTUAL/THEORETICAL	METHODOLOGICAL
(Thinking)	(Doing)

FOCUS/RESEARCH:

WORLD VIEW:

Black holes are giant vacuum cleaners in space. Black holes exist in our driers and feed on our socks.

QUESTIONS

RQ1 What are the clues to the existence of black holes?

RQ2 How does matter interact with them?

RQ3 How would we interact with them?

PHILOSOPHY:

Black holes are still theoretical but there are many clues pointing to their existence.

THEORY:

The gravitational forces of black holes are so strong that not even light can escape.

PRINCIPLES:

The equation for the event horizon.

The speed of light is finite.

CONSTRUCTS:

Event horizon.

CONCEPTS:

Black holes, event horizons, gravitational forces, redshifting, and singularities.

VALUE CLAIMS:

This research helps to clear up the myths and fears of black holes by learning the real evidence.

KNOWLEDGE CLAIMS:

There are many clues to their existence including x-ray radiation, gravitational redshift, gravitational lensing, and gravitational forces. Any matter going into a black hole would be vertically elongated and horizontally compressed.

TRANSFORMATIONS:

Concept maps and calculator program.

RECORDS:

Written notes, the electronic notebooks, diagrams, and our brains.

EVENTS AND/OR OBJECTS:

We shall research the subject of black holes using books, the Internet, videos, and scientific journals.

FIGURE 8.10. Black holes **V**: The final spaghettification.

Research Association Annual Meeting.[3] Their **V** diagram appears in Figure 8.10.

[3] Marino C. Alvarez, Geoffery Burks, Goli Sotoohi, Terry King, Bobby Hulan, and Adelicia Graham. "Students Creating Their Own Thinking–Learning Contexts." April, 2000, ED 441 037.

As part of their investigation they prepared three concept maps. The one shown in Figure 8.11 is their concept map on black holes.

This map was a second draft of a map previously submitted for review. Comments were made upon the map and sent back to the students electronically. This map formed the template from which Bobby and Addie wrote a story that incorporated the facts and of their research with a fictional account about Vincent and his journey into space in the year 2334 to explain the effects that black holes would have on matter such as humans. This imaginative story illustrated the importance of not only understanding scientific facts and ideas, but the ability of these two students to infuse them into a creative portrayal that includes their metaphor of "Spaghettification," which provides the reader with a better understanding of their research topic "black holes." This study was evaluated using the theory of educating and the four commonplaces of educating: teaching, learning, curriculum, and governance.

Third Graders using the V Research Process

In a study with third graders, the **V** was used to determine how this population would conduct an experiment with "sprouting plants" using lima beans under four conditions: water, no water, light, no light (Alvarez & Risko, 1987). Their teacher conducted the experiment and grouped her students in randomized groups that were stratified according to their reading stanine scores. An example of a **V** diagram constructed by a student is shown in Figure 8.12.

An inspection of this **V** shows that the knowledge claims related to the principles, but were not stated in the records (i.e., "the one with no air grew a leaf"). The teacher was able to see this discrepancy and asked the students in this group to set up this part of the experiment again. She noticed that a piece of cardboard was placed on the jar fitting loosely, therefore letting air into the jar. This portion of the experiment was repeated, and students then understood that air was needed for the seeds to sprout. This clarified their misconception and accounted for the notation under principles. In this case, the **V**s acted as an evaluation instrument for both the teacher and the students in determining how well ideas were represented among the component parts of the **V** diagram. Together, the teacher and the students were able to resolve uncertainties or misunderstandings that occurred during the experiment and make the educative event a meaningful learning experience.

An Action Research Study Using the V Research Process

Nikki Bethune (2003) used the **V** diagram with her ninth grade physical science students in an action research study in order to learn more about them

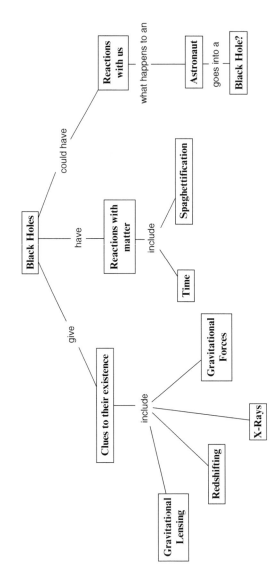

FIGURE 8.11. Concept map of black holes.

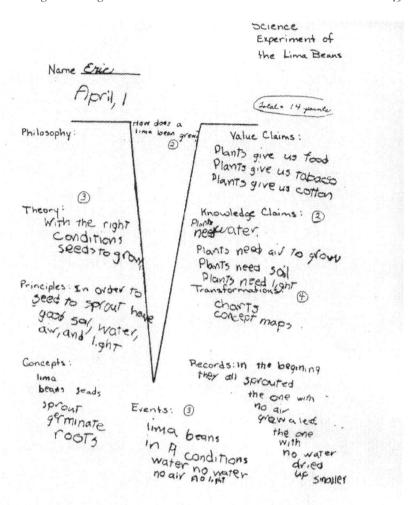

FIGURE 8.12. Third grade student's **V** diagram.

and then improve her teaching practices. She introduced her students to the **V** diagram to help them construct meaning during their laboratory investigations and used the four commonplaces of educating to assess her results. Her focus question was: "How does the use of the Vee heuristic as a nontraditional lab report influence the teacher in constructing meaningful learning during laboratory situations?" She also asked four secondary questions that were based on the four commonplaces of educating that she used to evaluate her research investigation. These questions were: "Does the use of the Vee diagram allow the teacher to facilitate meaningful learning during the lab activity?" "Do students like using the Vee diagram as a lab report and feel they learn the concepts through lab activities?" "Does the use of Vee diagrams advocate more student-centered lab activities in the curriculum?" "Does the use of Vee diagrams meet the state standards for 9th grade Physical Science?"

Ms. Bethune's students ranged in abilities from low to high achievement levels. After introducing the Vee to her students she asked them to answer two questions: "What did I learn?" and "How does this apply to the world outside of the classroom?" Her purpose was to focus the students' attention on the relevance of the data and to have them think about why they are learning these concepts in school. Students were given a focus question before each lab session and worked in groups. Each **V** diagram was scored individually by the teacher. Students were given a survey to assess their feelings and attitudes about the **V** and its components and the lab experience for each of the laboratory sessions. She also interviewed some of the students to get more of an indepth view of their thoughts and feelings with the **V** diagram and also to ascertain their knowledge of the science concepts being studied. During this procedure, Ms. Bethune also kept a journal of her feelings concerning student progress, and the practices she used with them during this process.

Although an experienced teacher of 12 years, Ms. Bethune used the results of her action research study to inform and change her teaching practice. Prior to this study she relied more on telling students what they needed to do, what needed to happen in lab sessions, and why the results occurred. She described this procedure as producing "cookbook" labs. Following the study she states, "The use of the Vee allowed me to facilitate activities and guide students to discover science for themselves. I learned to ask guiding questions and pull upon students' prior knowledge to lead them in the right direction as they acquire new knowledge."

Her analysis of the student surveys and interviews provided an evaluation of the study using the four commonplaces of educating. Evident within her analyses is the role of the societal environment and its influence in the learning process.

Learner: Students enjoy participating in lab activities. Not only does it give them a chance to get out of their seats, but they also have the opportunity to learn from their own experiences. The majority of the students like using the Vee diagram as a lab report. Many have stated that it does not waste their time copying procedures and materials lists. Those who do not like the Vee diagram, tend to not like it because of the challenge it presents. They focus on the difficulty of developing the concept map and base their overall feelings of the Vee on their troubles in one section. The students, who successfully struggle through the challenge, find satisfaction in the end because they accomplished a task. When questioned about which teaching method helps them learn the best, students rank lab activities the highest.

Curriculum: The days of using "cookbook" labs are gone. The Vee diagram creates an atmosphere where students are creating meaningful learning. Thus, the Vee diagram has and will replace "cookbook" labs in my curriculum. Implementing the Vee diagram and having the students develop their own procedures takes more time than handing them a canned experiment, but the depth of understanding makes up for lost time.

Governance: Additionally, the Vee diagram meets all of the Oklahoma PASS process standards. Therefore making it a welcome addition into the science classroom and curriculum. Through the use of the Vee diagram, students observe, measure, classify, experiment, interpret, communicate and model. They are actively engaged in "Inquiry," the latest addition to the PASS process standards. This helps achieve Oklahoma's educational goal to create scientifically literate citizens.

Teacher: [This section is extracted from the Discussion section of the study]. I have been forced to give up control of learning in my class during lab activities. This gives my students more freedom and responsibility to learn science. The Vee diagram has alleviated preparation time in setting up a lab activity. When using a "cookbook" lab, I had to be sure the directions or procedure was written clearly and precisely for the equipment that was available. It did not allow for the flexibility to change an experiment to better fit the learning of the individual student. The Vee diagram has helped me to be a facilitator of learning with the student at center stage, rather than a mere disseminator of information trying to cram knowledge into their brains. The focus is on the learning rather than the teaching. By learning the value of learning, students are more apt to seek knowledge for themselves.

Engaging in this action research project enabled Ms. Bethune to critically examine her teaching practices and skills. She exemplifies what a professional teacher does to improve the teaching and learning process that is needed in our schools. This is accomplished by teachers investigating their own student populations and sharing their findings with their colleagues. Teachers, like Ms. Bethune, listen to their students and plan and develop lessons and assignments that establish connections that better prepare students to become knowledgeable and responsible individuals.

A RESEARCH STRATEGY

This *research strategy* is a way to guide your research investigation (Alvarez, 2002a). It is a *strategy* for achieving understanding rather than a rigid framework. The components that comprise each phase interact to aid the researcher in planning, conducting, and reaching decisions of an investigation. A diagram of the research strategy appears in Figure 8.13.

As can be discerned from this visual each component directly corresponds to the elements arrayed on the **V** diagram. Adhering to these components ensures the completion of a research investigation and provides the researcher with a one-page **V** of the research report. Appendix II provides a detailed question guide that relates to elements shown in the research strategy.

RESEARCH FUNDING

Estimating the cost of constructing a valuable piece of knowledge is difficult. First, most authors of research grant proposals are not well-trained

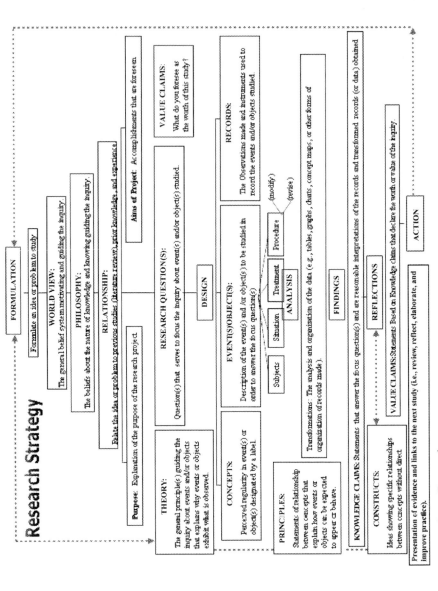

FIGURE 8.13. Research strategy.

to prepare them. Few would even think of connecting new knowledge to dollars and cents. Making knowledge is good in itself. It is so worthwhile and noble that considerations of its cost seem demeaning. Who can put a dollar cost to a new idea?

In academia, the tenured professor need not justify any work by appealing to cost estimates. These professors have earned the right to do their work in the context of academic freedom. Once their minds construct new knowledge, then its value in dollars and cents can be estimated by others. A university full of competent thinkers publishing qualified work is one of the most valuable institutions in a free society.

University administrators do think about money. University presidents are often chosen on a major criterion of their fund-raising talents. These talented individuals often have a rich history of academic productivity. Many have been highly successful writers of grants garnering large sums. A small number of such individuals have mastered the art of connecting their professorial knowledge making to research funding. It is to this group that we tip our hat. They value knowledge making first of all, and, second, they create specialized knowledge claims in drafting funding proposals. This second-order intelligence is very much like the metaknowledge claims of **V** diagrams.

Our task now is to show how **V** diagrams produce research proposals.

1. V Diagrams Save Time

For researchers drafting research funding proposals, estimates of time and money are crucial. Such estimates require an overview of the entire research program. The time the researcher spends on doing a **V** diagram of the entire research program can be worth a lot of money.

We know from our experience that students who learn to construct a **V** diagram before they enter a laboratory event use lab time efficiently. In a typical biology lab of three hours, these students will do the lab successfully in less than three hours. Some can complete writing the lab report and turn it in before they leave. Moreover, satisfaction scores are very high. They have made a genuine knowledge claim in a short period of time. **V** use saves time and increases productivity.

2. A Program of Research

Funding proposals are usually set in a context of a whole program of research. Research projects usually involve a small group of individual researchers, and each researcher brings specialized knowledge to one part of the whole project. These individuals must learn to share knowledge as they work to jointly create a set of knowledge claims. No one person is the complete master of the domain. The individuals must cooperate with each other, respecting each other's specialized knowledge. Team research requires researchers to share their thinking. When team members draw concept maps of their specialized interests and share these maps, then it becomes brilliantly obvious whose thinking is most relevant to the research work. It is at this point that the use of **V** diagramming techniques comes in handy. For a group of individual researchers facing the onerous task of preparing a research proposal, constructing a **V** is a great place to begin. Each can make their **V**, and share it. A large common **V** can be put on a white- or chalkboard. The committee's task is clear – work around the **V**. When all elements have been discussed, then connecting them takes only a little time. It is possible to construct a **V** for the whole project in a morning's work. We have experienced the joy that comes from releasing creativity to produce a research proposal.

For researchers drafting research funding proposals, estimates of time and money are crucial. Such estimates require an overview of the entire research program. The time the researcher spends in doing a **V** diagram can be worth a lot of money. If I were an administrator of research projects and programs, I would require **V** diagrams from *all* of my research workers. I would train them to estimate time and money precisely, and I would govern actions with the slogan "controlling the meaning controls the effort." Nothing controls meaning as well as time and money.

3. Programs of Research in Action

As time goes by, some parts of a research program are completed before other parts. Progress is variable. Reports of progress can be shared by individual researchers sharing an up-to-date **V** diagram. Each report can be exhibited around a room. Judgments of next steps to completion can be made jointly. The laggards can be stimulated by the front-runners. Time – a lot of time – can be saved by making interim **V** diagrams. The "Parade of **V**s" shown below (see Figure 8.14) and described in Chapter 6 is stimulating.

New knowledge, by definition, is an unknown. Surprises occur in research. Shocking surprises can interrupt everything, with joy or gloom.

We know from our experience that **V** diagrams reduce shocking surprises and greatly increase confidence in knowledge making. Not everything around a working **V** can be a shocking surprise. Good pieces are always available, and bad pieces can be recognized readily. In research, anything that saves your sanity is welcome.

4. The Final Report and the Making of New Proposals

Writing a competent final report usually takes a lot of talent and a lot of time. The final report, however, can be improved in many ways when prior **V** diagrams are available. The progress of knowledge making is readily evident by the "Parade of **V**s."

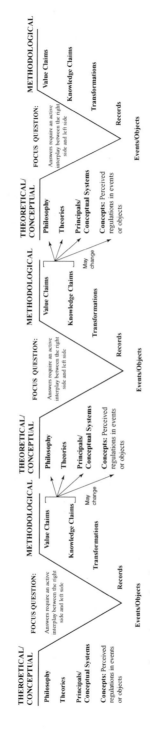

FIGURE 8.14. A parade of **V**s.

155

New proposals can often grow out of final reports. Completed **V** diagrams of finished research are a dandy source of new ideas and new proposals. A quick way to create a new proposal is to take the knowledge claims of past research and to turn them into questions. Whatever is uncertain about prior claims is a stimulus to new questions. New proposal writing can be done in half the time it usually takes when one is starting from scratch.

5. Interdisciplinary Research Proposals

The romance and dreaming about bringing different experts together to solve problems can be awesome anticipation. It just seems obvious that problems belonging to no specific discipline can be solved by experts from a variety of disciplines joining hands. The initial meeting of experts yields a lot of happy talk. The second meeting is the one to avoid, for then precise tasks are handed out to individuals. The journey from romance to precision can be frustrating and disappointing. This common outcome can be mitigated by the use of **V** diagrams.

An Example. A large university received money without any one person designated to receive it. It was a generous amount of money from a foundation with special interests. The foundation wanted research to be done on an issue of great concern to them. A university committee was given the task of designing the research. Specialists from different disciplines met. Each person expressed an interest in being involved in the proposed research design.

After a go-around with statements from each future participant, the discussion came to a standstill. No one knew what to do to guide the group into action. Since there was no intellectual leadership showing how to construct knowledge on the issue, the discussion turned into a power-grab (i.e., a grab for the free, available money based on social status, not on research merit). Sensing this turn, some professors just got up and left the room. One professor, however, proposed a new move. He suggested that each participant go to the chalkboard and write a list of the key concepts each thought relevant to the new issue. After six lists appeared on the board, he simply drew a circle around all the concepts held in common. Those with shared concepts saw clearly where their intellectual interests meshed.

This group met, drafted a working proposal, received the dollars, and got on with the needed research. Sharing explicit concept clusters can increase research efficiency by a factor of ten. Cost reductions should be obvious.

When members of a research group are "on the same page" then multiple errors are eliminated, much time is saved, and research productivity increases. We repeat: Research efficiency increases by a factor of ten.

Interdisciplinary research can be helped greatly by the use of **V** diagrams. "Working around the **V**" brings out the special value of each person's knowledge. Estimates of cost/benefit become more accurate when the time each person needs can be expressed in terms of what that person will contribute to making the **V** format active.

6. Risk–Reward

Comparisons of risks to rewards can produce insightful judgments. High risk and high reward judgments are more of an exciting gamble than productive value. Low risk and high reward is a very unlikely finding; if it were that easy, why has no one thought of it before?

How to determine risks? If a research proposal is framed in **V** format, then each element around the **V** can be evaluated for its potential risk. The most important risks are found in the events the researchers will make happen. Immediate actions have immediate consequences. Examine future events very carefully. Some exciting risks are connected to wild theorizing ("But is the theory wild enough?"). Sometimes the use of an unfamiliar method can excite interest and expose risk. Using **V** diagramming in writing research proposals gives a handle on exactly *what it is* that the research is risking.

7. The 3–1 Ratio of Thinking and Doing

In new research proposals, plan to spend 75 percent of your time thinking on the Conceptual side of the **V**, 25 percent on the methodological (doing) side of the **V**. Think it out before you do anything. "Do your damndest with your mind, no holds barred!" was advice a Harvard president gave to all who would listen. We believe formulating Telling Questions deserves a lot of thinking-before-doing. If a major change occurs in questions asked, then most prior methodological commitments may need to be changed as well. The costs can be more accurately estimated when the 3–1 ratio idea is used. Estimates of time are a good index to estimates of cost. "Time is money," said Benjamin Franklin.[4]

WRITING AROUND THE **V**

Once a piece of knowledge has been analyzed, it is relatively easy to use the **V** diagram to write a paper of the outcomes. A concept map of "Writing around the **V**" is shown in Figure 8.15.

---

[4] *Advice to a Young Tradesman, Written by an Old One.* The Writings of Benjamin Franklin: Philadelphia, 1726–1757, Volume II. B. Franklin and D. Hall, at the New-Printing-Office, 1748.

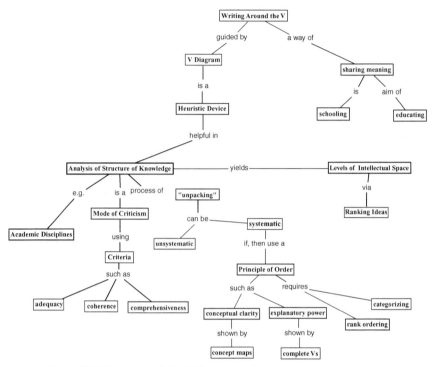

FIGURE 8.15. "Writing around the **V**."

"Writing around the **V**" analyzes the structure of knowledge in any discipline involved in schooling and educating. The curriculum is thought to
be the collection of disciplines. The analysis of each discipline is a mode of
criticism. The critical analysis tests the adequacy, coherence and comprehensiveness of deliberate efforts to construct knowledge.

It is a way to "unpack" knowledge and value claims. When we unpack knowledge, we do so under the principle of conceptual clarity, order,
and explanatory power. It is a way of ordering ideas into different levels of intellectual space. The analysis of unpacking is based on the notion
that some ideas are more important than other ideas. So, we learn to *rank*
ideas. When unpacking a suitcase we put, into piles, our socks, shirts,
pants, blouses, skirts, dresses, and hose and then separate them for the
laundry according to lights and darks, and then create a separate pile to
be taken to the cleaners. We do not rank order our socks, shirts, dresses,
and blouses – we list them. Just as we rank ideas, we also learn to connect one idea to another in contexts such that meaningful discourse is
possible. Discourse that is meaningful is a text that can be shared. Sharing meanings, so that we can explain things, is an aim of educating. Negotiating meanings such that we can settle conflicts, make peace, reach

satisfying and satisfactory mutual accommodations is an aim of living the good life.

Teaching students how to share meanings, how to explain things, how to create value, how to empower themselves such that they become self-educating is one of the highest goals of schooling and educating. In this complex process we see that facts and values ride in the same boat. Knowing and valuing are coextensive actions in our lives.

By "Writing around the **V**" we are better able to discern: (1) what events or objects are being observed; (2) what concepts are already known that relate to these events or objects; and (3) what records are worth making. We can then be guided in formulating focus or research questions that are directly based on the event(s)/object(s) to be studied.

All of the elements necessary in writing a comprehensive paper are contained within the **V** diagram. We are better able to visualize the merits or shortcomings of an experiment, a mathematical problem, a research report, or a textual reading by writing our reactions. Our analysis is more comprehensive as a result of using the **V**. The paper is more exact and contains far more pertinent information than simply listing the facts or results.

Part Three

Summary

All knowledge, a deliberate construction of human beings striving to know about nature and experience, has structure. We know this about knowledge because we can analyze constructed claims of knowledge. We can see what elements have to be brought together to make a structure. These elements (e.g., theory, facts, assertions, and assumptions) may vary in their roles and intensities in any particular set of knowledge claims. But some version of the key elements will always be present. One only has to provide an analysis of any purported set of such claims to see this structure. Thus what we know about the structure of knowledge can easily be seen as a sort of knowledge about knowledge. This kind of knowledge is more durable than any particular set of knowledge claims, some of which are consumed or made out of date, by the progressive ordering of new knowledge.

PHILOSOPHY OF EDUCATION

Philosophy of Education is an academic field that supplies publishable articles to educational theory. These philosophers write theories of education, and write philosophy that only a few educators read and understand as having immediate use and value in the practice of educating. Educating with **V** diagrams puts the word "philosophy" high up on the conceptual side of the **V** diagram. Teachers and students construct **V** diagrams from direct concern for sharing meaning, negotiating meaning, changing the meaning of human experience. A piece of philosophic knowledge can be integrated nicely with other pieces of knowledge in the process of constructing a **V** diagram. When this event happens, philosophy of education happens.

V VERIFICATION

Verification is the idea that truth can be tested by some explicit criteria of evaluation. Or, in different words, verifying is acting in a way that tests the truth value of some claim of knowledge. In Chapter 7 we wrote of two theories of Truth. The Correspondence Theory claims truth is made when a knowledge claim matches a piece of reality. Knowledge corresponds with reality. Most scientists hold this view of their work – their claims match up with reality. The Coherence Theory claims truth is made when a set of claims hang together without interruption or nagging doubts of how the claims fit together. Knowledge coheres with knowledge.

Pragmatism, as a philosophy, holds that the tests of truth are found in the ways things work out with each other. It is a functional view of truth, an engineer's view of making things work. In the phrase "truth is what works," the force is on the "what" – exactly what is it that works. The cry of expedience is that anything works and that's OK, and that view is rejected by Pragmatists.

V verification connects all three of these major ideas of truth. The correspondence aspect in the V is the tight connection between events and the records of events. We name this connection facts. The coherence aspect of the V is the tight connection between all the elements up and down the V. In a fully-fleshed V diagram, the elements can be seen as connecting to each other in a coherent way, like the parts of a good story that develops cumulative meanings. The pragmatic aspect of the V lies in the utility of V diagrams. How well the Vs are used is determined by how the people use and interpret the elements and the completed V.

Understanding the structure of knowledge afforded by the V reveals how past knowledge can be reconstructed and then forecasted into future learning and knowledge making. This furtherance of knowledge, learning, and understanding enables ideas to be tested in ways that go beyond traditional classroom expectations. Meaning escalates into value that comes about through deliberate intervention on the part of the researcher/learner.

The V points to the event to be studied, about which the research question is asked. The right side of the V illustrates methodological elements of the research – records, transformations of records into data, and knowledge claims and value claims resulting from interpretation of the data. The left side is conceptual, describing the concepts, principles, theories, and philosophies that guide the question asking, the event, and the activities of the right side. There is continual interaction among the components of both sides, helping to clarify and integrate the structure of the knowledge. Upon completion, the V helps your audience understand the meaning of a piece of research.

The Q-5 technique should be read in order to better understand the structure of knowledge being studied. This display enables the researcher to better prepare, focus, and follow through with the investigation at hand.

The V reveals visually the conceptual/theoretical and methodological process that explains the relevance, meaningfulness, clarity, stability, and the degree of integrativeness of an individual's mind with the evolution of a piece of knowledge. This piece of knowledge represented by the **V** provides the explanatory power necessary when analyzing and conducting research investigations; and also, during the normal practice when trying to make sense of emerging ideas or new information.

The benefits of using the **V** are many, such as guiding the design of research, to analyze and evaluate the quality of research reports, textbooks and curriculum material used when developing and improving the design of educative events; having students use the **V** with a lesson or laboratory experiment; and when planning a research investigation. The exciting aspect of using the **V** is that it helps us to see more clearly how knowledge is constructed, an insight that is empowering, useful, and lasting.

The continuous quality of educative events must include evaluation and research that supports continuity and interaction. We need to evaluate properly what the person and persons involved bring to the occasions of educating, including especially assessments of prior knowledge. **V** diagrams help in this evaluating. In addition we need some facts about how the meaning of events and experiences has changed, and some express anticipating of future events based on what present-time knowledge can suggest. Continuity of the past with the present leading to future events is a judgment of wise and experienced people.

Events and experiences take time. Learning that simplifies complexity takes a lot of time. Knowing ways to hold fast-moving temporary events together over time is important knowledge of governance of the social setting. How teachers control immediate events is significant. How knowledge gained from that experience contributes to future events is even more significant. Formatting this knowledge with **V** diagrams helps both teachers and students remember what happened. The teacher can use well-made **V** diagrams in future teaching. Students can use their well-made **V** diagrams as they progress into future learning.

The theory of educating contributes greatly to holding together complex events and experiences and simplifying them for future value. The case study by Nikki Bethune, cited in Chapter 8, is a clear example of the successful integration of educative practice, educational theory, and action research. Case-study methods can contribute to generalization of knowledge claims when **V** formatting is used. The **V** diagram form enhances generalization because it is the form that holds together the multiple details, the different events, and the significant questions and answers.

WHERE IS THE END IN EVENTS?

When we are hard at work on a project we feel good that we are doing the work. How do we feel when it is over? How do we know that we have actually come to the end? How do we, as authors of this book, know the end in the events of writing? We write with a deadline in mind – a date on a calendar – but we pass the deadline because we have not finished the writing. We then set another calendar date and work hard to meet our deadline. People who work in the field of advertising have real time deadlines because the work has to go out or not be used. Some of these creative people find that their creativity increases as the time grows short. They act like crisis junkies – they love the pressure, even seek it out. Others know when the work is done because a strong feeling of satisfaction occurs when completion, not just a deadline, is met. Completion and closure are important qualities of events.

"Art beholds the significance of outcomes. Well done!!! You've finished the job! There's nothing left to do on this project! So, start up another project, OK?" "Where something ends, something else begins," wrote John Dewey (1938). In our case, when one **V** is completed, and we behold the significance of its outcomes, then the next research effort can begin with the results of the prior work. The ending of events is transitory (but not ephemeral) and it signifies the beginning of the rethinking process. Create new questions from the answers; use data transformations to improve conceptual thinking; and imagine unrealized possibilities from the lofty levels of the conceptual patterns.

Continuity in educative events is a good thing for out of prior achievements new futures grow. "Growth is a fact of life," wrote Dewey.

We believe that artists create new meanings in their art, and compose them into a whole. An important event occurs of a dominating quality of whole, of completion, of satisfaction. At this point in time, one should stop and just admire what has been completed. Take a deep breath. Give time for the seratonium in your brain to release enough juice so you just feel great. You have finished what you started. Satisfaction is both earned and deserved. You feel satisfied.

We believe that the **V** diagrams provide criteria for completing a work of knowledge making. When you work around the **V** so that all the elements have been connected to each other – all the created meanings are composed into a whole – you know the job is done. Your **V** is a small work of art. Admire it. Feel a well-justified pride, for the work is both difficult and creative.

You can admire the fact that you did answer the questions you asked. You can take pride that the events became regular, reliable, and repeatable as the basis for the claims you call knowledge claims. You really do know something about reality.

REASONING WITH TECHNOLOGY

9

Electronic Educating

Principle 9. Electronic educating extends learning beyond the walls of the class-room or laboratory and enables meaning to be negotiated electronically in ways that go beyond the conventional paper-and-pencil formats.

Computer technologies have invaded modern societies in multiple ways. But as Professor Cuban concludes, computers have been "oversold and underused" in university life (2001). We believe his analysis is largely correct. The "killer applications" of computer technologies to university educating are still missing. We believe the failure lies in the lack of a coherent theory of educating. For the past eight years we have been using a theory to guide the changes in educative experience shared through email using reciprocal journaling. Electronic educating uses email – a computer-based interactivity between teachers, students, curriculum, governance, societal forces. Email is a powerful mode for negotiating meaning in ways that make educative events happen. Our theory of educating explains why some events are educative and most are not.

Electronic Literacy

Electronic literacy is a goal of electronic educating. Electronic literacy is grasping meanings expressed electronically. By electronic we mean information that appears in multiple formats on a screen in print and nonprint forms accessed via the Web. Electronic literacy requires the application of problem-solving and comprehension skills necessary to derive meaning and make judgments. Literacy is a word that represents events of using already-grasped meanings to grasp meanings not one's own. Reading a book is an example of grasping meanings in order to grasp new meanings. Electronic literacy is the same. Our computer screen is like the book pages that hold potential meanings.

Electronic educating uses email, as one form, to organize events of educating. Electronic literacy in the context of electronic educating is different from reading the newspaper on the computer screen. Electronic educating permits a sharing of information between two or more parties where feedback is possible. A sharing of information in order to negotiate a shared meaning permits educative events to happen. The event is like a good conversation, with back-and-forth dialogues between parties as a search for meaning is undertaken.

An ordinary classroom is a place where educative events can be created. An ordinary computer screen is a place where educative events can be created. A classroom can hold a small library of relevant books; so can a computer. The difference lies in the fact that Internet email can reach into libraries around the world, and specific books can appear and be downloaded onto a computer. Electronic literacy explains the many ways that new meanings can be made to appear on a computer screen, including access to chat rooms or blogs that provide spaces for multiple entries and dialogues. Electronic literacy assumes ordinary literacy is available as a means to expand into extraordinary literacy the Internet permits.

Challenges to Educators and their Classrooms

Technology is influencing the ways in which students are using metacognitive tools for learning new information. Changing are paper-and-pencil modes of communicating in favor of electronic interactions that are more efficient and foster collaborative dialogues. Teachers and students are using the Internet not only to access information, but also to share their thoughts, feelings, knowledge and meaning in creative compositions and reports (Alvarez, 1996a). Electronic literacy is affecting both the societal and formal school curricula (Alvarez, 1996b, 2001a; Reinking, 1998). Elementary, secondary, postsecondary, and adult students are using computers in the workplace, church, community, local and college/university libraries, community centers, and their home. Electronic literacy is changing the ways students are being asked to cope with interactivity that departs from passively receiving information via the radio or television or from a textbook that presents information in a linear format (Alvarez, 1997). The ways in which students are interacting with electronic text places a demand on the teacher to develop challenging lessons and assignments that make use of this type of information processing.

Information Technology spreads information. Information can be useful in educating, but one needs a theory of educating to tell us how to use information to make educative events happen. Information seldom carries with it meta-information codes that tell you how to use the information. Typically, information is not sufficient to change the meaning of the information. Educating changes meaning. If Information cannot be used to change meaning, then information is by definition non-educative.

Using computer-formatting to increase subtle and powerful meanings is not easy. Computer software relies on the SEQUENCE OF MARKS to create meaning. If one mark is out of place, the meaning is lost, or misunderstood. Most of us who use computers are well-aware of the failures in communicating caused by a mistyped email address (only one mark needs to be out of sequence for failure to ensue). Conceptual literacy, such as reading a book, is not based on one specific sequence of words. Language is yeasty; meanings multiply into many different forms. For those of us knowledgeable in reading literacy, we know how complex and difficult it is to develop functional literacy in human beings. The huge practical problem is how to meld the ordinary and customary practices of literacy in reading with the extraordinary potential literacy made possible by computer-formatting. **V** diagrams are one answer.

In our studies investigating the influence of metacogntive tools such as concept maps, interactive **V** diagrams, thematic organizers, timed writings, and electronic communications and their effect on teacher practice we find that informing practice through collaborative partnerships leads to a conceptual change approach to teaching and learning (Alvarez, 1993, 1995, 2001b, 2002b; Alvarez & Busby, 2002; Alvarez & Alvarez, 1998; Alvarez, & Risko, 1989; Alvarez & Rodriguez, 1995; Alvarez et al., 1999; Alvarez et al., 2000; Alvarez, Burks, & Sotoohi, 2003; Stockman, Alvarez, & Albert, 1998).

Teaching is an exchange of facts and ideas engaged under meaningful circumstances in an environment that goes beyond simply telling and assigning. These facts and ideas should relate to topics, problems, situations, and contexts of a given discipline that take into consideration the experience and world knowledge of the students. In addition, our position is that these facts and ideas should not be confined to one subject discipline in which the teacher and students are assigned, but rather serve as the anchor from which other disciplines are incorporated so that relationships among them can be readily ascertained, acknowledged, and assimilated.

Our view is predicated on our belief that monitoring student progress and understanding keeps us better informed about our teaching practice, the value of our course content, and takes into consideration Gragg's (1940) warning that "wisdom can't be told." It is also consistent with Gowin's (1981) theory of educating and Ausubel's (1968) theory of meaningful learning. Our theory guides us when interpreting the findings of our research projects and others so that better communication and understanding of the key concepts occur with the "live" audience who weigh the merits of their learning derived from these discussions, assigned readings, assignments, and their applications.

Alternatives to Conventional Instruction

No longer is the textbook the single resource for middle, high school, and postsecondary students. Students are now able to access the Internet through multiple pathways of inquiry. Most textbooks present information in a fixed chapter and linear format, while the Internet allows students to access information from multiple perspectives in a nonlinear format. Neither is the school library the major resource for housing materials. Libraries from all over the world can be accessed instantaneously via the World Wide Web. Students are using the Internet to access various directories that take them to numerous databases that enable them to sort through information and note category relationships. Directories serve as research tools for our students to solving specific problems and as a repository to publish their papers.

Students and teachers are actively involved with authentic tasks and materials couched in problem-oriented formats within meaningful contexts that foster thinking and learning. In our Exploring Minds project, students construct meaning from real data and are asked to make sense of the world around them. They pursue individual paths of inquiry using critical thinking (thinking about thinking in ways to bring about change in one's experience) and imaginative thinking (exploring future possibilities with existing ideas). Students engage in social and solitary contexts that involve them in writing, interviewing, and reflecting with ideas gleaned from their conversations and their readings. In our project, practitioners are facilitators rather than dispensers of learning. These teachers use their knowledge and skills to guide student inquiry by using the idea of a negotiated curriculum. Teachers and their students engage in research practices that affect the four commonplaces of educating: teaching, learning, curriculum, governance, and fortify the societal milieu. The situational context (e.g., classroom, field experiences, and electronic communications) in which these commonplaces occur takes into account the affective, connotative, and cognitive domains. These account for the feeling, "willing," and thinking activities.

Electronic educating takes place within the normal confines of the teaching and learning process. Lessons and assignments involve the use of technology as a "tool" for searching, storing, sharing, creating, and imagining; and become a natural part of the learning and communication process. In a Constructivist vein, the role of technology is to guide learners into new pathways that provide them with opportunities to make sense of new materials that they view and read. Our Exploring Minds project studies minding events. These events of minding can be studied by focusing on the idea of "changing meaning." Educating changes the meaning of human experience. Sharing meaning is basic to educating. The American philosopher John Dewey held that shared experience is the greatest human good.

At the Center of Excellence for Information Systems at Tennessee State University, meaning is shared by electronic means. The idea of electronic messages and journaling is a recent idea that for its users changes their life in important ways. Using electronic means of sharing meaning changes the process of educating. It changes the life of these teachers and students in very important ways. Every domain of educating is changed.

We define teaching as the achievement of shared meaning. In this domain of educating teaching is changed in powerful new ways. A kind of virtual reality takes over the ordinary reality of teaching. Through electronic communications, the time and place of shared meaning is radically changed. The teacher "teaching" and the student "studenting" can occur at any time or any place; they do not need to be socially together in one single classroom at a specified time of day or night. Classrooms may continue to function, but the usual assumptions about classroom time-and-space uses can fly out the classroom window as fast as an electronic communication becomes "sent mail." The idea of "social control of classrooms," administration, and governance changes as does the idea of a curriculum. A curriculum becomes the structure of knowledge of prior events used to make new events happen.

Surprisingly, the idea of true learning changes very little. Learning is a responsibility of the learner to learn. No one can learn for us; we must do our learning on our own. The most important achievement for students is their learning how to learn. Once they have a working idea of how they learn, then all subsequent learning will improve in speed, accuracy, comprehension. Learning about your own learning is like writers writing about their own writing – both pass the self-referential test.

Many, many students have deep trouble with their learning. Many are in denial; that is, many students do not seek help with their troubling learning problems. The more they learn, the more mislearning events can occur. Mislearning practices can be changed. For example, the heavy reliance on rote-mode learning can be supplanted with conceptual learning that is more effective. Much mislearning relies on different sorts of "social" learning required to "get through the system"; that is, students spend a lot of time on learning "swift" ways to pass tests (including study guides of various sorts; Cliff Notes, etc.). Students focus on how to get grades easily. Often students spend time and effort on learning how to pass the course instead of spending that same time on learning the instructional material of the course. We call these students "Teflon learners," – nothing sticks.

Conceptual learners spend much less time than do rote-mode learners and to greater effect. These students learn to ask real questions and find apt ways of constructing satisfying and satisfactory answers. They actually know something more than just how to get a passing grade. Electronic meaning sharing can change most of the ordinary activities of educating. The Exploring Minds project seeks to document, describe, and explain these significant changes.

Finding Out What Our Students Know and Understand

Keeping abreast of how our students perceive the course content is a key component of pedagogy. How are we, as professors and teachers, to know the

extent to which our students are processing new information in meaningful ways that are deemed to be acceptable rather than in ways that may be
misconceived, confusing, or relegated to rote memorization?

In order to promote learning and understanding that go beyond the
walls of the classroom and result in reflection, we use electronic exchanges
with our students to reveal their feelings and thoughts as well as our own
about the course content over a semester period (Alvarez, 2001b, 2002b;
Alvarez & Busby, 2002). The processes involved are social, political, and
organizational when negotiating the curriculum and adhering to politi-
cally driven mandates, while working within the organizational structure
of the school, college, or university.

Our students use the journaling component of the Exploring Minds
Network to monitor their understanding of class content, relate their world
knowledge and experience to what they are learning, and communicate
with the professors and teachers their thoughts, feelings, and reactions to
what is taking place. In turn, these journal exchanges serve as a mediating
process that negotiates the curriculum in such a way that new information
is meaningfully learned rather than relegated to rote memorization. The
four commonplaces of educating plus one: teaching, learning, curriculum,
and governance plus the societal environment are the conveyances that
take place in these dialogic exchanges as well as the undertakings of the
reports, projects, cases, lessons, and assignments that take place during the
course of the semester or academic school year.

Faculty and Student Use of Computers in the Classroom

A case study involving faculty at Stanford University indicated that computer use by professors primarily consisted of preparing documents used
for instruction (e.g., handouts and email listservs), and when researching
for personal writings. However, using this same technology in their daily
teaching was negligible (Cuban, 2001). The teaching faculty members at
Stanford University apparently lost their capacities to reason when dealing with computers in their classrooms. Changes in conventional teaching
did not occur with the computer revolution. Using information technology to improve the quality of teaching was not something they did very
much of – like many teachers elsewhere. The technology of the chalkboard
and chalk, the pencil and paper, the talk-for-others-to-listen techniques are
still the rule in most college classrooms. Videotapes do play a role. The
overhead projector is used sometimes. Even the Socratic method of asking
leading questions in order to expose the ignorance of students is uncommon in college teaching these days. It may be that any serious reasoning
about educating – enlightened teaching, coherent student learning, developing conceptually-sequenced curriculums, debating choices that rule

the governance of instruction – is not possible because intellectual frame-works and comprehensive theories of educating are thought to be missing altogether.

Computer access does not necessarily equate to computer classroom use, but it does indicate that students having computer access to the Inter-net does imply engagement for personal use and induces student learning brought about by the societal, informal, curriculum than by the formal, school curriculum. For example, Cuban (2001) found that students' use of computers was peripheral to their primary instructional tasks, and that less than 5 percent of the middle and high school teachers integrated com-puter technology into their regular curricular and instructional routines. When teachers in their classrooms used computers, these computers did little to alter the existing teaching practices already in place (see Cuban, Kirkpatrick, & Peck, 2001).

Perhaps it should be noted that technology systems that have been de-veloped for school use are by persons who have little knowledge or ex-perience of what it is like to teach at elementary, middle, secondary, or postsecondary schools. This position also encompasses the social, cultural, organizational, and political factors of the school environment that shape the complexities of what people do in this milieu.

The theory of educating in this book is a challenge to those who would desire to engage in serious reasoning about the uses of technology in edu-cating. The reasoning begins with clear cases of what counts and what does not count as "an educative event." We note a huge difference in the meaning of the word "education" and the meaning of the word "educating." *Educa-tion is a construct, not a concept.* Educating refers to events that happen, are made to happen, are subject to researching and knowledge making. This theory of educating serves to generate knowledge, very much like any sci-entific theory or theory of science. If there is to be a science of pedagogy, then this theory can guide and direct scientific research about events that are educative.

We believe the heuristics of **V** diagramming and concept mapping gener-ate serious reasoning about many relevant matters involved in elementary, middle, secondary and postsecondary learning, adult teaching, professo-rial competence, and what students can do to learn.

The feeling of knowing and understanding comes about through dia-logic exchanges focused on events. This feeling when teachers and stu-dents share their experiences and knowledge that shed light on a problem or topic of interest. It is a time when thinking on a level of conception becomes thinking on a level of realization: a powerful moment in ed-ucating occurs when grasping a meaning and feeling the significance of this act come together. This process evolves from a beginning event, which leads to a middle event, and reaches an ending event (product).

It does not necessarily signify the finite resolution, but instead reaches a state of "temporary completeness." Within our conceptual framework, this sharing and negotiating of meaning takes place only in a community of thinkers.

Communities of Thinkers

The building of communities of thinkers by students and teachers is vital if we expect meaningful learning to take place within our classrooms. For a decade or more we have experienced a community of thinkers defined as an active group of students and teachers striving to learn more about a discipline by engaging in the processes of critical thinking and imaginative thinking (Alvarez, 1995; 1996b, 1997; Alvarez & Rodriguez, 1995). Developing a community of thinkers focuses on the kinds of thought processes needed by the teacher and students to achieve learning outcomes. This is in contrast to focusing on ways that these learning outcomes can be accomplished expediently through literal questions, rote memorization, and lecture that results in provisional rather than meaningful learning.

During this inquiry, the teacher thinks about the facts and concepts that need to be understood by students, the supplementary reading materials and artifacts that need to be provided, ways to incorporate other subject disciplines into the inquiry, and the connections and interconnections that need to be threaded together so that new information can be learned and understood. The teacher selects from an array of teacher-directed/teacher-assisted strategies and meaningful materials that can be used to facilitate student thought. Likewise, the student becomes an active thinker in the learning process by engaging with the lesson by relating prior knowledge and world experience, informal and formal; selecting from an array of student learning strategies that are part of an individual's arsenal; and working with the teacher toward extending meaning and understanding with the subject matter.

Thinking for processes to achieve a learning outcome is different from thinking for a learning outcome. The former is a process of thinking moving from some initiation to a conclusion or solution. A learning outcome focuses on increasing a skill or on perfecting solutions (see Russell, 1956). In an effort to increase learning efficiency, we focus on the processes of thinking, selecting, eliminating, searching, manipulating, and organizing information. Emphasis is placed on thinking as a process involving a sequence of ideas moving from some beginning thought, through a series of a pattern of relationships, to some goal or resolution. Within a community of thinkers, teachers and students ask questions, seek answers, and reflect on their thoughts and feelings as they engage in problem solving and decision making.

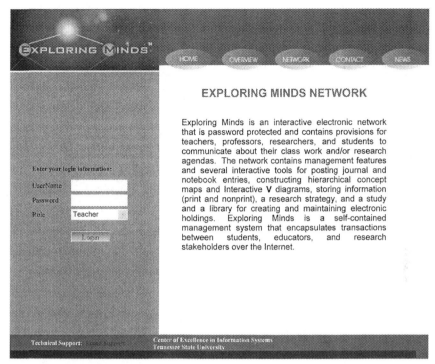

FIGURE 9.1. Exploring Minds Network.

EXPLORING MINDS NETWORK

Exploring Minds is a metaphor for a conceptual system and an electronic network that enables individuals to think about thinking in ways that differ from conventional forms. This thinking accounts for solitary, collaborative, and mindful learning that contributes to personal meaning that results in either intrinsic or instrumental applications. Exploring Minds allows both thinkers and tinkers to accommodate each other in the thinking/learning process. Tinkering with learning is rarely seen in conventional educational settings beyond kindergarten.

Our Exploring Minds Network (http://exploringminds.tsuniv.edu) was developed at the Center of Excellence in Information Systems at Tennessee State University, from a teacher's perspective with classroom experience at the middle, secondary, and postsecondary levels that includes management, interactive communications, monitoring, and metacognitive tools (Alvarez, 1997). Exploring Minds Network is an active electronic venue for professors, teachers, researchers, and students to reflect, negotiate, and evaluate the teaching/learning process that enables systemic changes to occur under meaningful and thoughtful circumstances (see Figure 9.1).

Ideas are revealed in narrative and visual formats through electronic journals, conceptual arrangement of ideas, and **V** diagrams so that metacognitive tasks such as self-monitoring, reflective and imaginative thinking, and critical analysis are a crucial part of the learning process. A visual **V** externalizes mind thinking. *The basic premise that underpins Exploring Minds is that the mind deals with meaning and meaning is the basis for conceptual understanding of facts and ideas.*

This network is password protected and contains provisions for teachers, professors, researchers, and students to communicate about their class work and/or research agendas. Students communicate via the electronic journal, concept maps and **V** diagrams that they develop and receive feedback. This network is designed as a venue for faculty and students (elementary, middle, secondary, and postsecondary) to reflect, negotiate, and evaluate the teaching–learning process almost exclusively over the Internet (Alvarez, 1997, 2002). The network contains several interactive tools for posting journal entries, constructing hierarchical concept maps and **V** diagrams, maintaining a notebook, a communication system, an electronic note taking procedure, and storing information (print and nonprint) in a backpack (portfolio). Exploring Minds is a self-contained system that encapsulates transactions between students and other learning stakeholders interactively over the Internet.

Management System

The management portion of the Exploring Minds site is divided into five consoles: *director, coordinator, teacher, student,* and *parent*. The director oversees the entire project, the coordinator oversees a cohort of teachers, administrators, and or other affiliated members, and the *teacher console* (see Figure 9.2) enables the teacher to assign passwords and usernames, create classes and subgroups, and maintain student records of assignments, examinations, journal entries, announcements, and other record-keeping data that are typically done through pencil-and-paper formats.

Students, once given a password and username by the teacher, have an account and are able to enter information of all sorts: construct concept maps, **V** diagrams, enter notations and thoughts into their electronic journal, notebook, and enter video clips, photographs, journal articles, drawings, simulations, and any other relevant information (print or graphic) into their own study/library.

Students also have a biographic file to enter any pertinent information about themselves, including a photograph. Students can change their password and username, enter relevant information (e.g., email address and telephone number), and anecdotal information including a photograph. Only anecdotal information is made public and can be viewed by any participant. The *profile* allows the teacher, coordinator, or director to access participant records.

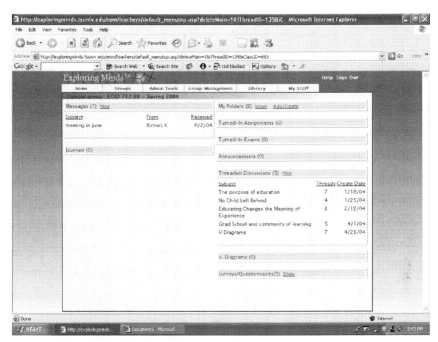

FIGURE 9.2. Teacher console.

When students log onto the *welcome* portion of the website, they are alerted to new messages, assignments, announcements, and threaded discussions (see Figure 9.3).

The *parent console* permits the parent/guardian of a student to communicate with the teacher(s) and access their child's records with teacher permission. The teacher is in charge of setting up accounts for students, parents/guardians, and guests.

Administrative tools appears in the teacher console and is designed for teachers to create, edit, and delete groups (classes) or subgroups within groups with participating members. The *group management* section contains several categories and subcategories and management tools that include calendars, communication (sending messages and announcements), assignments and examinations, gradebooks, records, journals, threaded discussions, **V** diagrams, concept maps, action research strategies, and a component creator that creates questionnaires and surveys (see Figure 9.4).

The *gradebook options* section permits access to student or participant records of transactions that occur during a semester or year (e.g., assignments, **V** diagrams, and journal postings). The records portion archives all transmissions that occur by students in a class.

A calculation feature, a subcategory of gradebook options, permits the selection for assignments and examinations to be either weighted or to

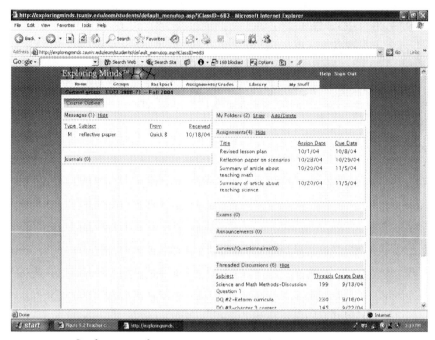

FIGURE 9.3. Student console.

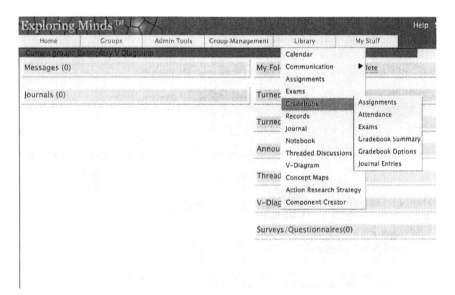

FIGURE 9.4. Group management features.

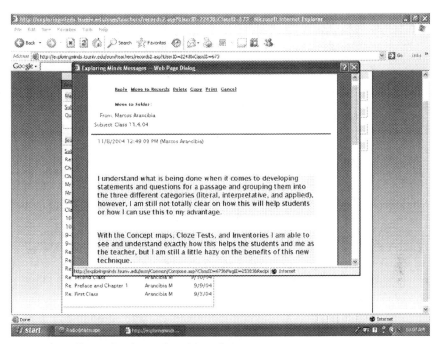

FIGURE 9.5. Example of a student journal entry.

be computed through a total point system. By selecting *percent system*, grades are calculated based on specified assignment/examination weights. Grades are calculated based on points (no weighting) and are entered as actual points, not the percentage. Two other functions of this subcategory are automatic attendance and gradebook summary display that, when selected, permit students and parents to view their respective individual grades of assignments and examinations.

Electronic Journal: Feedback for Shared Meanings

A prominent feature of Exploring Minds is a reflective portion containing journals and notebooks for students to enter their thoughts and feelings of course content (see Figure 9.5). The journal serves as an exchange section whereby ideas can be posted and *feedback* received from professors, researchers, and teachers. Once comments are made and sent back to them, the students then read the response by clicking on the message appearing on the *welcome page*. A record (date and time) of each transaction is automatically noted in the student's journal section and also in the records portion of the teacher console.

Dialogic Exchanges

Students are asked to enter their thoughts, feelings, and questions in their electronic journal following each class session. A rehashing of what transpired during the class session is discouraged. In other words, students reflect on the content of the class session and express their thoughts about the facts and ideas that appealed to both their thinking and feelings. Students also post reactions to their assigned class readings.

Informing Practice

After each class session and before the next class meeting, each journal entry posted by the students is read by the teacher. Teacher responses to the students' entries are predicated on the type of entry posted. For example, in several studies we were interested in the ways our undergraduate and graduate students reflected upon what was being taught both by their affective and cognitive responses as well as how well they understood the facts and concepts of a specific lesson. Three levels of reflection were classified and judged as follows:

1. How important were the facts and ideas perceived by our students;
2. If they reported that the facts and ideas were part of their prior knowledge and/or experience; and,
3. If they applied the facts and ideas of a topic to another relevant situation.

For example, if students reported that the facts and ideas that were presented in a class session or reading assignment were deemed to be important they were classified under Category 1. If students included in their journal posting information that was presented and/or which they actively participated sparked an association with a past experience (a school subject, or a former teacher, or a situational experience that occurred in their classroom, school, or community), then this part of their entry was classified as falling into Category 2. If their journal posting contained ways in which the information of this class session or reading assignment could be applied to another topic or relevant situation, then these comments were classified as Category 3.

As part of the analysis, we also read each posting to determine if any misconceptions related to the lesson or reading assignment were reported in these entries. This immediate feedback eliminates early conceptual confusion. These studies revealed certain patterns. The majority of the postings were entries that posed either direct questions about the clarity of meaning, the students' understanding of the class activities, specific questions, or their interpretations of the material.

For the most part, we responded to each student entry. The primary reason being that the postings were worded in such a way that *"asked"* either directly or indirectly for a response. Our responses took the form of *answering* a direct or indirect question/statement, offering encouragement, or asking them to share their concerns and revelations, by initiating a threaded discussion or sharing their ideas and/or materials with the members of the class. Many of the postings by the students contained embedded questions that were explicitly stated. One can question the sincerity of these postings since the students knew we were reading them. Nevertheless, the overall postings by the class, as a whole, together with their in-class discussions, indicated that their remarks were consistent with their thoughts and feelings of the course content and their interactions with us. This daily and weekly feedback clarified meanings.

It was clear that students maintained a dialogue with themselves and also with us that better enabled them to grasp meanings and to understand and integrate important facts and ideas. Simultaneously their electronic entries informed us of their level of understanding of each class session, thereby alerting us of any reteaching that needed to be done and also the planning of forthcoming lessons and reading assignments that could be better learned and understood. Based on the students' completed assignments, in-class discussion, and journal records, each of us teachers changed the format of our course as it was taking place. Our final examinations reflected this negotiated curricula by including questions and problems that arose from these electronic dialogues.

It is important to note that these dialogic exchanges are most valuable when they occur in concert with a teacher in a classroom and the subsequent reflections that occur in the journal postings. Face-to-face interactions promote the dialogic exchanges and are the basis from which these interchanges occur and misconceptions are clarified and further elaborations, if needed, reach fruition.

Electronic Notebook

An *electronic notebook* is provided to students. This notebook helps to organize notes taken for a class, a report, or paper (see Figure 9.6).

This notebook acts as a storage area of records and events and serves the same function as does a regular hand-written notebook. The difference is that an electronic notebook can be accessed through wireless communication systems such as a laptop computer and information can be gathered from various Internet sources and locations.

Teacher and Student Library/Study

Formerly physical space is required for libraries and study rooms. In this network, electronic space is much more useable and economical. The Teacher's Library provides a venue by which the teacher creates the reference materials needed for a particular class (see Figure 9.7).

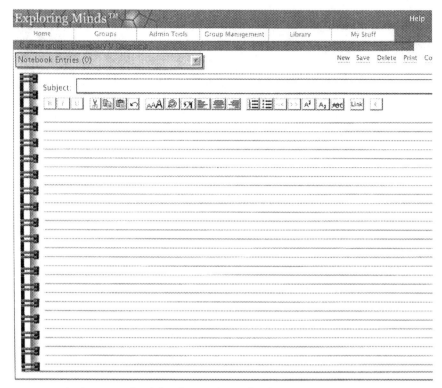

FIGURE 9.6. An example of the electronic notebook.

FIGURE 9.7. Teacher's library.

FIGURE 9.8. Teacher/Student Study.

Sections of the teacher's library include the files section, reference documents, photo gallery, electronic journals, Internet links to relevant sources, movies, articles, and reports. These items are stored in the Teacher's Library for student access and retrieval. By students clicking on each respective category a display of the requested materials appears and can be viewed or downloaded to their study.

Both the teacher (researcher, administrator) and the student have a study. This personal study for both teachers and students can house video, photographs, document files, and other digital materials. It is a place that provides the user with opportunities for assemblage of different types of print and nonprint materials. This area electronically stores and categorizes pertinent information relevant to a specific work within a class or research project (see Figure 9.8).

It is a sanctuary within an electronic medium that provides a place to pause, think and reflect.

Action Research Strategy

The *action research* page contains the following phases: problem/situation, plan/strategy, course of action, resolution, and action.

Research Phases

|

Problem/ ⇨ Plan/Strategy ⇨ Course of Action ⇨ Resolution ⇨ Action
Situation

Each phase takes the user through the research process (see Figure 8.13 in Chapter 8). The researcher is asked to *think* about the respective questions under each heading. Researchers are asked to think about each of the headings, to include their *feelings* about what is taking place, and to also respond to the questions posed in each of the phases. Each phase has a series of questions to be answered and sent to the teacher or mentor for review and comments. These interactive dialogues serve as feedback to the student and a record of transactions that occur during the research process.

The elements contained within this action research strategy correspond to those arrayed on the **V** diagram (see Chapters 3 and 4). This entry page provides the researcher with three options (see Figure 9.9).

One is to select and begin a new project; another is to continue working on an existing research project; and there is a provision to select an editing feature.

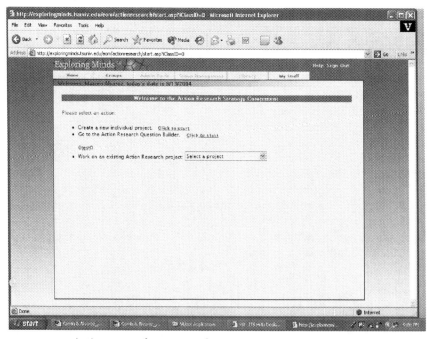

FIGURE 9.9. Action research strategy phases.

Questions that appear in each of the phases can be edited and rewritten to correspond to the action research strategy described in Chapter 8 and also in Appendix II. Since these questions can be rewritten they can be crafted to meet the educational method and design of a researcher (e.g., experimental, correlational, casual-comparative, historical, qualitative, and mixed quantitative and qualitative). The nature of the research strategy enables collaborative groups of students or teachers to be established, or groups of students and a teacher or mentor, or a student (such as a master's or doctoral) and a group of mentors. Each response entered in the phases is archived and made available for review by the cohorts. This serves as a record of what is transpiring during the development, carrying out, and finalizing of the research investigation. A *management* section displays the names of the participants and the name of the research project that each individual or group is affiliated. The teacher or mentor can monitor a student's progress during each phase of the action research process.

Concept Maps

Hierarchical concept maps enable students to reveal their ideas with a theme or target concept under study (see Novak, 1990, 1998; Novak & Gowin, 1984). Students can use a software program (e.g., Inspiration 6.0 or CMap http://cmap.coginst.uwf.edu) to construct their concept maps. In our project, students send their maps electronically via the Exploring Minds Network for review. This concept mapping feature is used by a student, saved as a file, and then it can be printed or submitted to a teacher as an electronic communication. Students can work individually or in a group where their maps are collaboratively constructed, reviewed, and revised. Each revision is archived and versions are saved to their individual records file once the map is reviewed by their teacher and/or a researcher. Teacher/researcher comments are then sent to the student where the file is viewed and the comments are read. The student views these comments appearing on the map, reflects on these comments, and thinks about how to incorporate these comments in revising the map. The map is then redrawn and submitted again for review. Like the *Interactive V Diagram*, each version of the concept map that is revised is archived. When students redo their concept maps, they reconceptualize their ideas and these ideas become more meaningful. Student thinking can be directly shared.

These maps are very helpful for negotiating ideas not only with the teacher, but also with one's peers. The connections shown on the map together with the linking words determine the extent to which ideas are meaningfully represented. Cross-links (broken lines showing relationships between ideas portrayed on one part of a map with ideas portrayed on another) provide valuable insight into the visual display.

Procedures for making concept maps are given in Chapter 8. There are times when students use the concept mapping technique to map portions of their textbooks or as an evaluation instrument to determine knowledge of a given topic. Appendix III contains a *Scoring Criteria for Concept Maps* protocol that we use to rate student maps (Alvarez 2002a). However, cautions should be taken to use these scores carefully. Arbitrary assessments with these maps are not advised. Instead, we recommend the user of this protocol to read the scoring criteria.

Interactive V Diagram

The *Interactive V Diagram* has been designed with several features (Alvarez, 1998). A *quick help* menu and a link describing the **V** components with explanations of the epistemic elements is available, together with instructions for entering information on the **V**. Information is entered onto the *interactive V diagram* by clicking on the respective field of the arrayed elements and then typing the data. Once the fields on the **V** template have been completed, the user can review the entries and then electronically submit the information to our base site by clicking on *ready for review*.

The teacher has the option of selecting from the following: *teacher review, student review*, or *move to records*. When the teacher or professor receives the **V**, it is reviewed and comments are made directly onto the submitted **V**. The reviewer then sends these comments back to the sender who is then able to read the comments. A **V** can be sent to four reviewers, and comments can be made by each of these four reviewers on one or more of the **V** components. Each reviewer's name appears at the top of the **V** with a color code along with a respective color check mark that identifies the reviewer and his or her comments that appear on each revised **V**. The precision and validity of constructed knowledge increases greatly. The initiator of the **V** looks on the **V** and by either moving the cursor over the check mark or clicking on the "+" is able to read the remarks. These remarks can be printed and incorporated into a revised version of the **V** and sent again to the reviewer. Once the **V** is finalized it can be archived in the student's *records* folder under the heading of Group Management.

The interactive **V** diagram has several distinguishing features. When opening the **V** diagram page the following visual appears (see Figure 9.10).

On the left side is a panel that names the **V**s that have been created in this personal section of the Exploring Minds Network. On the right side are options to select a "new" **V** when starting a new project, a "quick help" screen, and some information "About **V**s."

When selecting a "new" **V** the following screen appears that prepares the user to initiate the process. By clicking on "click to begin" the initialization of the **V** Diagram is started (see Figure 9.11).

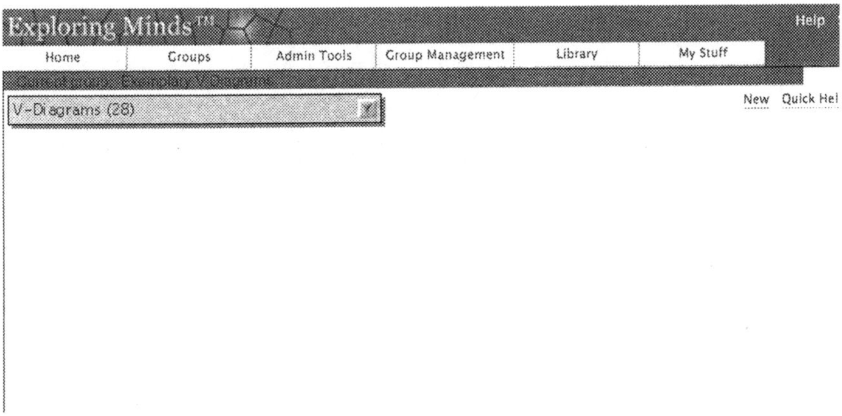

Exploring Minds™   Help

| Home | Groups | Admin Tools | Group Management | Library | My Stuff |

Current group: Exemplary V Diagrams

V-Diagrams (28)   New   Quick Hel

FIGURE 9.10. Opening a **V** diagram page.

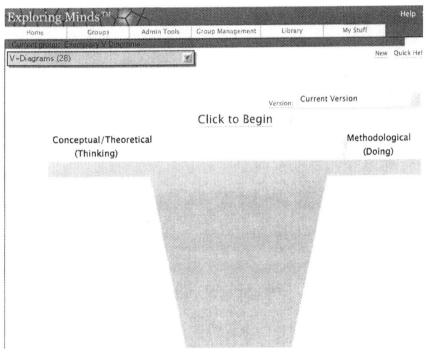

Exploring Minds™   Help

| Home | Groups | Admin Tools | Group Management | Library | My Stuff |

Current group: Exemplary V Diagrams

V-Diagrams (28)   New   Quick Hel

Version: Current Version

Click to Begin

Conceptual/Theoretical   Methodological
(Thinking)   (Doing)

FIGURE 9.11. Selecting a new **V**.

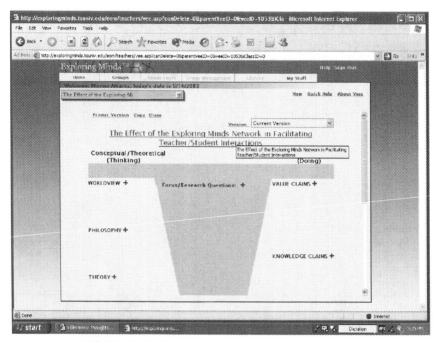

FIGURE 9.12. "Click to begin."

Notice that on the right side is an indicator prompting the "version" that this particular **V** is being formulated. "Current version" means that the **V** is in its first attempt. Once the **V** is submitted to be reviewed by another collaborator or a teacher and feedback on any or a combination of elements arrayed on the **V** are provided, the version then is recorded as "second version." Subsequent submittals and reviews then are archived and numbered to indicate the degree of thought that was involved in its reconceptualization. Again we see an increase in the precision and validity of shared meaning.

"Click to begin" displays a title to be inserted for this project. Once the title is saved the rest of the elements arrayed on the **V** are displayed (see Figure 9.12).

Notice the items that now appear on the left side of the screen. Clicking on "Printer Version" extends the length of the **V** to its full view. "Copy" allows the **V** to be copied to another location, and "Close" saves the work in progress. Clicking on any of the elements provides the user with a screen to enter the information that is pertinent and relevant.

The user is able to enable the computer to print the shaded **V** area by selecting "printing options" and following the directions. The "print" selection prints a hard copy of the **V**. Clicking on "Return to Normal View" returns the user to its previous format and provides additional options.

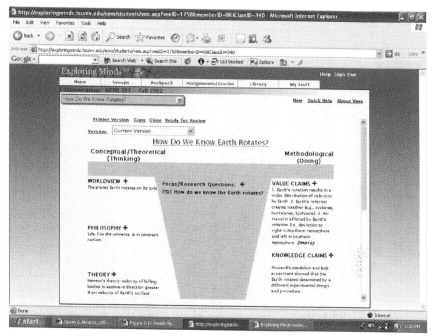

FIGURE 9.13. "Ready for review."

"Ready for Review" sends the **V** to another for review (see Figure 9.13). This other person is usually a teacher or university professors on a master's or doctoral committee, or other teachers working collaboratively on an action research project, or research scientists collaborating with one another, or students working with other students on the project. As in reviews of scientific research, knowledge construction gains more value through review. By clicking on the "+" symbol to the right of each element, the reviewer can type in comments or suggestions that need to be clarified or addressed. Once completed, the reviewer sends the current version back to the sender. Upon receipt the originator of the **V** is able to see the name(s) of the reviewer(s), which are individually color-coded and match the check marks that appear on each element that was commented upon on the **V** (see Figure 9.14).

In this example, the name of the reviewer is shown with a blue check mark. Viewing the check mark beside *theory* indicates where the comment was made. The user can either roll the cursor over the check mark to read the comment or can click on the "+" symbol and read and print the comments of the reviewer. If more than one reviewer responds, the names appear and the color-coded check marks of different colors are next to their names. The user is then able to distinguish who made the comments and make revisions as deemed necessary. When the user reconstructs the

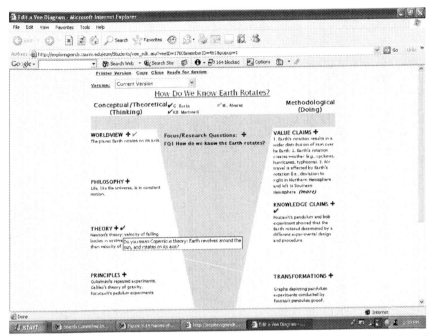

FIGURE 9.14. Names of reviewers with designated color-coded check marks of areas with comments.

V incorporating the ideas of the reviewers, the reconceptualization process begins and ideas begin to be negotiated, concepts and facts are clarified, and the precision and validity of knowledge claims are enhanced.

The Exploring Minds Network provides faculty with a system to communicate more effectively with their students. In addition to the management features (class assignments, class roll, calendar, announcements, grade book functions, and course material), the teacher or professor is able to react to student journal postings on a regular basis and thereby monitor students' thoughts and feelings instead of waiting for end-of-the-semester evaluations. These interactive dialogues, together with visual displays of the concept maps and V diagrams, serve to negotiate the learning process and better serve meaningful understanding between the professors, teachers, and students during the semester or school year.

The uniqueness of Exploring Minds is the active engagement that occurs between teachers, professors, and their students afforded through the use of the journal, concept maps, and interactive V diagrams. In essence, teachers and professors are active learners with their students, and facilitate the learning process by guiding student inquiries, evoking discussions, and involving their students with other affiliated schools whose students may be engaged in similar research/study topics.

At the university level, Exploring Minds is used with postsecondary minority students at three universities who are affiliated with our NASA and NSF grants. In the classroom we use Exploring Minds with undergraduate and graduate students in education methods, administration, and research classes and with undergraduate students in physics and astronomy classes. Our students post their class and text-reading reactions in their notebooks, their concept maps that they construct revealing how they perceive certain topics and their conceptual relationships, and use the **V** diagram to analyze and critique documents, plan lessons, and to initiate, carry out, and finalize their research. We respond to their journal postings and also to their representations of their respective maps and interactive **V** diagrams. Ideas are shared and meaning is negotiated as we and our students discuss class topics either biweekly or weekly depending upon the number of meeting times of each respective class. Our students have immediate feedback and are in close contact with us through an electronic process that takes them beyond the time constraints and walls of the classroom.

Another function of the Exploring Minds Network is to provide supervising and cooperating teachers of elementary, middle, and secondary schools to make use of this technology to communicate and monitor their respective student teachers. Since there is a parent component associated with this network package it lends itself to better home/community access and cooperation with classroom teachers, administrators, and support personnel of a given school.

The sharing of ideas using this network has been an integral educational component with middle and high school and university students and their teachers/professors in our Exploring Minds program. Co-authored papers have resulted from conference presentations where teacher and student voices have been heard concerning their research endeavors with case-based instruction. Exploring Minds provides a learning context that encourages students to *think about learning* and enables them to learn principles that may help them to better understand and apply new information instead of learning prescriptions that may be either misconstrued or vaguely meaningful.

Part Four

Summary

Electronic literacy environments differ from traditional classroom reading and writing activities. This type of environment is challenging teachers, administrators, and test makers in ways never before confronted. Students are versed in electronic literacy from their early years. As they progress through school their experiences in computer literacy become more sophisticated.

Electronic journaling creates shared and mediating learning contexts and invites multiple connections across contextualized information. Questions, thoughts, and feelings are exchanged after students have an opportunity to reflect on each class activity and assignment through electronic journals that take place beyond the walls of the classroom. Student reflections are dependent upon how important they perceive the lesson, whether they have experienced the lesson in their world experience and/or the knowledge of the facts and ideas being studied, and/or their ability to apply newly learned methods to other situations. Their queries inform us of any information that needs clarification or elaboration to which we can respond directly and, if warranted, make the rest of the class aware of an issue, fact, or concept that needs further explanation at our next class meeting.

VALUE JUDGMENTS

Value judgments are always a significant part of the process of making knowledge claims. For example, concepts are sharpened by their close connection to real events and their regularities; facts – so basic to claims – are sharpened by the explicit recognition of facts as *records* of events. Further up the V, the questions are sharpened by acute concept specification, and knowledge claims have increased reliability and validity as they become more tightly connected to events and records of events.

Our studies indicate that when you ask students to conduct journal entries as a "dialogue with oneself," the entries are written in such a way that evokes a valuable reflective stance within the person. This stance differs when one is asked to record what transpired during the class session. That stance results in a "report-like" response that is similar to a note-taking type of entry. This type of "report-like" entry does little to stimulate thought or evoke feelings because reflection on the class session is minimized and one is relegated to writing down the information and then repeating it again either from notes or memory into a journal entry.

The Exploring Minds Network facilitates teaching and learning of our course content. It also provides a means whereby meaningful learning of ideas is shared, negotiated, and continued beyond the walls of the classroom. These electronic exchanges enable us and our students to negotiate the curriculum in ways that traditional lecture and college teaching does not. This negotiating creates an emergent curriculum.

The uniqueness of the Exploring Minds Network is the active engagement that occurs between teachers, professors, and their students through the use of the journal, concept maps, interactive **V** diagrams, and research strategies. In essence, teachers and professors are active learners with their students, and they facilitate the learning process by guiding students in their queries, by promoting discussions, and involving their students with affiliated schools whose students may be engaged in similar research/study topics.

Interactive electronic **V** diagrams are included in this book to show that their use in a technological format is being conducted by secondary and postsecondary students. These **V**s are part of the Exploring Minds Network and are featured so as to portray their use in an electronic venue. Ideas are shared and negotiated in ways that cannot be achieved through traditional formats. An individual can formulate a **V** and share it with others either in a group or with a mentor or another student within or beyond the walls of the classroom. Replies are viewed and thoughts are reconceptualized when a new version of a **V** diagram is reconstituted. Such manipulations stimulate thought in ways that demand more than just "answers." These comments stir one's imagination and enhance the thinking and learning process to greater heights, leading to greater expectations and accomplishments.

We have developed a stand-alone version of this **V** that can be installed on a personal computer that has the capabilities for educators, students, researchers, and administrators to formulate, conduct, and finalize research investigations; plan lessons; analyze documents; and share these **V**s with others electronically. For information on this stand-alone **V**, contact our Exploring Minds Project (http://exploringminds.tsuniv.edu), or the Center of Excellence in Information Systems, Tennessee State University, Nashville, TN 37209.

Epilogue

If you have read this far, then we know you have grasped many meanings not formerly your own. If you comprehend a major thesis of this book, then you know that a grasped meaning is what you learn. This principle of grasping a meaning in order to learn the meaning is therefore a guide to inquiry itself, whether purely scientific inquiry, or practical problem solving in everyday life. You probably understand how important the idea of meaning is to our getting smart; and that getting smart, to a depth of wonderful human understanding, is a major event in our lives.

Inquiry and learning have sometimes been thought to refer to the same events. People who engage in inquiry do learn, and learners do use inquiries in their learning. However, inquiry and learning are significantly different when inquiry refers to constructing knowledge and learning refers to an individual's reorganizing his or her own meanings. Learning occurs after an individual has grasped a meaning; meaning is what the learner learns.

The significant fact is that science itself can gain power from the focus on meaning. The connection between scientists and educators is "What do they have in common?" V-diagram analysis will show they have much in common – events, records of events, and concepts naming regularities in events. It is not a matter of "translating" from one isolated domain (science) into another domain (education). It is profoundly a matter of identifying shared events.

We devised a theory of educating. Not a theory of education, or educational theory. This semantic shift aims to highlight events-that-are-happening anywhere, anytime as educative events. The criterion of validity must be satisfied before we begin our serious inquiries. A theory is a general heuristic that explains events. A coherent theory puts together principles, conceptual structures, constructs, concepts connected to events. Scientific theories derive explanations from causal laws (empirical generalizations) and use theories to predict possible events in precisely-constrained contexts. Theory in this sense of a scientific theory is far too narrow in its scope of inquiries to cover events that interest us.

We believe we have a theory of educating that does explain educative events. The book gives you knowledge claims, value claims, principles of action, action research, concept maps, and, of course, the key feature, **V** diagrams. **V** diagrams are the general heuristic that works across the board of our interests in educative events.

PART 1. THE ART OF EDUCATING

The art of educating with **V** diagrams can be called art because completion and consummation are felt. Art does simplify complexity and it connects parts into wholes. An educative event increases in value when it creates these felt-qualities. Art and science are both creative, as is educating, and both art and science show the good effects of educating artists and scientists.

Teaching is both an art and a science, but it is in the art of teaching that the educative event is shaped so that it stimulates the palate and stirs a learner's curiosity and imagination. The teacher who thinks about a lesson and makes available relevant resources is similar to the artist who anticipates the form, color, and texture of a painting when creating a work of art. The world of teaching and the world of art both require learning from the future in ways that make sense to the learner or viewer. The stronger the connections between the new educative event and the learners' prior knowledge and world experience the better the thinking–learning process.

The theory of educating espoused in this book directs teaching to focus on changes in the way students organize their expectations of what they will be doing in school. For this to occur, students must first grasp the meanings with which they are unfamiliar; a sense of surprise is expected. They must "get the point" before deliberate learning can occur. Within the context of educating, educational value is evident in those moments when grasping the meaning and feeling the significance of that meaning come together. When cognition is educative, then it is never separable from emotion. Feelings embrace thinking. When cognition occurs without emotion, then it is always cognition that does not matter. It is learning and knowing that are not truly educative. This theory stresses the centrality of the learner's experience.

The formulation of a theory of educating encourages a solution to the classic theory–practice problem. Practitioners and researchers are concerned with educative events, and the theory of educating espoused in this book is a guide to thinking (and feeling and acting) about these events. Just as writing is always rewriting, educating is reeducating. It is a continual process of working and reworking and structuring and restructuring – the qualities of human experience interacting with nature. As a theory it should be tested through practice and research.

The Art of Educating: Simplifying Complexity without Denying It

The key to unlocking the simplicities that make up the complexities of life is the human mind. It is this tool that enables the individual to seek resolutions to complex phenomena. The **V** diagram is a tool that provides a venue for the thought processes to reach fruition and expand the knowledge with a given topic or idea. It is an enabler that helps the user to think new thoughts. Ideas are stimulated so that reconciliation can be forged in the pursuit of knowledge making.

Thinking about and conceptualizing the components arrayed on the left side of the **V** combined with the methodological elements on the right side bring together new insights with previously known information in ways that allow the user to think new thoughts about past knowledge. The middle of the **V**, with its Telling Question and Focus/Research Question and the events to which they are directed, actively tie both sides together into an arrangement that evokes cognitive dissonance as well as synchronization of the ideas. The abilities to question, make judgments, reason, reconcile, rethink, reflect, reorganize, make predictions, and engage in unrealized possibilities are part of this learning and evaluation process signified by the **V** diagram.

We believe that simplifying complexity is not a task to be approached superficially, but rather one that requires serious thought and inquiry so as to conjure new ways of thinking about past happenings, to critically examine current happenings, and to imagine future happenings that can become realities. This occurs when users of the **V** diagram formulate their own questions regarding the event under study. The way a question is posed influences the way in which the event is examined, the records selected and the concepts needed to explain the conditions. Question formulation is a neglected activity for most students at elementary, middle, secondary, and postsecondary education levels. Too often questions are already given either by the teacher or in prepackaged materials, therefore providing little opportunity for ideas to be initiated by the teachers and their students.

The four commonplaces of educating (teaching, learning, curriculum, and governance) form the foundation of the educational theory, practice, and knowledge. These commonplaces encompass a theory of educating that is comprehensive and can be measured in multiple ways to determine achievement and academic success in the classroom, school, district, state, and national arenas. These four commonplaces of educating need to be considered when planning an investigation or when analyzing a document. Teaching, learning, curriculum, and governance serve as categories from which to group and assess what is going to happen such as when planning an investigation, or analyzing what has happened under each of these areas, when evaluating a document or completing an educational research study. A better understanding of the worth of a document or research study is achieved when these commonplaces of educating are part of the planning and evaluation process.

The societal environment influences the way in which an individual acts, accommodates, and relates the formal school curricula to these societal and world experiences. This societal educative environment is playful, philosophical, academic, recreational, heartwarming, heartbreaking, endearing, distrustful, debilitating, as more societal values are created by communities of thinkers. It is important to realize that just because a person lives in a particular societal environment, it does not follow that this person is like another person or shares common beliefs, aspirations, knowledge, or experience within the same environment. Proximity does not make a society.

The degree to which formal school educates is congruent with the degree of the societal factors that have shaped and guided an individual to accept, reconcile, or refute the academic curriculum and policies that are mandated. This complexity needs to be simplified through the melding of the formal school curricula and that of an individual's societal curricula. The two may not be compatible, but they can be mediated through meaningful learning that consists of teachers using educative materials, students taking responsibility for their own learning, a curriculum that is emergent, not fixed, and a governance procedure that permits this learning process to evolve without mandated restrictions.

As learners we need to have the opportunity to relate what we know to what is new. Making connections with new ideas enables us to better enhance our mental models with a given topic and thereby increase our ability to make new knowledge with unknown phenomena. As teachers and parents we need to do the same connection making of the known to the new with our students and offspring. When learning is reduced to memorization of complex ideas, then it becomes an artificial process that neither instills an intrinsic desire to learn, know, and understand nor promotes the idea of a primary aim of educating: learning for oneself by reducing complexities – simplifying the notion of learning through creative, imaginative, caring, reasoning, and critical thinking and understanding.

With the publication of *The Art of Educating with V Diagrams* we find ways to bring coherence of judgment to all fields. Just "Lay the **V**" on exemplar studies in any field and the criteria of excellence will emerge. With explicit criteria of excellence, then specific case after case can be judged. Coherence will develop, along with impatience with sloppy and undisciplined disciplines. Time and money will be less expensive and more effective. Value grows.

To test these claims, do the **V**. Construct **V**s of currently important research reports. Major defects in knowledge construction will be spotted directly.

The science of educating with **V** diagrams begins to emerge as we focus on research. Given time and more work a new science of pedagogy could be constructed and pursued with good effect to improve schooling. From the ending of this book the beginning of a project to develop valid educational research that is anchored and ingredient in the process of educating is both a real and unrealized possibility.

Science is the backbone of our work. **V** diagrams were created to explain scientific knowledge. Any scientific research paper, when analyzed thru **V** diagramming, can be displayed on one page in the **V** format. This format shows the structure of knowledge. Scientists construct knowledge of events they make happen. The scientists use theories and conceptual structures to ask Telling Questions. They use refined techniques to make records of events. Knowledge is constructed by connecting events, concepts, and records of events (facts).

Students' learning is focused on constructing knowledge. Scientific inquiry and individual human learning overlap; they share many of the same events. Scientists are also learners and their learning (inquiry) leads to constructing knowledge professionally. A large part of our *society* is organized to support and develop the best *science*. **V** diagrams show us that both scientists and students focus on events they make happen, on records of these events that are the facts of the case, and on concepts that name regularities in the focused events. **V** diagrams of the work of scientists and the work of students has the same *form*; only the *content* varies. When students from the first grade in elementary school learn to use **V** diagrams, they learn to expect new knowledge to have the same form. Every grade, K through 12 and postsecondary, has curriculum and instruction events of **V** diagramming. There is continuity in events of constructing knowledge.

Learning that all knowledge has structure is a powerful piece of human learning. The age or sophistication of the learner makes no significant difference to the great transformative effect on the learners. Expecting structure of knowledge and constructing your own knowledge are educative events of major significance.

A theory of educating is the brain of our work. The theory, first published in 1981, has been well-used in a variety of settings. Today this theory is embedded in the technology of electronic educating. Reasoning with Technology is achieved through the use of a coherent theory. New technologies (e.g., computers, digital cameras with documentary films, and telephonic devices of all sorts) initially promise practical value for educating but their use value is marginal because there is no theory of educating that guides their effective development. Chapter 9 on electronic educating clearly shows the functional integration of interactive communicating in teaching, learning, basic-in-use researching of educating, scientific inquiries (e.g., in astronomy, astrobiology, and physics), and administration of institutional practices. The theory brings coherence to a variety of thinking in what we name "the communities of thinkers."

V diagramming helps us to be tightly-focused on a very few of the highest priorities. Getting smart about deep human understanding is the top value. The **V** formatting sets a high standard for constructing and reporting knowledge claims in science. It contributes to advancing scientific literacy at all levels of understanding. It provides sharp focus in scientific research evaluation and in writing new proposals for large funding. The **V** format saves a lot of time and a lot of money in science projects. At the same time it saves students otherwise lost to learning.

Grasping a meaning not our own and then using that grasped meaning for learning is an event of deep human understanding. It is not, however, a topic of self-evident importance. That meaning is the fuel of learning was overlooked by scientists trying to discover scientific laws of learning. No such laws were discovered. What is now self-evident to us is that learning how to learn is a special sort of learning that guides all subsequent learning. The individual person is the cause of learning. Our students learn about managing their own learning. They experience situations where they must ask questions first and construct answers on their own. Self-efficacy is a goal.

One way to describe self-efficacy in learning is to understand what learning around the **V** means. This learning is difficult, and it takes a lot of time to figure out what learning to mastery really involves. The irreducible fact is that no one can learn for us; we must learn for ourselves. We can get help from teachers and other learners, but it is our task and it creates both freedom and power to those who achieve that understanding.

The functional interaction between the four commonplaces of teaching, learning, curriculum, and governance set in a broad societal context gives high leverage for educating. Each separate element has its own value. For example, we work with teachers about their teaching. We work with administrators about how they share meaning in order to run things. We check to see what curriculum is emerging from multiple **V**s. All of these values feed into conditions for individual learning; value multiplies with the interactions. High leverage is a result.

Coherence is a top value also. **V** diagrams connect a dozen separate components. The stories and the storeys – tall stories – show these working connections. The email records express the individual struggles of learning. This work is not easy, nor conventional; it is difficult and novel. Each individual takes a different path. All of them show up in the communities of thinkers.

How do we describe the nexus of scientific opportunity and practical need? The simple, direct answer? Use **V** diagramming! We know a major nexus of science and educating involves human learning guided by the structure of the knowledge **V**.

Scientific opportunity can start at any place on the **V**. Opportunity can begin with a change in philosophy of science, as we see today with the passing of Positivism and the progress of Constructivist views. The major discovery of DNA is shaping scientific opportunity and practical need in Life Sciences in incredible and astonishing ways. The President of Stanford University, Dr. John Hennessey, writes glowingly of what the Clark Center (powered by the potential values of DNA science) is doing to change the educating events (*Stanford Alumni Magazine*, 2004). They changed the construction of offices and big tables to change the ways human meaning is shared, and educating is enhanced.

Continuity in scientific research grows as each piece of new research opens up possibilities for the next, new thing. Old knowledge perishes when new knowledge grows. It is like the healthy organism – old skin perishes as new skin grows. Organic progress of live creatures shows waves of changes, some of which are destructive. Conceptual change can be abrupt. Technological change can be very sudden – the car replacing the horse.

Continuity of attention occurs in a program of research. Unsolved problems grab our attention. Stability amid functional instabilities requires our attention. Continuity of a pattern of inquiry is governed by the left side of the **V**, the thinking side. The commitment to Telling Questions organizes change.

The continuous invention and verification of our knowledge is a prime condition for our survival.

Educational Research, Theory, and Practice

Educational research is a multifaceted effort involving research on education and educators, collaborative university/school partnerships involving researchers and educators, and research conducted by educators on programs, practices, methods, and mandated policies. Teachers and administrators should become involved in research practices that not only test and evaluate programs and practices, but also determine whether what is possible is desirable from an educational point of view.

Biesta and Burbules (2003) caution us to be aware of efforts that narrow the scientific focus of educational research by defining science as a fixed set of methods; the result of which is a reduction to an "unscientific" state. This notion of reductionism does more harm than good in an educated and free society. It leads to fixed practices that curtail the processes of imaginative and critical thinking and reasoning. Restricting what counts as research also continues to spawn the favor of memory. This emphasis on memory as an intellectual measure of school success is changing as advances in technology enable individuals to move from linear thought and reliance on memorization to a higher standard of intellectual prominence: imagination. Technology is the organized energy and the intellectual focus that will spur imagination. The degree to which an individual's imagination can be revealed will serve as the future intellectual standard for cognitive ability and educational value.

Democracy in educational research depends upon educators, researchers, and administrators trying to experiment with new ideas and educational practices; and to be free to examine the effectiveness of mandates decided for them by others. With freedom comes power to alter the roles of educational decision makers. To be denied the opportunity to pursue such a democratic freedom is undemocratic.

We invite you as educators, administrators, and researchers to exercise your imagination. Test our theory of educating when planning and evaluating educational materials, curricula, assessments, programs, methods, and practices.

The Science of Educating

We began this book thinking about the art of educating, not the science of educating. We end this book with an astonishing recognition of the possibility that maybe we are on the cusp of inventing the science of educating. We are surprised, of course. Science has such a major place in the modern world. It is surprising that the science of educating has not already been invented. Philosophers John Dewey, Alfred North Whitehead, and William James published widely on science and education. Their followers used conceptual goggles of modern philosophy and filled journals with writing on various aspects of science, education, schools. No science of educating emerged, so far as we know.

We invite the readers of this book to consider if we have described events of educating in sufficient detail and elaboration so that a new science of educating can be constructed. We know we have not built the science, but we believe now that it can be constructed. Its promise requires a lot of dedicated talent and a lot of money. The conceptual entertainment of unrealized possibilities is a good place to begin.

So, Now What Is Possible?

Anticipating possibilities can seem an endless process of futile speculation. Given this distracting thought as something we all experience occasionally, we believe that the "conceptual entertainment of unrealized possibilities"

(Whitehead, 1938) can be recommended in the context of a book full of realized possibilities. The presentation of a seasoned theory that guides several years of practice is an excellent context for asking, *"So, now what is possible?"*

Events and facts, events and concepts, events and events are our metaphysical reality. We rub together these three golden coins – events, concepts, facts – as we anticipate the future and our fitness to live from the future. We prepare through education and we grow through educating. When we connect concepts, facts and events together in a coherent fashion, then we get a feeling that we understand. We have organized a small piece of our world.

It has been said of the Scientific Method, that if a better method can be developed, then using the scientific method itself will develop the new method. We believe if a better method for improving the creation of knowledge making in science, law, and poetry can be found, using the **V** will invent it.

The reason: **V** making is self-referential. It uses itself to improve itself. It can improve other fields as well.

Give it a try!

Appendix I

V Diagram Scoring Protocol

Teacher	_____	Student's Name	_____
School	_____	V Title	_____
Scorer	_____	Submission #	_____
Date	_____		

Directions: Circle the value that best represents each category.

Category	Value	Total	Comments
Research Question	0 1 2 3		
Events/Objects	0 1 2		
Concepts	0 1 2 3 4		
Records	0 1 2 3		
Theory	0 1 2		

Principles	Stage 1	Stage 2		
	0	0		
	1	1		
	2	2		
		3		
		4		
World View	0			
	1			
Philosophy	0			
	1			
Transformations	0			
	1			
	2			
	3			
	4			
Knowledge Claims	0			
	1			
	2			
	3			
	4			
Value Claims	0			
	1			
Total				

Appendix II

Research Phases and Questions

The research phases and questions are presented as an example of those used with high school students using this electronic research strategy when conducting their case-based action research. The Exploring Minds Network has provisions for designing questions that are more suitable to other research methods and designs through an editing feature.

PHASE I. PROBLEM/SITUATION

Students are first presented with a case or a topic to be studied by the teacher or mentor. We have written cases on CDs that have included the use of thematic organizers with electronic links associated with interpretive statements designed to activate students' schema with topic; provided background information with hyperlinks to relevant source materials on the Internet; described key concepts that needed to be understood; and provided associative linkages to Internet sites that further elaborates on each of these concepts with either descriptions, examples, simulations, audio reports, video clips etc.

Directions to Students

Select either a problem that needs to be resolved or a situation that needs to be addressed that stimulates your interest. Relate the circumstances of the problem or situation to your own prior knowledge and experience. *Reflect* on this problem/situation by asking yourself:

1. How important is it to know more about this problem/situation?
2. Have I read about this situation/problem before?
3. Based upon what I have read or experienced how can I apply what I already know or have experienced to this problem/situation?
4. How can I make this problem/situation *interesting* for me?

PHASE II.   PLAN/STRATEGY

Formulation

Formulate an idea or a problem. Write it on a sheet of paper. Begin by asking yourself questions that need to be answered. Ask yourself:

1. Is this an interesting idea or problem to investigate? If so, what are the key reasons for engaging myself? (List them underneath the idea or problem on your paper.)
2. What questions need to be answered?
3. What focus/research questions need to be asked?
4. What are some of the resources that I can access?
5. What materials will I need?
6. Who are the persons I need to consult?

Starting Points:

1. Brainstorm ideas.
2. Begin developing a concept map of your study.
3. Relate the ideas of the problem or situation to previous studies (literature review), prior knowledge, and experience.
4. Begin using the **V** diagram to plan your investigation.
5. Start formulating your Research Questions relating them to your events/objects.

Relationship. Relate the idea or problem to previous studies (literature review), prior knowledge, and your experience.

1. Read about your idea or problem in journals that report related studies.
2. Use the **V** diagram to analyze a seminal report by "Laying the **V**" on the document (see Q-5 technique and **V** diagram components).
3. Make notations of a given study:
   a. convert the answers in the findings into questions. Are these questions related to the ones that were hypothesized or asked in the research questions at the beginning of the study?
   b. the sources they discuss in the introduction;
   c. the purpose or the problem being studied;
   d. the kind of method used in the study;
   e. the ways in which the information was gathered to answer their research questions;
   f. how the information was analyzed when reporting their results or findings; and
   g. what the author(s) said about these findings.

4. What information in this report relates to your questions or concerns?
5. Was it written in a readable fashion?
6. Can you relate your prior knowledge and experience to this report?
7. Are there any questions that you feel are not answered in this report? If so, what would you have done to make the report more understandable?

Purpose: What is the major focus of your research investigation? Why do it?

1. Based upon your understanding of what you already know coupled with what you have read or viewed, give an explanation of what you are trying to know.
2. Is your purpose to the point?

Aims of the Project: Direction of the study.

1. At this point what do you foresee the direction your case investigation taking?
2. What *course of action* are you thinking about?
3. Does it give you direction for accomplishing your *purpose*?

Value Claims: Statements that declare the *worth* or value of this inquiry.

1. What potential value do you see resulting from your study? "What's it good for?"
2. "What is the good of it?"

Research Questions: Question(s) that serve(s) to focus the inquiry about event(s) and/or object(s) studied.

1. How do you plan to go about designing your study?
2. Write a Research Question (RQ1) that directly relates to what you want to find out.
3. Is it stated in a clear fashion? If a few peers or colleagues were to read your Research Question would they agree on the meaning of the key words?
4. Do you need to write a second Research Question (RQ2) that relates to your *Purpose and Aim*?
5. Limit the number of Research Questions you ask. It is better to answer one, two, or three well-thought Research Questions than to make an extensive listing.

During this phase of your *Research Strategy* it is important that the event(s) and/or object(s), concepts, and records correspond directly to the Research Question(s) you are asking.

Event(s)/object(s): Describe the event(s) and/or object(s) to be studied in order to answer the research question(s).

1. Keep in mind the meaning of these terms: *event* and *object*.
   Event: Anything that happens, can be made to happen, or is within the realm of possibility to happen.
   Object: Anything that exists and can be observed.
2. How are you going to arrange the purpose or focus of your study in a way(s) that answers your research question(s)?
3. Would a consensus of judges (e.g., teachers, scientists, professors, and experts) agree that this is an educational event?
4. Write a brief description of the design or plan of the events or objects.
5. Does your description of the event(s) and/or object(s) clearly state what you will be investigating?
6. Is your description clearly stated so that it correlates with the research question(s) you asked above?
7. Do you need to restate the research question(s) so that they directly relate to these event(s) and/or object(s)? If so, rewrite these questions now.
8. Compare your research question(s) to your description of the event(s) and/object(s). Do you feel satisfied that this description will answer your question(s).

Concepts: Perceived regularities in event(s) or object(s) designated by a label. A concept is a sign or symbol that points to regularity in events or objects.

1. Concepts are usually identified by words, but they may be numerical or symbolic, such as musical notations, chemical notations, iconic symbols, and mathematical symbols.
2. List the terms that need to be operationally defined in your paper.
3. Do these terms directly relate to the Research Question(s) you have asked, and to the description you have written under event(s) and/or object(s)?
4. The key concepts and telling questions become the tools for thinking both about the events and the claims made about the events.

Records: The observations made and instruments, techniques, and devices used to record the events and/or objects studied.

1. Are the instruments you have listed going to accurately make a record of what you are asking and what you are doing in this study?
2. Do you need to add or discard any of your instruments?

Constructs: Specific relationships between concepts that serve to organize your ideas. Make a concept map showing these concepts and their relationships.

World view: *A world view is the general belief system motivating and guiding the inquiry. Think about your idea or problem. Ask yourself:*

1. What are my views about this idea or problem? List them.
2. How do others perceive this idea or problem? (Students, parents, administrators, teachers, researchers, community members, members of the local board of education, members of the state department, federal government, state and national organizations, and other countries). List them.

Philosophy: *The beliefs about the nature of knowledge and knowing guiding the inquiry. Ask yourself:*

1. What are my beliefs about this idea or problem as it relates to the direction that this inquiry will take? List them.
2. What do others think and feel about this idea or problem? List those that you know about as well as those philosophical entries that you perceive others hold.

Theory: The general principle(s) guiding the inquiry about event(s) and/or object(s) that explains *why* events or objects exhibit what is observed.

1. What idea(s) is guiding your study?
2. What assumptions are you testing?
3. Are these assumptions related to the event(s) and/or object(s) that you are studying?

PHASE III. COURSE OF ACTION

Be systematic in answering your own questions, when gathering materials, and interviewing persons. Where do you need to visit? Who are the persons you need to interview or consult (e.g., other teachers, librarians, community persons, or family relatives)? Where can you locate the information you need (e.g., school library, public library, college/university libraries, databases, community agencies, newspapers, state departments, government agencies, museums, archives, and information on the World Wide Web)?

Design

You are now ready to finalize your research design. *Review* your event(s) and/or object(s). Does the Research Question(s) directly relate to these events/objects? Do the concepts, and records correspond directly to the Research Question(s) you are asking and what you are going to do under events?

1. Do you need to restate the research question(s) so that they directly relate to these event(s) and/or object(s)? If so, rewrite them now.

2. Compare your research question(s) to your description of the event(s) and/object(s). Do you feel satisfied that this description will answer your question(s).

Records: Review your records.

1. Are the records valid and reliable?
2. Do the concepts, principles and theories relate to your record making devices that assure validity and reliability?
3. Do you need to add or discard any of your instruments?

CONCEPTS. 1. Look at these terms again. Do these terms relate to the Research Question(s) you have asked, and to the description you have written under event(s) and/or object(s)?
CONSTRUCTS. 1. Make a concept map of the left side of the V diagram.

Design

1. Write a description of your design or plan.

PHASE IV.   RESOLUTION

Analysis

Analyze the event(s) and/or object(s) conceptually. Use your records of the event/object to analyze your findings.

1. Make sense of the event. Ask yourself: "What's happening?"
2. What ideas (concepts) are taking place?
3. Does the idea arise from new knowledge?
4. What key idea is surfacing that can be connected to the event, or part of the event you would call a fact?

Transformations: The analysis and organization of the data (e.g., rankings, tables, graphs, charts, concept maps, or other forms of organization of records made). Take these facts and put them in some order.

1. Make a summary judgment of these facts by writing them in a paragraph. Be sure to include in this summary how the concepts, principles and theories guide your record transformations. The choice of any graph or table, or the choice of certain statistics, should be influenced by your guiding principles.
2. Make a judgment on the criteria used and the way you *selected, ordered*, and determined *significance* from the collected data.
3. Be sure to make reliability checks at each point: selection, order, and significance.

4. If you use some kind of statistical or descriptive analyses you need to transform the data into a table, graph, or chart.
5. When interpreting your records think of the best way this information can be displayed to show what you have found.
6. Does your visual record accurately display your findings?

Findings

Knowledge claims: Statements that answer the research or focus question(s) and are reasonable interpretations of the records and transformed records (or data) obtained.

1. For each Research Question (RQ) there must be an answer.
2. Carefully evaluate your knowledge claims in relation to the Research Question(s) asked and your events(s) and/or object(s), records, and transformations.
3. Ask yourself: "What rules need to be followed when answering the Research Question(s) in light of what I have learned from the event(s) and/or object(s), records, transformations, and knowledge claims?"
4. Does your answer correspond directly to the question(s) asked?
5. Do you understand your answers to the Research Question(s) asked?

CHECK PRINCIPLES
1. Review your *knowledge claims*. Have your previously stated *principles* changed?
2. Do the principles show *how* your event(s) and/or object(s) appear to behave?
3. Do you need to rewrite the principles?
4. Do the principles still relate to the *theory* you stated?

CHECK THEORY
1. Have your *knowledge claims* altered, supported, or negated your *theory*?
2. How will you report this theory that guided your inquiry in your research report or paper?

Reflections

Value claims: Statements based on knowledge claims that declare the worth or value of the inquiry.

1. State the significance of your research findings.
2. Does your research have practical implications to the area you studied?

3. Do your research findings help you to have a better grasp of the topic?
4. Will someone else reading your case report learn from your work?
5. What do you consider to be the primary meaning of this investigation?

PHASE V. ACTION

Presentation of evidence and links to the next study (i.e., review, reflect, evaluate, and improve practice or extend knowledge of the event(s) or object(s)).

RETHINKING PROCESS

1. What new questions do the data make you think of?
2. Can the key concepts be redefined?
3. Use the evidence that you have gathered and link it to a follow-up investigation.
4. As you reflect on the outcome of your research study, *think* and *imagine* what can be done to advance the knowledge and understanding of your findings.
5. What unrealized possibilities can you imagine?

WRITING YOUR REPORT OR PAPER. When finalizing your research report or paper check to see that you have answered the following questions to your satisfaction:

1. Are you using the **V** as a template from which to write your report or paper?
2. Are your interpretations presented in a coherent and organized manner?
3. Do you think that someone else reading your interpretation of the report or paper can learn something as a result of your work?
4. What further action should be recommended to extend this research? Be sure to review and include your thoughts in the action phase when writing this section.

Appendix III

*Scoring Criteria for Concept Maps**

Hierarchy. The map shows hierarchy by displaying different levels of space. It moves from most inclusive concept, to less inclusive concepts, to least inclusive concepts: superordinate, coordinate, and subordinate. Five points are awarded for each level of space. Examples and nonexamples *do not* constitute a level.

Relationships. Each concept is linked by a line which signifies a *proposition* (a meaning relationship) between two concepts. In order to receive points the concept should be connected to the other and be meaningful. If the relationship is valid and the word or a word phrase is labeled on the proposition (line) 3 points are awarded. If the relationship is valid, but is not labeled, 1 point is awarded. Crosslinks, examples and nonexamples are *not* counted as relationships.

Branching. This occurs when a coordinate or subordinate concept has links to several specific concepts. *Within* each hierarchical level, points are awarded for each coordinate, subordinate, and specific concept listed

---

* Total points may exceed 100 depending upon the number of valid and significant entries portrayed on the concept map. A word of caution concerning scoring of hierarchical maps. Scoring is secondary to the purpose of constructing concept maps. The rater uses scoring as an ancillary record. The primary use of scoring is to aid the developer by clarifying conceptual ambiguities, faulty linkages, and extending his or her knowledge with the target concept. Scoring criteria are not shared with the learner. Instead, the scoring by the rater allows more in-depth review of the map and provides points of discussion with the learner. The difficulty establishing a static scoring system lies with the organic nature of the map itself. The map is a visual representation of an individual's thought processes and therefore, by its nature, evolves into various states. The stage at which the map is scored and analyzed represents a slice of the condition with the target concept as it exists at the time it was developed. The teacher may wish, in some instances, to construct an exemplar concept map and use it as a basis for comparison scoring. However, caution is advised due to students being able to construct a map that may differ from that developed by the teacher, but which includes pertinent and relevant information associated with the key target concept.

within a grouping: Level 1 = 5 points; Level 2 = 4 points; Level 3 = 3 points; Level 4 = 2 points; Level 5 and beyond = 1 point. Examples and nonexamples are *not* counted as branches.

Cross Links. Ten points are awarded when one meaningful segment of the map is connected to another segment of the map (shown by a broken line in the *scoring model*). This cross link connection needs to be both valid and significant. Cross links indicate thought, creative ability, and unique awareness.

Examples. Specific events or objects that are valid instances of a designated concept are awarded 1 point *within* the listing regardless of the number. These examples are *listed*, not circled, since they represent *specific items* of the labeled concept. For example, under the subordinate concept "reptiles" a listing appears such as: 1. Snake. 2. Lizard. 3. Alligator. Even though three examples are *listed*, the total is 1 point.

Nonexamples. Specific events or objects that are *invalid* instances of a designated concept are **stated** *as nonexamples*. One point is awarded *within* the listing regardless of the number.

Deductions

Faulty Links. Linkages to concepts that are *invalid* or are *misconceived* are deducted from the total number of points for each category. These faulty linkages are very important in the learning process. They serve as points to discuss with the learner for clarification and further understanding of the target concept.

Scoring Protocol for Hierarchical Concept Maps

School: _____   Student: _____
Teacher: _____   Date: _____

Points are awarded for **each** of the following categories **as many times as they are represented** on the hierarchical concept map. *Points are deducted for invalid or misconceived linkages and* **representations.**

Categories	Valid	Not Valid (−)	Total Valid Score	Comments
Relationships to each link 1 = not labeled $1 \times \underline{\quad}_{(not\ labeled)} = \underline{\quad}$ 3 = labeled $3 \times \underline{\quad}_{(labeled)} = \underline{\quad}$				
Hierarchy 5 points each level $5 \times \underline{\quad}_{(\#\ of\ Levels)} = \underline{\quad}$				
Branching **Level 1 = 5 Points** $5 \times \underline{\quad}_{(\#\ of\ Branches)} = \underline{\quad}$ **Level 2 = 4 Points** $4 \times \underline{\quad}_{(\#\ of\ Branches)} = \underline{\quad}$ **Level 3 = 3 Points** $3 \times \underline{\quad}_{(\#\ of\ Branches)} = \underline{\quad}$ **Level 4 = 2 Points** $2 \times \underline{\quad}_{(\#\ of\ Branches)} = \underline{\quad}$ **Level 5 &** **beyond = 1 Point** $1 \times \underline{\quad}_{(\#\ of\ Branches)} = \underline{\quad}$				
cross links 10 points each $10 \times \underline{\quad}_{(\#\ of\ cross\text{-}links)} = \underline{\quad}$				
Examples 1 point each $1 \times \underline{\quad}_{(\#\ of\ examples)} = \underline{\quad}$				
Nonexamples 1 point each $1 \times \underline{\quad}_{(\#\ of\ examples)} = \underline{\quad}$				
Total	▓▓▓	▓▓▓		

Scoring Model

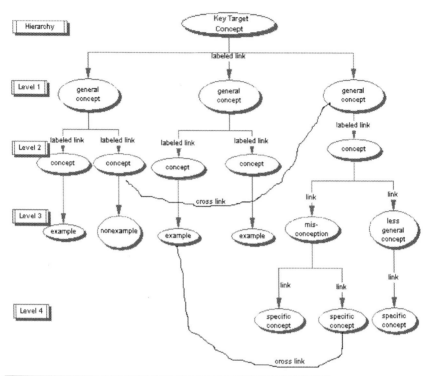

Categories	Total	Not Valid	Total Valid Score
Relationships to each level **1** = not labeled **1 × 5 = 5** **3** = labeled **3 × 5 = 15**	20	1 × 3 = −3	17
Hierarchy 5 Points each Level 5 × 4 = 20	20		20
Branching **Level 1 = 5 Points** 5 × 3 = 15 **Level 2 = 4 Points** 4 × 5 = 20 **Level 3 = 3 Points** 3 × 2 = 6 **Level 4 = 2 Points** 2 × 3 = 6 **Level 5** **& beyond = 1 Point** 1 × 0 = 0	47	3 × 1 = −3 2 × 2 = −4	40
Cross links 10 Points each 10 × 2 = 20	20	1 × 10 = −10	10

Examples 1 point each			
$1 \times 4 = 4$	4		
Nonexample			
$1 \times 1 = 1$	15		5
Grand Total			92

---

*Note:

In the column labeled "Total" calculate the total number for each category using the formulas.

In the column labeled "Not Valid" determine how many in-valid or misconceptions exist and using the formulas on the left column calculate how much needs to be deducted in each category (use minus sign).

In the last column labeled "Total Valid Score" simply subtract the total score from the "not valid" for each category to calculate the grand total.

Bibliography

Abrams, Max H. (1953). *The Mirror and the Lamp: Romantic Theory and the Critical Tradition*. New York: Oxford University Press.

Adams, Gladys A. (1998). *Forgotten Voices: Why We Left High School*. Unpublished doctoral dissertation. Tennessee State University, Nashville, TN.

Allgood, W. P., Risko, V. J., Alvarez, M. C., & Fairbanks, M. M. (2000). "Factors that influence study." In R. F. Flippo & D. C. Caverly (Eds.), *Handbook of College Reading and Study Strategy Research* (Chapter 8, pp. 201–219). Mahwah, NJ: Lawrence Erlbaum Associates.

Alvarez, Marino C. (2002a). *Researcher's Notebook*. 3rd Revision. Center of Excellence in Information Systems. Nashville, TN: Tennessee State University.

Alvarez, Marino C. (2002b). "Informing Professor Practice and Student Learning." Presented at the Annual Meeting of the American Educational Research Association, New Orleans, LA.

Alvarez, Marino C. (2001a). "Developing Critical and Imaginative Thinking within Electronic Literacy." In J. A. Rycik & J. L. Irvin (Eds.), *What Adolescents Deserve: A Commitment to Students' Literacy Learning* (pp. 191–197). Newark, DE: International Reading Association.

Alvarez, Marino C. (2001b). "A Professor and His Students Share Their Thoughts, Questions, and Feelings." Paper presented at the American Educational Research Association Annual Meeting, Seattle, WA.

Alvarez, Marino C. (1998). "Interactive Vee Diagrams as a Metacognitive Tool for Learning." In S. McNeil, J. D. Price, S. Boger-Mehall, B. Robin, & J.Willis (Eds.), *Technology and Teacher Education Annual, 1998, Vol 2* (pp. 1245–1248). Proceedings of SITE 98. 9th International Conference of the Society for Information Technology and Teacher Education (SITE), Charlottesville, VA: Association for the Advancement of Computing in Education (AACE).

Alvarez, Marino C. (1997). "Thinking and Learning with Technology: Helping Students Construct Meaning. National Association of Secondary School Principals." *NASSP Bulletin 81*, (592), 66–72.

Alvarez, Marino C. (1996a). "Explorers of the Universe–Students Using the World Wide Web to Improve their Reading and Writing." In B. Neate (Ed.), *Literacy Saves Lives* (pp. 140–145). Winchester, England: United Kingdom Reading Association.

Alvarez, M. C. (1996b). "A Community of Thinkers: Literacy Environments with Interactive Technology." In K. Camperell & B. L. Hayes (Eds.), *Literacy: The Information Highway to Success* (pp. 17–29). Sixteenth Yearbook of the American Reading Forum. Logan, UT: Utah State University.

Alvarez, M. C. (1995). "Explorers of the Universe: An Action Research Scientific Literacy Project." In K. Camperell, B. L. Hayes, & R. Telfer (Eds.), *Linking Literacy: Past, Present, and Future* (pp. 55–62). American Reading Forum, Volume 15, Logan, UT: Utah State University.

Alvarez, Marino C. (1993). "Imaginative Uses of Self-Selected Cases." *Reading Research and Instruction 32* (2), 1–18.

Alvarez, Marino C. (1989). "Hierarchical Concept Mapping." Invited portion included in the chapter "Thinking Visually." In Walter Pauk. *How to Study in College,* 4th ed. Boston: Houghton Mifflin Company, pp. 212–219.

Alvarez, Marino C. (1983). "Using a Thematic Preorganizer and Guided Instruction As an Aid to Concept Learning." *Reading Horizons 24,* 51–58.

Alvarez, Marino C., & Alvarez, Christopher M. (1998). "Thinking about Learning: Progenitor and Progeny." In R. Telfer (Ed.), *Finding Our Literacy Roots* (pp. 97–113). American Reading Forum, Volume 18, Whitewater, WI: University of Wisconsin-Whitewater.

Alvarez, Marino C, Burks, Geoffrey, King, Terry, Hulan, Bobby, & Graham, Adelicia. (2000). "Students Creating Their Own Thinking–Learning Contexts." Paper presented at the American Educational Research Association Annual Meeting, New Orleans, LA.

Alvarez, Marino C., Burks, Geoffrey S., & Sotoohi, Goli. (2003). "High School Students Using Electronic Environments for Informing Learning and Practice." Paper presented at the National Reading Conference, Scottsdale, AZ.

Alvarez, Marino C., & Busby, Michael R. (2002). "Two Professors Share Their Thoughts and Feelings with Their Students." In D. A. Willis, J. Price, & N. Davis (Eds.), *The Society for Information Technology & Teacher Education International Conference (SITE 2002). Volume 4* (pp. 1961–1964). Albuquerque, NM: Association for the Advancement of Computing in Education (AACE).

Alvarez, Marino C., & Risko, Victoria J. (2002). "Thematic Organizers." In B. J. Guzzetti (Ed.), *Literacy in America: An Encyclopedia of History, Theory, and Practice. Volumes I & II* (pp. 653–655). Santa Barbara, CA: ABC-CLIO.

Alvarez, Marino C., & Risko, Victoria J. (1989). "Using a Thematic Organizer to Facilitate Transfer Learning with College Developmental Studies Students." *Reading Research and Instruction 28* (2), 1–18.

Alvarez, Marino C., & Risko, Victoria J. (1987). "Using Vee Diagrams to Clarify Third-Grade Students' Misconceptions during a Science Experiment." In J. D. Novak (Ed). *Proceedings of the Second International Seminar, Misconceptions, and Educational Strategies in Science and Mathematics, Volume I* (pp. 6–14). Ithaca, New York: Cornell University Press.

Alvarez, Marino C., & Rodriguez, William J. (1995). "Explorers of the Universe: A Pilot Study." In W. M. Linek & E. G. Sturtevant (Eds.), *Generations of Literacy* (pp. 221–236). The Seventeenth Yearbook of the College Reading Association, Commerce, TX: Texas A&M University – Commerce.

Alvarez, Marino C., Stockman, Stephanie A., Rodriguez, William J., Davidson, Bobby, & Swartz, Katie. (1999). "Informing Practice through Collaborative

Partnerships." Paper presented at the American Educational Research Association Annual Meeting, Montreal, Canada.

Alvermann, Donna E. (1981). "The Compensatory Effect of Graphic Organizers on Descriptive Text." *Journal of Educational Research 75*, 44–48.

Ausubel, David P. (1968). *Educational Psychology: A Cognitive View.* New York: Holt, Rinehart, and Winston.

Ausubel, David P. (1963). *The Psychology of Meaningful Verbal Learning.* New York: Grune & Stratton.

Ausubel, David P. (1960). "The Use of Advance Organizers in the Learning and Retention of Meaningful Verbal Material." *Journal of Educational Psychology 51*, 267–272.

Ausubel, David P., Robbins, L. C., & Blake, E. (1957). "Retroactive Inhibition and Facilitation in the Learning of School Materials." *Journal of Educational Psychology 48*, 334–343.

Baker, Linda, & Brown, Ann L. (1984). "Metacognitive Skills and Reading." In P. D. Pearson (Ed.), *Handbook of Reading Research.* New York: Longman.

Bandura, Albert. (1986). *Social Foundations of Thought and Action: A Social Cognitive Theory.* Englewood Cliffs, NJ: Prentice Hall.

Best, John W., & Kahn, James V. (1989). *Research in Education.* 6th edition. Englewood Cliffs, NJ: Prentice-Hall.

Bethune, Nikki. (2003). "Vee Diagrams: An Action Research Project on Its Implementation in 9th Grade Physical Science." Unpublished master's thesis. Montana State University, Bozeman, MT. A synopsis of the master's thesis can be viewed at http://arexpeditions.montana.edu/articles/nikki/introduction.htm.

Biesta, Gert J. J., & Burbules, Nicholas C. (2003). *Pragmatism and Educational Research.* Lanham, MD: Rowman & Littlefield.

Bode, Henry Boyd. (1971). *How we learn.* Westport, CT., Greenwood Press, Publishers, p. 288. Originally published by D.C. Heath & Company, 1940.

Chaille, C., & Britain, L. (1991). *The Young Child As Scientist: A Constructivist Approach to Early Childhood Science Education.* New York: Harper Collins Publishers.

Cortes, C. E. (1986). "The Education of Language Minority Students: A Contextual Interaction Model." In *Beyond Language, Social and Cultural Factors in Schooling Language Minority Students.* California State Department of Education.

Cortes, C. E. (1981). "The Societal Curriculum: Implications for Multiethnic Education." In J. A. Banks (Ed.), *Education in the 80s: Multiethnic Education* (pp. 24–32). Washington, DC: National Education Association.

Cuban, Larry. (2001). *Oversold and Underused: Computers in the Classroom.* Cambridge, MA: Harvard University Press.

Cuban, Larry, Kirkpatrick, H., & Peck, C. (2001). "High Access and Low Use of Technologies in High School Classrooms: Explaining an Apparent Paradox." *American Educational Research Journal 38* (4), 813–834.

Dewey, John. (1958). *Art As Experience.* New York: G.P. Putnam's Sons.

Dewey, John. (1938). *Experience & Education.* New York: Macmillan Publishing Company.

Dewey, John. (1933). *How We Think.* Boston: Houghton Mifflin Company.

Dewey, John. (1902). *The Child and the Curriculum.* Chicago: University of Chicago.

Donham, W. B. (1949). "Why experiment? The Case System in College Teaching of Social Science." *Journal of General Education 3* (January), 145–156.

Earle, Richard A., & Barron, Richard F. (1973). "An Approach for Teaching Vocabulary in Content Subjects." In H. L. Herber & R. F. Barron (Eds.), *Research in Reading in the Content Areas: Second Year Report* (pp. 84–100). Syracuse, NY: Syracuse University, Reading and Language Arts Center.

Erickson, F. (1984). "School Literacy, Reasoning, and Civility: An Anthropologist's Perspective." *Review of Educational Research 54*, 525–546.

Fry, Edward. Fry's readability graph: Clarifications, validity, and extension to level 17. *Journal of Reading 21*, 242–252, 1977.

Goodman, Yetta M., & Haussler, M. M. (1986). "Literacy Development in the Home and Community." In D. R. Tovey & J. E. Kerber (Eds.), *Roles in Literacy Learning* (pp. 26–32). Newark, DE: International Reading Association.

Gowin, D. Bob. (1981). *Educating*. Ithaca, NY: Cornell University Press.

Gowin, D. Bob. (1970). "The Structure of Knowledge." *Educational Theory 20* (4), 319–328, 1970.

Gowin, D. Bob., and Green, Thomas. (1980). *The Evaluation Document: Philosophic Structure*. Portland, OR: Northwest Regional Educational Laboratory, Publication No. 30.

Gowin, D. Bob., & Millman, Jason. (1969). "Research Methodology–A Point of View." *Review of Educational Research 39* (5), 553–560.

Gragg, Charles I. (1940). "Because Wisdom Can't Be Told." *Harvard Alumni Bulletin 43*, 78–84.

Graves, M. F., Cook, C. L., & Laberge, M. J. (1983). "Effects of Previewing Difficult Short Stories On Low Ability Junior High School Students' Comprehension, Recall, and Attitudes." *Reading Research Quarterly 18*, 262–276.

Hall, Nigel. (1987). *The Emergence of Literacy*. Portsmouth, NH: Heinemann.

Hopkins, Charles D., & Antes, Richard L. (1990). *Educational Research: A Structure for Inquiry*. 3rd ed. Itasca, IL: F. E. Peacock Publishers.

Huck, Schuyler W., & Cormier, William H. (1996). *Reading Statistics and Research*. New York: HarperCollins.

James, William. (1911). *Some Problems of Philosophy: A Beginning of a Introduction to Philosophy*. New York: Longmans, Green and Co.

Kelly, George A. (1955). *The Psychology of Personal Constructs*. New York: W.W. Norton & Company.

Langer, Ellen J. (1997). *The Power of Mindful Learning*. Reading, MA: Addison-Wesley.

Leahy, Robert. (1986). "Educating for Authenticity." *Counseling and Values 30*, 175–182.

Leedy, Paul D., & Jeanne E. Ormrod. (2001). *Practical Research: Planning and Design*. 7th ed. Upper Saddle River, NJ: Prentice-Hall.

Lipman, Matthew. (2003). *Thinking in Education*. 2nd ed. Cambridge, UK: Cambridge University Press.

Mayer, Richard E. (2003). "Theories of Learning and Their Application to Technology." In H. F. O'Neil, Jr., & R. S. Perez (Eds.), *Technology Applications in Education: A Learning View* (pp. 127–157). Mahwah, NJ: Lawrence Erlbaum Associates, Chapter 6.

Millman, Jason., & Gowin, D. Bob. (1974). *Appraising Educational Research*. Englewood Cliffs, NJ: Prentice-Hall.

Mintzes, Joel J., Wandersee, James W., & Novak, Joseph D. (1998). *Teaching Science for Understanding A Human Constructivist View*. San Diego: Academic Press.

Neumann, Anna, & Peterson, Penelope L. (1997). *Learning from Our Lives: Women, Research, and Autobiography in Education*. New York: Teachers College Press.

Novak, Joseph D. (1998). *Learning, Creating, and Using Knowledge: Concept Maps As Facilitative Tools in Schools and Corporations*. Mahwah, NJ: Lawrence Erlbaum Associates.

Novak, Joseph D. (1990). "Concept Maps and Vee Diagrams: Two Metacognitive Tools to Facilitate Meaningful Learning." *Instructional Science 19*, 29–52.

Novak, Joseph D., & Gowin, D. Bob. (1984). *Learning How to Learn*. New York: Cambridge University Press.

Reinking, David. (1998). "Introduction: Synthesizing Technological Transformations of Literacy in a Post-Typographic World." In D. Reinking, M. C. McKenna, L. D. Labbo, & R. D. Kieffer (Eds.), *Handbook of Literacy and Technology: Transformations in a Post-Typographic World*. Mahwah, NJ: Lawrence Erlbaum Associates.

Risko, Victoria J., & Alvarez, Marino C. (1986). "An Investigation of Poor Readers' Use of a Thematic Strategy to Comprehend Text." *Reading Research Quarterly 21* (3), 298–316.

Russell, D. H. (1956). *Children's Thinking*. Waltham, MA: Blaisdell Publishing Company.

Sarason, Seymour B. (1990). *The Predictable Failure of Educational Reform*. San Francisco: Josey-Bass Publishers.

Scriven, Michael. *Reasoning*, New York: McGraw-Hill, 1976.

Stockman, Stephanie A., Alvarez, Marino C., & Albert, Jr., T. J. (1998). "Bringing Mars exploration into the K–12 classroom: The Mars Orbiter Laser Altimeter Education Program." *Proceedings of the 29th Lunar and Planetary Science Conference*. Houston, TX.

Tizard, B., & Hughes, M. (1984). *Young Children Learning: Talking and Thinking at Home and School*. London: Fontana.

Wertheimer, M. (1959). *Productive thinking*. New York: Harper & Row.

Whitehead, Alfred North. (1966). In W. H. Auden and L. Kronenberger, *The Viking Book of Aphorisms*. New York: Penguin Books.

Whitehead, Alfred North. (1938). *Modes of Thought*. New York: Macmillan Company.

Whitehead, Alfred North. (1929). *The Aims of Education & Other Essays*. New York: The Macmillan Company.

Name Index

Subject Index

Printed in the United States
By Bookmasters